CURIOSITIES SERIES

New Hampshire
CURIOSITIES

QUIRKY CHARACTERS, ROADSIDE ODDITIES & OTHER OFFBEAT STUFF

ERIC JONES

INSIDERS' GUIDE®

GUILFORD, CONNECTICUT
AN IMPRINT OF THE GLOBE PEQUOT PRESS

The prices and rates in this guidebook were confirmed at press time. We recommend, however, that you call establishments before traveling to obtain current information.

To buy books in quantity for corporate use or incentives, call **(800) 962–0973, ext. 4551,** or e-mail **premiums@GlobePequot.com.**

INSIDERS' GUIDE®

Copyright © 2006 Morris Book Publishing, LLC

All photos by the author except the following: Pages 26, 28: Jennifer Seavey; pp. 64, 101, 103, 107, 112, 119, 128, 137, 150, 189, 194, 321: Erica Bleeg; p. 68: Helen Dalbeck; p. 91: Robert Mitchell; p. 192: Rob Bossi; p. 195: Tracey Bragdon; p. 224: The Mount Washington Resort at Bretton Woods; p. 259: Lowe Family; p. 263: Robert Kozlow.

Text design by Nancy Freeborn
Layout by Debbie Nicolais
Maps by Rusty Nelson © Morris Book Publishing, LLC

ISSN: 1931-3969
ISBN-13: 978-0-7627-3979-0
ISBN-10: 0-7627-3979-7

Manufactured in the United States of America
First Edition/First Printing

For Megan and Shannon
(aka Princess Monkey and Shorty Puppy)

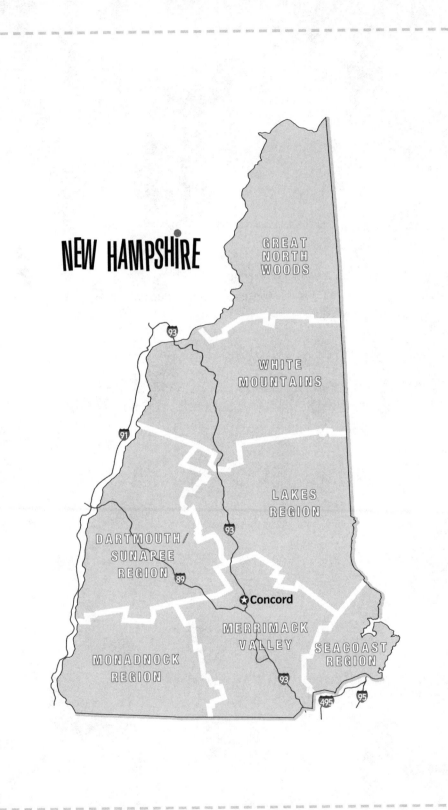

NEW HAMPSHIRE

GREAT
NORTH
WOODS

WHITE
MOUNTAINS

LAKES
REGION

DARTMOUTH/
SUNAPEE
REGION

Concord

MERRIMACK
VALLEY

SEACOAST
REGION

MONADNOCK
REGION

Contents

Acknowledgments

For me, the best part of being a travel writer is that you need lots of help from strangers to get your job done and, better yet, few of them expect to be paid. While writing this book, I found help not only on the roadside when I was lost but also in town halls, libraries, and newspaper offices; at historical societies and radio stations; and in homes and workshops from Pittsburg all the way down to Portsmouth. I extend my gratitude to all.

I thank the following folks for treating me to especially generous helpings of help: Ron Garceau at *SooNipi Magazine* on Lake Sunapee for his help with curiosities in the Dartmouth/Lake Sunapee Region, including the story about Charlestown's poor old James O'Neill, who was boiled post-mortem, and nobody knows why; Charles J. Jordan, editor of *Northern New Hampshire Magazine,* whose book of mysteries and odd happenings, *Tales Told in the Shadows of the White Mountains,* helped guide me to curiosities in the White Mountains and beyond; and Joe Citro and Diane Foulds, whose wonderful chapter on New Hampshire oddities in their book *Curious New England* also served as a particularly rich resource.

Journalists from all over New Hampshire were tremendously helpful. In the far north, I'm especially grateful to John Harrigan, outdoor columnist for Manchester's *Union Leader* and former owner and editor of *Colebrook's News and Sentinel,* who sight unseen invited me up north for a guided pickup truck tour of the area and dinner at his camp, where I got a gourmet meal and five-star hospitality in a log cabin 2 miles from the nearest road. I also found a mother lode of New Hampshire history, legend, and lore on J. Dennis Robinson's wonderfully rich and varied Web site, www.seacoastNH.com, for which I've been immensely grateful, both as a writer and as a Seacoast-area resident. Dennis was also kind enough to point me in the direction of a particularly elusive skinny house, as well as offer me some pointers on the ethics of good journalism. At New Hampshire Public Radio, the news director, Mark Bevis, and *The Front Porch* host, John Walters, offered numerous media contacts and entry ideas.

Many, many local historians have generously shared their time, research, and stories, but none more so than Fremont's Matthew Thomas, who met with me in his home, gave me a tour of Fremont's local historical museum, and loaned me the 1,000-plus-page Fremont town history that he himself researched and wrote. I would never have known about the delightfully kinky eighteenth-century practice of "bundling" had it not been for that weighty and wonderful tome.

I'd also like to thank my editor, Gillian Belnap, for her patience and kindness. Elissa Curcio is the best copy editor a travel writer could ask for, and I'm grateful for the many ways she made this a better book. (Of course, it should go without saying that any errors I can't blame on my troubled adolescence, I'll begrudgingly claim as my own.) And finally, I thank Erica for cheering me on through those dark nights of the soul when I didn't think I had a single quip or bad pun left in me.

Introduction

For the past nine months, I've driven all around the state of New Hampshire asking perfect strangers questions like, "How far to the little church on the boulder?" or "Which way to the giant pumpkin chucker?" Sometimes people responded so quickly it was as if they could read my mind—a sign perhaps that they'd been asked the same question many, many times before. When I went searching for Willa Cather's grave in Jaffrey Center, I didn't even have to ask: A man saw me wandering the Old Burying Ground in the rain with my head down and called out from the road, "You lookin' for Willa?" How did he know I wasn't searching for a lost contact lens or contemplating my own mortality?

Other times I would see a person working in the yard and stop to ask directions to, say, a 60-foot-tall intermediate-range nuclear missile on a town green somewhere nearby, and we would chat for a while about the snow, or the rain, or the conditions of the roads as a result of said snow or rain, or, if the conversation took a certain turn, about the drinking and/or hunting and/or junk-collecting habits of a particular neighbor down the road a piece, who certainly didn't remain nameless.

Every now and then, when people I met heard I was looking for weird, wacky, and offbeat people, places, and events in New Hampshire, they'd ask me to name one or two of my favorites. And each time someone asked, I would have to stop and think as if I were hearing the question for the first time. Was it the outboard motor museum in Gilmanton? How about Frances Glessner Lee's gory little crime scene dollhouses? Or Larry Davis's 2,850 consecutive daily ascents of Mount Monadnock? Maybe the Giant Pumpkin Regatta in Goffstown where they hollow out 600-pound pumpkins and pilot them down the Piscataquog?

The truth was, just like some proud parent, I liked them all, not because they were all equally odd, but because they were all pretty darn . . . curious. And the more I scratched beneath the surface of each little New Hampshire oddity and anomaly, the more interesting and downright weird each of them became.

To give just one example, as far as I can tell, New Hampshire is the only state in the union with a rock that no longer exists featured prominently on its license plate, state quarters, highway signs, and official stationery. Odd, right? Even more curious, though, is the fact that had it not been for a father and son team of cliff-dangling caretakers who performed what amounted to yearly facials on the Old Man of the Mountain, the 40-foot-tall Neanderthal-browed profile probably would have fallen from his cliff a lot sooner. Odder still, now you can pay a quarter to look up through a special viewfinder to the spot where the Old Man used to be, 1,200 feet above Profile Lake, and see an Old Man of the Mountain mirage.

I've enjoyed learning that Captain Samuel Jones buried his amputated leg in Washington (New Hampshire, not D.C.), that the real-life progenitor of our national icon Uncle Sam was born in Mason, that there's a horse named Old Tom buried in the middle of Alton's cemetery, and that there's a 3,200-square-foot mural in the basement of Dartmouth's Baker Library that features some of the scariest academics you've ever seen, even if you happen to work in academia. These curiosities and the peculiar stories behind them have connected me to New Hampshire—its history, its places, and its people—in new and surprising ways. Taken all together, they've made this great Granite State seem more real, more complex, more interesting, and certainly more weird. In short, each and every rock profile resembling a human head I've visited, each and every erratic boulder I've gazed upon and thought, "Wow, that's a BIG rock . . ." has made my home feel more like home. And it's hard to pick a favorite when you're feeling *verklempt*.

SEACOAST REGION

Give Me a New Blue Eye and a Ceramic Leg—Stat!
Dover

Patricia Aveni has been doctor, nurse, diagnostic expert, therapist, receptionist, and um, finger replacer at her clinic for over thirty years, and she doesn't show any signs of burnout yet. Maybe that's because it's not often that she has to deal with what cops like to call the "Tough Cases," the little tikes who have been neglected or mistreated or, even worse, forgotten. On the contrary, Aveni says, most patients who end up at her clinic have been "loved to pieces."

Sound a bit macabre? Don't worry. Pat's kids aren't alive. Her clinic at 12 Stark Avenue is called the Dover Doll Clinic, and all her patients are dolls—literally. Aveni, a renowned doll expert, is the equivalent of a hotshot doc when it comes to doll repair and restoration, from the simplest outpatient procedure—say, a quick stitch job on some overalls—to the most complicated surgery, like a combination face-lift and double eyeball transplant on a seventy-eight-year-old infant.

What are some of the most common doll injuries? According to Aveni, older ceramic dolls can have damage to noses, limbs, fingers, toes. And, of course, the older a doll is, the more likely it is to need significant work and the more difficult and delicate that work tends to be. Sounds all too familiar, doesn't it? Turns out that doll care isn't that different from people health care after all. Only Pat doesn't take Blue

Cross/Blue Shield. And, come to think of it, your doctor probably isn't going to have a go at your face with a tiny brush and some solvent to remove discoloration.

For minor surgeries or major makeovers (for dolls, that is), call Patricia Aveni's Dover Doll Clinic at (603) 742–6818.

Local Currents Compete for World Title (Maybe)
Dover

Just off Dover Point, under the highway bridges that span the bottle-neck where the waters of beautiful Great Bay merge with the Piscataqua River, you can find some of the swiftest and strongest, if not *the* swiftest and strongest, tidal currents in the entire world. At least that's what Seacoast tourist brochures claim. *Some of the strongest tidal currents in the world . . .* But if there's one thing I've learned researching this book, hometown boosterism can sometimes get the better of facts.

To get the facts right, I spoke to M. Robinson Swift, professor of mechanical and ocean engineering at the University of New Hampshire in Durham. So just how fast are the currents off Dover Point, and how do they fare in head-to-head competition with top-ranked currents from around the world? "The speed varies, of course," he told me, "and this is just off the top of my head, but when tidal currents get reinforced with freshwater flow from melt-off or rainfall they can be as high as four knots." Hah! So there you have the facts: Four screaming knots barreling down on you like a Kenworth without any brakes! What a tidal current! What a river, oh mighty Piscataqua, what a great Great Bay!

"The fastest currents occur where the tide has to flow through a narrow opening to fill and empty a large basin or estuary, like the Great Bay," the professor went on. "Now, as far as how the currents here compare to others around the world, I'm not so sure about that. Let's just say there are a lot of other places you'd have to check out before you could make any claims: the Bay of Fundy, the Alaskan coast, San Francisco Bay, and that's just for starters." But then the professor eased up on the academic skepticism a little bit. "But don't get me wrong, four knots is really cooking," he said. "It's fast enough to pull ordinary mooring buoys right under, and the random turbulence associated with that kind of current can make navigation really difficult in smaller boats." I think he was trying to make me feel better.

These currents may not be the fastest in the world, but we think they're alright.

It didn't work. Within minutes of speaking with the professor, I did a brief Web search and found three locations on this continent alone with faster tidal currents. In fact, the current speeds in a place called Surge Narrows, British Columbia (even sounds like a dangerous place, doesn't it?), which regularly clock in at a whopping 7.5 knots, are almost twice as fast as ours.

So all you Seacoast Region tourist brochure writers, now is the time to come clean. May I suggest a revision: "If you want to get all scientific about it, they probably wouldn't even make a list of the top ten or even twenty fastest tidal currents in the world. But the currents off Dover Point, where the Great Bay empties into the Piscataqua, those are our currents, darn it, all four knots of 'em, and we think they're alright."

You can witness Dover's pretty fast tidal currents at Hilton Park, just off westbound exit 5 of the Spaulding Turnpike, on Route 16 in Dover.

A Museum with Wonderfully Low Standards
Dover

Maybe you'll head to Dover's Woodman Institute for its extensive collection of nineteenth-century natural history specimens, from the towering stuffed polar bear, to the cuddly-looking manatee, to the last mountain lion shot and killed in New Hampshire (1847), down to the gaggles of stuffed birds, pinned moths, and pickled reptiles scattered throughout the museum. Or perhaps you'll come for the human history, including an entire seventeenth-century garrison house, impeccably preserved under a large open-walled shelter; Abraham Lincoln's saddle; and a suit of Japanese medieval armor.

Or you can come for the real curiosities. For starters, check out the 6-foot-long stuffed iguana, found dead by the side of the road right here in Dover (don't even ask), or the two-headed snake suspended in formaldehyde, or some other cloudy preservative, in an old-fashioned glass canning jar. He's hard to spot among his pickled compatriots, from bullfrogs to toads to rattlers, each in its own Ball jar of decades-old . . . juices, but if you bend down close enough to read the handwritten index cards, you'll spot him. Perhaps the museum's most famous animal oddity is the four-footed chicken—just a baby chick, really, with both front-wheel and what looks to be less functional rear-wheel drive.

But, if you're like me, you'll come for the oddest oddities: the glass display case of botanical curiosities that includes specimens like an ingrown branch (think ingrown toenail in the form of a tree branch); wood growing around a stone; a "natural cloth" that resembles a loosely woven stocking tied at one end, donated by an anonymous collector who harvested it from "some species of palm tree" (the collector didn't sweat the details, so why should we?); a 32-inch-thick wedge of bark from a redwood; and, my personal favorite, a "piece of wood badly eaten by ants," the gift (if you'll permit me to call it that) of one Mr. E. M. Bailey of Andover, Massachusetts.

The Woodman Institute's great strength is that it accepted such donations, and many more like them, because its directors lacked funds for acquisitions and so never had the luxury of saying no. Established in 1916 to encourage the study of local history, natural history, and art, the Woodman has accepted donations ranging from the original 1675 colonial garrison house, to a blackjack used to kill a local cashier in 1897, to a man-killing Australian clam. The eclectic collecting continues to this day. "We rarely say no to a donor," Thom Hindle, the current director, told me, "not only because we don't have money, but because we never know what else a donor might have tucked away in the attic."

The Woodman Institute, located at 182 Central Avenue in Dover, is open Wednesday through Sunday, except holidays. The museum drastically reduces its hours in December and shuts down entirely January through March. Admission is charged. For more information call (603) 742–1038.

A Parade for Those of Us with ADD

Durham

The first thing Mrs. Nobel Peterson gave me was a warning: "Now, if
you come this year and just plan to watch from the curb, well, I can
guarantee you'll be back next year marching in the parade, and then
the year after that you'll be the one cheering the loudest." The parade
she's talking about is Durham's Leif Eriksson Day Parade, and her warning to me was based on twenty-four years of experience. "We have people come back every year from all over the country, from Texas to
California to Michigan, just to march in our little parade," she told me.

Take special note of Mrs. Peterson's phrase "our *little* parade." The
parade isn't very big——there are no floats or marching bands or giant
inflated Disney characters—just a large group of people marching
down the street. And it just may be the shortest parade route in the
world. "We gather in front of the Laundromat around 6:00 A.M., admire
each other's Scandinavian flags, practice our cheers, then study the
parade route to be sure no one gets lost," she explained to me. "Then
at exactly 6:30 A.M. we march 25 feet to Young's Coffee Shop, where we
all have breakfast." And that's it. Throw in thirty seconds of singing
each Scandinavian national anthem followed by "The Star-Spangled
Banner" (in its entirety, of course), a brief Parade of Beautiful Sweaters,
and a scripted question-and-answer session about the parade itself—
including the questions "Why is the parade so early?" and "What proof
is there that Leif Eriksson discovered North America in A.D. 1000?" in
response to which the whole crowd shouts out the answers—and
you've got the entire program of Durham's Leif Eriksson Day Parade.
(Take note: Young's serves free coffee and free Viking cake, but each
marcher buys his or her own breakfast.)

The event takes place each year on the Sunday closest to October 9,
the date President Lyndon Johnson declared Leif Eriksson Day way back

in 1964. In a bit of explorer coincidence, Leif Eriksson Day coincides with Columbus Day weekend, but, according to Mrs. Peterson, divided loyalties aren't a problem. "The only requirement for participating in the parade," she says, "is that you be an admirer of Leif Eriksson's that morning. In the afternoon, you're free to march in some other explorer's parade, of course." And, of course, with Leif's modest 25-foot parade route, you'll have energy to spare.

For information or to make reservations, call Mrs. Nobel Peterson at (603) 868–9692.

"Give Me a Burger, Hold the Suds"
Durham

You've probably heard it said that good help is hard to find. Not so for Franz Guest, owner, cook, and grocery buyer at Franz's Food on Main Street in Durham. Durham, of course, is home to the University of New Hampshire, with its population of 10,500 potential cooks and counter helpers between the cash-starved ages of eighteen and twenty-three, and Franz's Food just happens to be a gourmet sandwich and burger joint located inside a Laundromat. "Most of my hires have happened right here," Franz said as he perched atop one of the top-loading commercial washing machines lined up no more than six paces from the register. "Skye was sitting right where I am, on this washer," he said, gesturing toward a young woman behind the counter with a 200-watt smile, "and I said to her, 'Hey, you want a job?' And she's been here three years—right, Skye?"

The Laundromat, it turns out, is under different ownership, hence Franz's relative indifference to people sitting on the washers. But the restaurant is Franz's and so is the food. The best in town, some locals say, and he doesn't even have a single table or chair in the place—there isn't any space among the Maytags. The whole restaurant looks to be about the size of a large bathroom. In the warmer months you're able to sit outside at one of the sidewalk tables and people watch. In the colder months you can do takeout or fight for space on top of one of the washers. Such limited space demands both creativity and a little extra work: For dry-goods storage, Franz installed cupboards beneath the Laundromat's folding counters, and he goes grocery shopping twice a day on average, since demand for dishes like his ChewWOWahhh (a chili dog) and Dog and Pony Show (a big hot dog with a horseradish, mayonnaise, and garlic "Pony Sauce") outstrips his fairly limited refrigerator space.

The day I visited, I ordered a scrumptious veggie burger. To go, of course. And hold the starch. Franz's Food is at 41 Main Street. For orders call (603) 868–3800.

Give me a veggie burger and hold the starch.

Exeter's Little Incident

Exeter

The Seacoast's preponderance of UFO sightings is a little vexing for area residents, especially since coastal Graniteers like to believe that they're at least as sane as citizens in the White Mountains or (please, oh please let it be true) the Great North Woods. As of August 2005, though, there had been more than 145 reported UFO sightings in the Seacoast's Rockingham County, a figure that makes it the state's undisputed county champion of alleged extraterrestrial visitations.

Perhaps the most famous of the Seacoast's many UFO sightings (could it have something to do with proximity to Massachusetts?) happened on the night of September 3, 1965, in and around the town of Exeter. Of the five UFO witnesses that night, two were Exeter police officers: David Hunt and air force veteran Eugene Bertrand. Largely as a result of the patrolmen's credibility, the United States Air Force later acknowledged that the sightings, which have come to be known as the "Incident at Exeter" (the title of John G. Fuller's 1966 best-selling book about the sightings), involved an unidentified flying object.

As the story goes, Norman Muscarello, an eighteen-year-old navy recruit from Exeter, was returning home on foot from his girlfriend's house in Amesbury, Massachusetts, when an object, which he later described as being "as big as a house" with bright red pulsating lights, suddenly appeared in the sky before him. The object silently "wobbled" closer and closer toward Muscarello until, utterly terrified, he dropped into a ditch beside the road. After the UFO backed away and disappeared over the horizon, Muscarello flagged down a vehicle and asked the driver to take him to the Exeter police station, where he told his story to officer Gene Bertrand, who just an hour earlier had interviewed a Seacoaster who claimed she had been chased in her car by a large low-flying object with flashing red lights for a distance of about 12 miles.

Muscarello joined Officer Bertrand in his cruiser and led him back to the field on the Dining family farm where the young man had first seen the object. After a brief investigation yielded nothing, Officer Bertrand heard Muscarello scream and turned to find what he would later describe as "a huge, shapeless object with five sequentially pulsating-from-left-to-right bright red lights" slowly rise above a stand of pines. The object seemed to tilt back and forth and float toward them with a motion that reminded Bertrand of a falling leaf. As Officer Bertrand made a hasty retreat toward his cruiser with a petrified Muscarello in tow (poor Norm!), officer David Hunt arrived on the scene. All three then watched as the UFO disappeared in the direction of Hampton, where an object of similar description was allegedly observed just minutes later by an anonymous motorist.

5-O and UFOs once met in this field.

Officials at Pease Air Force Base and at the Pentagon offered various explanations, including glare from airfield lights and nighttime refueling exercises, but both explanations seemed highly unlikely, especially the latter, since Officer Bertrand had been an air force refueling specialist. The mystery went unsolved, and remains so to this day, making Exeter's incident one of the few government-certified UFO sightings.

To see the field where the UFO sighting occurred, travel out of Exeter toward Kensington on Route 150 or Amesbury Road. Once you cross the Exeter line, it's about a half mile to the field (now surrounded by a white fence) on the east side of the road where Brewer Road intersects with Amesbury.

The Worst Band You Didn't Know You'd Love
Fremont

The Shaggs, a '60s-era rock act, were three teens from Fremont whose father withdrew them from the local high school, scraped together money for musical instruments and lessons twice a week in Manchester, and designed for his daughters a rigorous daily schedule of morning practice, afternoon mail-order home schooling, more practice, and then dinner. Oh, and to finish out the evening, the girls performed a round of calisthenics and, you guessed it, rehearsed one last time.

One would think all that practice and self-sacrifice might turn Helen, Betty, and Dot Wiggin into rock virtuosos, but the fruit of all those jam sessions and leg lifts was far more interesting than mere virtuosity. Described as "primitive," "raw," "unpolished," and "aboriginal" by their more generous reviewers, the Shaggs inspire in their listeners extremes of either appreciation or disgust. To wit: Frank Zappa reportedly said the Shaggs were better than the Beatles. And Lester Bangs, a music critic for the *Village Voice*, claimed that their harmonies sounded like "three singing nuns who've been sniffing lighter fluid." Their music must be heard to be believed.

The Shaggs started small and, much to their father Austin Wiggin's chagrin, they stayed small. For five years, beginning in 1968 and ending in 1973, the Wiggin sisters played in public almost exclusively at Saturday evening performances in the Fremont Town Hall, where as many as a hundred of their peers gathered to chat, dance, and, on occasion, heckle the sisters on stage. Dot led the group through sets that included a song celebrating parents ("Parents are the ones who are aaalwaays there!" she croons) and a number about Dot's lost cat named Foot Foot

Austin spent most of his savings on the recording of a Shaggs album in the spring of 1969, *Philosophy of the World*. Neither the girls nor the studio producer felt the group was ready to record, but Austin reportedly said he wanted to "get them while they're hot." The record didn't make any splash at all. A few years later, Austin brought the girls down to Boston for another recording session, but by 1973 Fremont had put a stop to the Shaggs' town hall performances and the sisters, by then in their twenties, were beginning to bristle under their father's strict managerial style. In 1975, when Austin died suddenly of a heart attack at the age of forty-seven, the band died, too.

End of story, right? Wrong. In the 1970s collectors got hold of copies of *Philosophy of the World,* and over the next three decades the album was rereleased a couple of times. With each rerelease the Shaggs got a little more attention and acquired a whole new crew of puzzled, bemused, but often adoring fans—slowly but surely the Shaggs were becoming an outsider music sensation. After best-selling author Susan Orlean wrote an article titled "Meet the Shaggs" in the *New Yorker* in 1999, Tom Cruise's production company optioned the film rights. As of this writing, a musical called *The Shaggs: Philosophy of the World* is opening off-Broadway after a successful run in Chicago. Really. The Wiggin sisters, who all still live within a dozen miles of Fremont, seem as surprised by their new fame as their fans, but they're just as sweet and good-natured as ever. Austin would be shocked to learn how long he really had to get the Shaggs while they're hot.

Grass Drag Championships
Fremont

Just in case you've ever wondered (and I know some of you have), snowmobiles don't really need snow to go mobile. A grassy field, some dirt, even a small pond will do in a pinch. In fact, once you've attended the New Hampshire Snowmobile Association's Grass Drags and Water Crossing Championships, held each Columbus Day weekend on Phil Peterson's Brookvale Farm in Fremont, you might even begin to wonder if there's any surface out there a true snowmobile fanatic wouldn't at least try to ride. (A gravel road? A rocky beach?) Still, just because you can do something doesn't necessarily mean you *should* do it—you little ones at home take note.

First held in 1985, the three-day snowmobile event has grown by leaps and bounds each year and is now billed as the nation's largest Grass Drags and Water Crossing Championships. Not to brag or anything, but here in New Hampshire we're able to draw bigger crowds of people than anywhere else to an event consisting of men and women drag racing their snowmobiles on grass and dirt and, oh yeah, over water, too, at speeds in excess of 110 miles per hour. It's an accomplishment of sorts, don't you think?

Need a little more explanation of the sport? A grass drag race is held on a 500-foot-long straight-line grass and dirt track. Each heat consists of four snowmobile racers lined up side-by-side on the track. When they're given the green light, the racers tear off down the track, dirt and grass flying from the sleds until they reach speeds as high as 115 mph on their way to the finish line. Each race is over in about five seconds.

The water cross component of the event is just about what you'd expect: a snowmobile race around a small island in a pond located in the middle of a farmer's field. Racers get a running start on an acceleration track and then try to see who can do the best job of making his or her snowmobile act like a boat. Obviously, sinking is an undesirable side effect, since snowmobiles aren't boats, but most riders make it around on sheer speed and guts.

Lauren, a grass drag fan from Concord, tried to describe the appeal of the sport for me: "There's so much about it that just feels off—the warm fall weather, the grass track, the water and the mud. It's like doing something your mother told you not to do with a bunch of your friends and getting away with it." Oh, now I get it—Snowmobile Free or Die.

The New Hampshire Snowmobile Association's Grass Drags and Water Crossing Championships are held each year in the middle of October at Phil Peterson's Brookvale Farm on Martin Road in Fremont. For directions and information go to www.nhgrassdrags.com or call (603) 237–8449.

George Washington's Naughty "Girl"
Greenland

Wouldn't it be great if one of George Washington's slaves had escaped, fled to the north, and settled here in New Hampshire? And wouldn't it be even better if, instead of taking his loss of free help in stride, old George wrote numerous whiney letters to a polite, ever-diplomatic, but less-than-cooperative New Hampshire official in a failed attempt to get his slave (actually, former slave, now free woman) put on a ship and brought back to Virginia? Wouldn't there be some kind of New Hampshire pride in that?

Well, it's a great story, and even all the more enjoyable because it's true. Ona Maria Judge, a house slave of George Washington's, escaped from Philadelphia by ship to Portsmouth in the summer of 1796, toward the end of the second term of Washington's presidency. In a letter sent to Joseph Whipple, Collector of the Port of Portsmouth, Washington said that "the girl" was a particular favorite of Mrs. Washington's and "handy and useful to her, being a perfect Mistress of her needle." Washington went on to say that "the ingratitude of the girl, who was brought up and treated more like a child than a Servant . . . ought not to escape with impunity if it can be avoided." He suggested she be seized and "put on board a vessel bound immediately to this place [Philadelphia]."

Washington and Whipple's correspondence stretches over a period of months, with Whipple remaining ever polite, ever diplomatic, but somehow ever unable to carry out the president's requests. In his first letter to Washington, he is happy to report that Ona "declared her willingness to return & to serve with fidelity during the lives of the President & his Lady if she could be freed on their decease, should she outlive them." Washington writes back to explain to Whipple that it would simply be unfair to reward "Oney's" ingratitude with special favors and "thereby discontent . . . the minds of all her fellow-servants who are far more deserving than herself of favor." The president again asks Whipple to seize Ona and put her on a ship, preferably one bound for Virginia, but to be careful not to incite a mob or a riot. When Whipple writes back to the president, he again reports only "failure," claiming it was impossible for him to tell whether seizing Ona would incite a riot since "so far as I have had opportunity to perceive . . . different sentiments are entertained [among the public] on this subject [of slavery]."

The Washingtons persisted in their attempts to retrieve Ona but to no avail. She married John Staines in 1797, and the couple had two daughters, Eliza and Nancy. The family settled in Portsmouth, but Ona Maria Staines lived out the last decades of her long free life on Dearborn Road in Greenland, either an ungrateful escaped servant girl, if you want to take George's view, or the epitome of a New Hampshire woman, one who chose freedom even at the risk of death.

Dearborn Road is just off Route 33 in Greenland. To read the full text of the letters excerpted above, visit the Weeks Public Library in Greenland at 36 Post Road (two doors down from the Greenland Central School) and pick up the manuscript "A Quiet Abiding Place," by Paul Hughes. For hours of operation and information call (603) 436–8548.

All Aboard the Trolley Cottage!
Hampton

Admittedly, the little stone house at 303 Mill Road doesn't really look like a trolley car. Neither does it act like a trolley car nor sound like a trolley car nor smell like one, if trolley cars can be said to have their own particular odor (crowded trolley cars perhaps . . .). But I, the author, assure you that the gray fieldstone and mortar walls of the little cottage on Mill Road are but the candy shell to the home's Tootsie Roll center of a trolley car. And I've got pictures to prove it.

The trolley car cottage was the brainchild of Ernest L. White, a Hampton stonemason and carpenter who, in 1934, purchased an 1897 Briggs trolley car body and had it moved to the Mill Road site. He then set to work pillaging stone walls in the area for building materials, carting the stones to the trolley by wheelbarrow, and cementing them in with great care and precision all around the car. By the time White was finished, the entire trolley, with the exception of the windows and doors, was completely encased in stonework and hidden from view, a trolley car entombed behind thick gray walls of granite. And his wife was impressed by the results. "You wouldn't think an old trolley car would make such a cute little place," Mrs. White noted in her diary, though originally she must have had her doubts.

The White family no longer owns the home. In fact, when I visited in the fall of 2005, a contractor was renovating the house for its current owners, who live in California and are planning to rent the place out. (That's right—the trolley house is for rent!) The contractor was kind enough to give me a quick tour inside. The ceiling's a little low in the kitchen, and the windows in front are shaped the same as a trolley's, wider than they are tall, and

Definitely the very last stop for this trolley.

there's a slight bow to the walls at the front of the house, where Ernest built around the nose and tail curves of the trolley, but beyond that, it's just your average comfortable cottage. A cute little place, just like Mrs. White said. And it all could be yours, to rent anyways, if you're in the market for a once-mobile home.

A Fake with a Long Shelf Life

Hampton

Some lucky fakes can get so famous, it doesn't matter that they're phony—no matter what, they'll always be stars. As a case in point, I submit Hampton's Viking rock, best known as Thorvald's Rock. Legend has it that Thorvald's Rock, which now sits on the grounds of the Tuck Museum in a shallow well with iron bars across the mouth to protect the stone from souvenir seekers, once marked the Boar's Head burial site of the Viking explorer Thorvald Eriksson, brother of the more famous Leif Eriksson and son of Erik the Red. Those scratches visible on the rock, legend also has it, are ancient runes.

The legend probably started on July 4, 1902, when Hampton district court judge Charles A. Lamprey published a piece in the local newspaper making the case that a strangely gouged stone on his family's coastal property marked the grave of the Viking explorer Thorvald. According to Viking sagas recorded in medieval Icelandic manuscripts, Thorvald was retracing his brother's discovery of Vinland (what is now known as North America) in A.D. 1004 when he found a stunning rock outcropping that reminded him of the fiords back home. Shortly thereafter he came ashore, skirmished with local Indians, was mortally wounded by an arrow to the armpit, and with his last gasping breaths requested burial ashore. Those rocks in the legend, Lamprey argued, had to be Boar's Head, the rocky promontory just north of Hampton

Beach, even though, truth be told, there are more than a few rocky out-croppings along the 3,000 or so miles of coastline between here and Canada. And the strangely gouged stone on Lamprey's property, it stood to reason (for reasons not altogether clear), marked Thorvald's final resting place.

Somehow the highly unverifiable and extremely unlikely, almost certainly totally untrue legend got spread by way of tourist brochures, real-estate developers, and newspaper accounts alike, and the rock became famous. It had a particularly eventful twentieth century: Sometime in the 1950s, it was moved to make way for new construction in the area. Then in 1973 local amateur archeologists reportedly searched for Thorvald's remains at the site where the stone once lay and came up empty-handed. Tourists sought out the rock on visits; some even chipped off pieces to take home as souvenirs. According to one report, an

Could a Viking rock get a restraining order on a man from Massachusetts?

enterprising but unethical man from Massachusetts even tried to take the whole rock home with him in his truck. Finally, in 1989 Thorvald's Rock was moved to the Tuck Museum where it rests to this day, safe—albeit behind bars—from amateur archaeologists, souvenir hunters, Viking fanatics, and a certain guy from Massachusetts with a pickup truck and a plan.

The Tuck Museum is located at 40 Park Avenue in Hampton; Thorvald's Rock is on the museum grounds close to Park Avenue. For museum hours and other information call (603) 929–0781.

Pardoned 300 Years Too Late

Hampton

Goody Cole's crimes, if she was in fact guilty of them, weren't necessarily of the cruelest, most blood-curdling variety. A young girl alleged that Goody had spoken to her through a cat. A couple of neighbors accused her of putting a curse on a cow. Oh, and two women claimed that they heard moaning in the wind whenever they spoke Goody's name. Such was the "evidence" that put Goody Cole, New Hampshire's only convicted witch, behind bars for the last few decades of her life.

It was 1656, decades before the Salem witch trials, when Eunice "Goody" Cole of Hampton was tried and convicted of witchcraft and sentenced to life imprisonment in Boston. In her eighties she was released and lived a pauper in Hampton her remaining years, depending on care and support from the very citizens who had imprisoned her. Legend has it that when she died, townspeople drove a stake through her heart before burying her on unconsecrated ground in an unmarked grave. Talk about getting shafted.

In 1938, the year of Hampton's tricentennial celebrations, a local group called the Society in Hampton for the Apprehension of Those

Falsely Accusing Eunice "Goody" Cole of Having Had Familiarity With the Devil (whew, that's a mouthful) formed for the sole purpose of rehabilitating Goody's good name. The town issued a proclamation exonerating her of all witchcraft charges but, surprisingly, not specifically apologizing for the years of false imprisonment or the whole stake-through-the-heart thing. Members of the group with the long name then burned copies of Cole's seventeenth-century court records and placed them in a tin along with samples of soil from her supposed home and burial sites. According to reports, citizens planned to erect a stone monument to Goody Cole and bury the ashes of her court records beneath it. For some reason the plan never materialized, and the ashes still remain, unburied, sitting at the Tuck Museum.

Goody got imprisoned for witchcraft, and all she got was this rock.

(Maybe that's why Goody's ghost is said to roam the town green on moonless nights.) You can also find an odd-looking unmarked erosion stone that's said to honor Goody on the Tuck Museum property, right near Thorvald's Rock.

The Tuck Museum is located at 40 Park Avenue in Hampton. For hours of operation and other information call (603) 929–0781.

Pro Sand Castle Builders Compete to Justify Dubious Career Choice
Hampton Beach

Greg Grady's serious about sand. So serious, in fact, that he's one of only about 250 master sand sculptors worldwide who can make a living "in sand," attending sand-sculpting competitions and creating commissioned sand sculptures for individuals, municipalities, and businesses. "A bunch of us sat around trying to figure out how many of us there were, and we came up with about 250," Grady said. "Now, of course, that's not set in stone, but it's a pretty good estimate." Don't you think it's kind of funny for a sand sculptor to say, "That's not set in stone?"

Grady is the organizer of the Hampton Beach Master Sand-Sculpting Competition, held each year at the end of June. A dozen master sand sculptors have twenty-one hours over a period of three days to create original works of art out of their individual allotments of ten tons of sand and all the water they want. "One of the biggest misconceptions people have," Grady told me, "is that we do something tricky to the sand [to create sculptures]. There are no tricks: just sand and water, that's it." (Only after the sculptures are finished can artists spray them with a 10 percent glue and water solution to help prevent damage.)

By the looks of things in 2005, sculptors shy away from castles. Creations that year included Adam and Eve on opposite sides of a towering apple tree and two mill workers wrestling with a piece of cloth jammed up in the huge gears of a factory loom. Judges choose first- through fifth-place winners based on artistic merit, technical difficulty, and overall design, and, with over $10,000 in prize money, the stakes are high. There's also a people's choice award, so you can vote for your own favorite.

While sand sculpting may sound like a great career, don't quit your day job just yet. There are risks beyond sunstroke and premature wrinkling. In the 2005 competition, one of the sculptures fell only an hour before judging, no laughing matter for the sculptor, Fred Mallet of South Padre Island, Texas, or for Greg Grady. "Ten tons of sand is no joke," he told me. "Someone could get really hurt." Luckily, Fred escaped unharmed, but others aren't so lucky. As a case in point, Grady recalled a competition down in Fort Myers when an inebriated spring breaker tried knocking down a competitor's sand sculpture to get a laugh out of his friends: "He kind of ran and tackled the thing, and then he just lay there, crying. An ambulance came and took him away—I think he dislocated his shoulder." That's one college student who won't miss his GREs to go build castles in the sand.

The Hampton Beach Master Sand-Sculpting Competition is held at the end of each June right on Hampton Beach. For information go to www.hamptonbeach.org or, if you'd like to volunteer at the event, call (603) 926–8718.

Round Up Those Breakdowns, We're Having a Wrecker Rodeo!
Hampton Beach

If you don't get a proper warning that the New Hampshire Towing Association is coming to town, you might mistake their wrecker parade—wherein hundreds of tow trucks large, medium, and small, yellow lights flashing, drive down the Hampton Beach strip—for a tow truck convoy headed off to clear some massive freeway pile-up. Of course, that's not the case. But watching tow truck after tow truck (and tow truck driver after tow truck driver) parade by, one can't help but stop and wonder: Who's going to come to the rescue if some poor soul does break down and needs a tow?

Each year in the middle of May, hundreds of tow trucks from all over New England parade through Hampton and down Ocean Boulevard, lights flashing and horns honking. While it's fun to get a close look at all those wreckers, especially without the anxiety of actually needing one, the parade is just a preamble, really, to the tow truck rodeo at Hampton Beach State Park. Drivers in the rodeo compete in four different classes—light duty, medium duty, flatbed, and heavy duty—for prizes and all-important bragging rights.

Events include the Timed Tire Change, the Barrel Race Round-Up, the Rolled-Over RV Removal, and the Customer Chitchat and Chow Down (a duel event consisting of an idle-chitchat-in-the-cab competition followed by a chili-dog-eating contest). Actually, I made those events up, but the competitions at the Wrecker Rodeo are just as fun. Okay, almost as fun. There's a timed obstacle course and a timed hitch and ride event, as well as a beauty pageant for the most attractive wreckers. Just for the sake of clarity, that's a beauty pageant for the trucks, not their drivers. Of course, a driver beauty pageant (would there be a swimsuit round?) really would be something to see. Something to see and then forget very, very quickly.

For information about the New Hampshire Towing Association's Trade Show and Wrecker Rodeo, visit www.nhtowingassociation.com. The location of the trade show and rodeo may change year to year, so be sure to confirm beforehand.

Buried Treasure Discovered

Isles of Shoals

Take an archipelago of tiny rocky islands about 9 miles off the coast of New Hampshire, add one isolated eighteenth-century village of fishermen and their families, sprinkle liberally with a couple of centuries worth of visits from curious tourists, shake well, and what do you get? More legends, lore, and ghost tales than you can shake an oar at.

Technically, only four of the nine islands that comprise the Isles of Shoals are in New Hampshire. The other five, including the wonderfully named Smuttynose and Appledore Islands, fall under the jurisdiction of a state to our north that will remain nameless. And if you think state borders wouldn't mean so much to people living on a group of small islands out in the cold, deep waters of the Atlantic Ocean, then think again. The famously uncivilized and hard-drinking eighteenth-century fishing village of Gosport on New Hampshire's Star Island was founded when our northern neighbor decided to tax the hundreds of fishermen living on Appledore and Smuttynose. Rather than pay taxes, the fishermen dismantled their homes and moved the quarter mile or so to Star Island, where they remained, untaxed and largely ungoverned by authorities until the Revolutionary War.

Books have been filled with Isles of Shoals history and lore, but the tales that seem to best capture the imaginations of tourists and locals alike are the ones about buried treasure. According to one famous local legend, Captain Samuel Haley, one-time owner of Smuttynose Island, found three or four bars of silver under a rock sometime around 1815. Unverified though the story is, it seems to give credence to other tales of buried treasure on the Isles of Shoals. Most famous among them is the legend of the pirate Blackbeard, aka Edward Teach, who in the early 1700s is rumored to have stashed some booty on Lunging Island (or is it Star Island, or maybe Smuttynose?) and then left behind his thirteenth wife to guard it. Oh, and need I mention that this thirteenth wife is said to roam the Isles in a white gown on moonless nights, waiting for her husband to return? The legend has prompted speculation, historical research, and even on-site scientific investigation, but so far no one has turned up a shred of evidence that Blackbeard's treasure was ever buried on the Isles.

But treasure hunters take solace. The first verified discovery of buried treasure was made on Star Island in the summer of 2005. Those who made the find won't divulge where the treasure was unearthed for fear of drawing unmanageable crowds of middle-aged men with metal detectors and headsets. The booty? An old penny from 1853 with a profile of a female liberty surrounded by a circle of stars. Does a penny leave you . . . underwhelmed? But it's the first verified discovery of money on the island. Who knows how many more pennies are yet to be uncovered? And, more importantly, who knows what unquiet souls might still be wandering the Isles of Shoals on moonless nights, searching for all that petty cash?

There's no telling how much petty cash might be buried on these Isles.

The Isles of Shoals Steamship Company, located at 315 Market Street in Portsmouth, offers twice-daily sightseeing tours of Portsmouth Harbor and the Isles of Shoals from May through October, with close views of the Isles but no disembarking. For information call (603) 431–5500. If you'd like to visit Star Island, there are a number of different charter companies to choose from, but I'll list only two here. Sail Amaryllis offers summer sunset sailing cruises aboard a 45-foot catamaran with dinner at the nineteenth-century Oceanic Hotel on Star Island. Call (603) 205–0630 for details. Island Cruises, which sails from Rye Harbor in Rye, offers both lunch and dinner visits to Star Island throughout the summer and early fall. Call (603) 964–6446 for more information.

Looks Like a Job for "Really Annoying Man"!
Isles of Shoals

This may take the prize for one of the most unusual jobs in the state, and it's a government job no less: Official Gull Harasser. Since 1997 the state's Nongame and Endangered Wildlife Program, in partnership with the Audubon Society of New Hampshire and other state and federal organizations, has been working to reintroduce, manage, and protect a population of common terns on the Isles of Shoals. In order to give the terns their old home back, though, tern biologists first had to scare off a whole gang of gulls that had moved in and taken over the place. And they had to keep scaring them so that the terns could nest, lay eggs, and multiply. Their efforts are paying off: In 1997 only six pairs of common terns bred on the Isles. Just five years later, there were over 1,700 pairs, and the numbers have increased even more since then. (Needless to say, the gulls, in typical NIMBY fashion, are not happy about what's become of the neighborhood.)

Your mission, should you accept it, is to annoy the heck out of these gulls.

One pivotal part of the
program is what biologists like
to call a "continuous human presence"
on Seavey Island to ward off gulls, but what I choose to call "gull harass-
ing." So how do you annoy a gull? (Now that's a question that sounds like
it deserves a punch line.) "Gulls are sensitive to some of the same stimuli
we are," John Kanter, the head of Nongame and Endangered Wildlife,
told me. "They don't like to be startled; they don't like loud noises."

So state and Audubon Society biologists shot off lots of fireworks in
early April of the first year of the project to prevent gulls from nesting on
the island; they clapped their hands and waved their arms when the fire-

works began to seem like overkill; and rumor has it that some staff even took to constantly nagging the seagulls to move out in the way parents are wont to do. Then they laid decoys and set up a sound system that played tern calls day and night to attract migrating terns to nest on the island. The gulls phoned in other requests, but to no avail—it was all-tern-calls-all-the-time. (Seems they wanted to hear gull cries instead, or, better yet, the mellow thud of a garbage can toppling to the ground.) And what did the biologists get for all this annoying and antisocial behavior? A paycheck. Sometimes life is so much more than fair.

 The tern reintroduction project is taking place on Seavey Island, which at low tide is connected to White Island and its 1859 lighthouse. Both islands are inaccessible to tour boats since they lack navigable landings, but they and the terns are quite visible during sightseeing tours of the Isles of Shoals. See the preceding Isles of Shoals entry for information about charter boat operators and tours, or visit www.wildlife.state.nh.us to learn more about the wildlife program.

UIO: Unidentified Immobile Object

Kensington

Look, what's that, over there, in front of the American Legion? It's a tank! It's an amphibious vehicle! It's an overgrown fuse box on tracks! Now, wait a minute . . . What the heck is that?

 The, um, "vehicle" parked outside Kensington's Legion Post 150 is certainly not your ordinary tank in the grass. If I were pressed to give my humble opinion, I'd have to say it most closely resembles an armored car that's been flattened a little and then set on top of double snowmobile tracks. All you World War I and World War II buffs needn't even bother writing in to tell me how ill-informed I am regarding twentieth-century war machines. I wouldn't know an amphibious assault vehicle from a Sherman tank, even if one of each rolled over me in quick succession and left perfectly visible track marks on my back.

For help with identification, you might think we could go to the members of Kensington's American Legion, but some of them don't even know when the vehicle appeared on their property, let alone how it got there or what it is. According to various reports, the whatchamacallit is either an M29 Studebaker Weasel tracked cargo carrier (an amphibious snowmobile and jeep combo originally designed for fighting in Nazi-occupied Norway) or a United Defense LP Lynx Command Amphibian. Or it could just be a little-known Volkswagen model from the '70s, some close cousin of the Volkswagen Thing painted a nice army green. Hey, it's possible. Have you ever seen a Volkswagen Thing? They definitely look like something you might drop from an airplane.

The vehicle, whatever it's called, is located in front of the Kensington American Legion Post at 195 Amesbury Road (or Route 150).

It's a tank, no it's an amphibious vehicle, no it's a—wait, what the heck is that?

The Garbage Man's Dilemma: Trash Art at the Curb

Lee

Former Marine Corps sergeant Peter MacDonald is a man who makes a statement with his art. Denied a permit to build a barn on his own property in 1989 after a neighbor allegedly registered a complaint with the town planning board about possible disruptions to her view, MacDonald decided to create a giant trash art installation in his front yard instead. He couldn't put a pony in it, but at least a work of art would be exempt from zoning laws under a little clause in our Constitution protecting freedom of speech. And that includes trash talking.

He went to the dump; picked up cast-off household appliances, broken furniture, and other unsightly rejectementa; and then just listened carefully to his muses, placing this old rusty piece of metal here, that three-legged chair there,

Junk art with a message, a very long message.

and presto, he had his very own work of junk art, displayed right where everyone could get a good view, including the neighbor who had filed the complaint: at the very edge of his property along Packersfalls Road.

If you're not the type who enjoys reading abstract, highbrow, or somewhat confusing artist statements (I've never read one that wasn't at least a little confusing), just feel free to ignore the many plywood boards filled with commentary that lean pell-mell against Peter's masterpiece for the edification of the public. MacDonald's been teaching what he calls "trashformation art" to schoolchildren for almost thirty years, so he's got a lot to say; in fact, he claims his credentials as an artist have helped him block attempts to have the art removed.

While the junk art installation may not seem like the most neighborly of gestures, MacDonald takes a very philosophical approach to conflict and claims that he has no beef against his neighbor: "She was just exercising her rights," he said. In fact, he even shoveled out said neighbor's mailbox for years, just because he felt it was the right thing to do. Come to think of it, maybe the state motto could use a little amending: "Live Free or Die, yes, but don't forget to be decent to your neighbor."

You can find Peter MacDonald's trashformation art at 465 Packersfalls Road in Lee. From downtown Durham follow Mill Road west for a little less than 3 miles, and the objet d'art will be on your right.

This Divided House Won't Fall

Portsmouth

Strawberry Banke is the name of both the original settlement that later became the city of Portsmouth and a wonderful museum restoration of an almost 400-year-old ten-acre waterfront neighborhood over on the northeast side of town. In the 1950s the neighborhood was slated for the wrecking ball, proclaimed a slum by city officials, its land taken by eminent domain, its inhabitants forced to find new homes. Luckily, citizens concerned about saving Portsmouth's history formed a nonprofit, bought the land back from the city, and founded the Strawberry Banke Museum.

SKINNY HOUSE ENVY OF NEIGHBORHOOD

Inquiring houses want to know: What's the skinny on how to get thin and stay thin? The secret is in the building. Right on Main Street in downtown Newmarket, there's a house so skinny, it's the envy of all the duplexes and McMansions in town. Only about 12 feet wide (and some spare change), the brick building is a standard two stories tall but very, very long, which enables it to house not only a small street-front tattoo parlor on the first floor, but two apartment units in the back.

The building is for sale as of this writing, but it turns out you can't even buy a skinny place in the Seacoast area without having a pretty fat wallet: In the winter of 2006, it was listed for sale with Shanley Realty for a little under $300,000. A small plaque just beside the front door identifies it as the Edward Smith Building and gives a ballpark construction date: prior to 1830. Beyond that, no one I've spoken to knows anything about the history of the building or why it's so darn skinny. Most folks agree, though, it's got quite a sleek figure for a 175-year-old.

I had been told that the skinny house was in Portsmouth, but Seacoast writer and historian Dennis Robinson, creator of the Web site www.seacoastnh.com, directed me to this skinny house at 98 Main Street in downtown Newmarket, right next to Wheelies Restaurant.

A skinny building that's the envy of every duplex in town.

One of Strawberry Banke's many charms is that it's not a historical re-creation like other colonial museums. Instead, it's composed of more than thirty-five restored buildings, thirty of which sit right on their original foundations. Of course, you'll find old houses at Strawberry Banke, filled with all the antiques you might expect, from lumpy beds to looms. And you'll get to talk to historical re-enactors who never break character, dressed up in full period costume. But one of the most unusual features of the museum is that instead of representing only one distant historical period, the buildings and furnishings trace pivotal moments in the neighborhood's evolution over three centuries.

The strangest example of this historical medley is the Drisco House, a dynamic duplex that is half 1950s and half 1795. Think Dr. Jekyl and Mr.

A house with a centuries-long rift.

Hyde. At the front of the house on the east side you'll find a re-creation of a shop run by the building's very first inhabitants, the Shapleys, with wares including dried fish, tobacco, and grain. And on the western front half of the house you'll find a 1950s-era living room, intended to show what the home might have looked like when it was last occupied, complete with Howdy Doody on TV, some scary-looking TV dinners, and a Technicolor picture over the mantle of Jesus with his twelve disciples at the Last Supper. Oh yeah, and some mid-twentieth-century American wallpaper that'll really knock your socks off.

The Strawberry Banke Museum is located on Marcy Street in downtown Portsmouth. The museum's so-called self-guiding season, when Strawberry Banke is open seven days a week, runs May through October. The museum's guided tour season begins on the first of November and runs through the end of April, with tours on weekends and during Christmas and Thanksgiving week holidays. Call (603) 433–1100 for hours of operation and tour times.

Hauntingly Memorable Tours
Portsmouth

Take a walk around Portsmouth with ghost-tour guide Roxie Zwicker (go ahead, I double dog dare you!), and it won't be long before you'll start to wonder whether there just might be more ghosts than people in this old seaport. Founded in 1623, Portsmouth is one of the oldest towns in the original thirteen colonies, so old that ancient bones, and the ghosts that tend to go along with them, have had lots of time to pile up—and not just in the graveyards that are clearly marked. Fourteen eighteenth-century coffins were unearthed by accident a few years ago by a crew doing excavation work at a busy intersection downtown, and some historians believe still more remain under the feet of downtown strollers.

Portsmouth's Music Hall? Haunted, possibly by a woman who once lived at the almshouse that stood on the site and who reportedly caused the great fire of 1813. The newly renovated Rockingham Hotel? Yup, haunted too, by a woman who's rumored to smell like the sea (hopefully not at low tide). The John Paul Jones House, the Sise Inn, Point of Graves Cemetery, and the Portsmouth Harbor Lighthouse? Haunted, haunted, haunted, and, you guessed it, haunted like nobody's business. (A friendly warning: You may want to avoid room 204 in the Sise Inn if an amorous ghost trying to give you a hug or pull you into the closet is a big turnoff.)

The stories of these sundry hauntings will not only send shivers down your spine, they'll also give you a better understanding of the people who used to live here and what their lives were like before they died and picked up the habit of scaring the bejesus out of us.

Roxie, dressed all in black and carrying an old-fashioned lantern, will lead you to these and a whole slew of other places in town where normal, not so normal, and flagrantly paranormal activity all seem to go hand in hand on a surprisingly regular basis. She does a number of graveyard walks and a couple of different haunted lighthouse tours, as well as the downtown tours along Portsmouth's quaint cobblestone streets. And if you want to tour local watering holes where abnormal events, both explicable and inexplicable, occur on a regular basis, you can take Roxie's "Haunted Pubs of Portsmouth Walk," including a stop at Molly Malone's Pub, where the waitress who brings you your Guinness can also tell you about her most recent sighting of the ghost in the white coat. Of course, not all strange happenings at Molly Malone's can be blamed on the unquiet dead, but it's always nice to have a ready excuse at hand.

For more information about Roxie Zwicker's historic and ghostly walking tours, visit www.newenglandcuriosities.com or call Roxie at (207) 439–8905.

Exclusive Military Tower by the Sea

Rye

If the home at the small point near Rye Beach along coastal Route 1A between Hampton and Portsmouth looks a little strange to you and you want someone to start doing some explaining, well, then, you've come to the right place. If we're talking about the same strange house, the one located at 2565 Ocean Boulevard that looks like a child's creation with blocks writ large, then its first incarnation was as a World War II military tower, called a base-end station, built to protect Portsmouth Harbor and the Portsmouth Naval Shipyard from enemy surface ships.

After the bombing of Pearl Harbor, towers sprung up all along the coastline to help thwart any future surprise attacks on American soil. Operating in concert, the towers on the New Hampshire seacoast would have enabled the military to track enemy surface ships and provide precise targeting coordinates for long-range artillery fire intended to sink them. Some people will tell you these towers were intended to help lookouts spot enemy submarines, but

All hands (and other parts) on the nude deck! It's a beautiful day!

that's categorically false. (A tower on the shore, even a tall one, wouldn't give you a very good view of a submarine. Actually, it wouldn't give you any view of a submarine.) Thankfully, the guns the towers were intended to aim were never fired, since no surprise ship attacks occurred.

The U.S. Navy built the 72-foot-tall tower near Rye Beach in 1940, along with an attached barracks disguised as a colonial-style ocean cottage. In 1966 Edward Samara bought the tower at military auction and began renovations—including nightmare-inducing home improvement projects such as cutting a 15-foot window in the concrete tower and then siding the whole thing top to bottom in shingles—eventually transforming this lynchpin of World War II–era homeland security into a 3,300-square-foot, ten-room, five-bedroom, three-bath luxury home. One particularly striking feature of the house is what Lisa Ross, Samara's daughter, calls the "Nude Deck." A large walled platform atop a narrow concrete support that sits high above the home's main living space, it's the perfect place for sunbathing in the nude, if you're into that kind of thing, you cheeky little devil, you.

The home had been on the market, but has recently been sold. The asking price? Let's just say, if you have to ask you couldn't have afforded it. But look at it this way: By military standards, $1.9 million for a whole house, and with ocean views to boot, is dirt cheap. Let's just hope that toilet seats were included.

Croquet Anyone?

Rye

When it comes to sports equipment in the yard, most people like to keep it simple: maybe a basketball hoop on a pole out front, a trampoline beside the house, perhaps even a volleyball net out back. Not so Marie and Jim McLaughlin. Drive by their home in Rye on some sunny summer afternoon, and you're likely to see men and women dressed all in white swinging wooden mallets at little colored balls on a huge patch of artificial turf in the backyard. Anyone up for some regulation, United States Croquet Association–approved croquet?

Jim and Marie built the croquet field, or court, or lawn—I'm not sure what the proper terminology is here—after Jim's retirement. Jim had been a longtime marathon runner, but he and Marie wanted to find a pastime they could do together without so much . . . discomfort. It was

This is my idea of exercise.

Marie's idea to go with croquet, a nice civilized sport that, unlike marathon running, doesn't involve pounding pavement, sweating profusely, and ingesting copious amounts of that awful energy goop.Croquet typically involves wearing white clothes and gently swinging a wooden mallet, and then finishing things up by drinking champagne and eating strawberries. Which would you choose?

A local croquet club uses the McLaughlins' backyard for playing Six Wicket Croquet, a rather complicated tournament version of the game that seems to involve as much strategy as waging a world war. Thomas Kennedy, a club member, happened to be practicing on the McLaughlins' lawn when I drove by, and he was kind enough to explain the game to me as he quite expertly moved his balls around the Astroturf and through the narrow wooden wickets. "The game is a sort of hybrid of billiards, chess, and golf," he told me, "which is why I enjoy it so much. You really need to strategize and play the angles and execute your shots." And the rest he told me, about shot sequence and ball colors and stuff, kind of went through one ear and out the other. But it looked like a whole lot of fun—and I don't think Mr. Kennedy came even close to breaking a sweat.

Marie and Jim McLaughlin live at 115 Pioneer Road in Rye. Their croquet court is clearly visible behind the house.

ATLANTIC CABLE AND SUNKEN FOREST GET TOGETHER

The green historical marker across from Jenness Beach on Route 1A in Rye states that the receiving station for the first Atlantic telegraph cable is located nearby, but that's not entirely accurate. According to Anton A. Huurdeman in his book *The Worldwide History of Telecommunications*, the Rye cable was actually the fourth transatlantic submarine cable to be laid, but it has the distinction of being the first *direct* transatlantic cable, stretching all the way from Ballinskelligs Bay, Ireland, to Halifax, Nova Scotia, before making its way down to the Rye receiving station, located in what is now the beautiful 330-acre Odiorne Point State Park.

Even if you're used to dial-up, the first true transatlantic cable, laid in 1858, was a little slow. It took a whopping sixteen hours to send a ninety-five-word message of congratulations from Queen Victoria to President James Buchanan upon the cable's completion. (And you thought you had a hard time communicating with members of the opposite sex.) A few weeks later, when the cable's chief electrician tried to rectify signaling problems by increasing signal voltage, he cooked the cable and that was the end of the e-flirtation between the Queen and Mr. President.

If you visit Odiorne Point State Park at low tide, sources claim you can still find remnants of the fourth transatlantic cable among a group of tidal tree stumps and roots known as the Sunken Forest, the remains of an ancient forest dating back almost 4,000 years.

Odiorne Point State Park is located on Route 1A in Rye. From Portsmouth, follow Route 1A South about 5 miles, and the park will be on your left. The Sunken Forest is directly south of the Seacoast Science Center, an educational center that houses a petting tide pool and a 1,000-gallon aquarium. For more information go to www.nhstateparks.org or call (603) 436–7406.

Storage Fit for a King

Seabrook

Maree Gregoire and her husband, Al, have the keys to the castle, but unfortunately they don't own it—they're just the resident managers. "I wish we owned it," Maree told me, when I popped in for a quick visit on my way to check out the nature center and hiking trails at the Seabrook Station Nuclear Power Plant. (By the way, it turns out the nature center has dramatically reduced its hours of operation to what appears to be . . . never.) And who *wouldn't* want the keys to the castle and the castle as well? It's only normal, right?

The castle is Seacoast Mini Storage, a storage facility with a false-front castle motif located on Route 107 just east of Interstate 95. Truth be told, I'm not a big fan of storage facilities. But the castle on Route 107 is different: It's playful, it's pretty, it's got those cutouts along the tops of the walls that look like perfectly shaped jack-o'-lantern teeth (What the heck are those called?). It is certainly not just a bunch of metal sheds with row upon row upon row of stuff waiting to be moved.

But why did the owner decide to turn his storage sheds into a castle? "He wanted people to feel that if they stored their things here, they would be as safe as if they were locked away in a fortress," Maree explained. She said she liked the castle front, but she seemed to like the flowers the owner had planted in front of the castle even more. "He does such a nice job with it. You'll have to come back and get a picture of all the peonies in the spring."

Are there any other benefits to working in a castle? "Well, one nice thing is that when people ask for directions, I get to tell them, 'You cross over 95 on 107, and then we're the first castle on the left.'"

The Seacoast Mini Storage castle is on Route 107 in Seabrook, about a half mile west of I–95.

Storage fit for small kings and queens.

Seacoast
**MINI
STORAGE**
— 24ᴴᴿ· Surveillance —
CLIMATE CONTROL

MERRIMACK VALLEY

Here's to Snowmobiling and Roughing It with the Kids

Allenstown

You'll certainly come away from the New Hampshire Snowmobile
Museum with a heightened appreciation for the history and evolution
of the personal motorized snow vehicle we call the snowmobile, or, if
you're a real North Country type, the "snow machine." But you might
also walk away with some questions. When it came to naming their
snowmobiles, for example, why were manufacturers so dead-set
against using the letter *w*? Among the many vintage snowmobiles in
the museum's collection, you'll find the Sno Cub, the Sno Pony, the Sno
Ghia, and the Sno-Traveler, all lacking the *w*, of course, and all featuring
designs so pared down and, well, retro, they look as much like children's toys as they do real machines built for cruising over the sno,
I mean snow.

Crammed in among its wall-to-wall rows of Arctic Cat and Ski-Doo
and Polaris sleds from the 1960s and '70s, the New Hampshire Snowmobile Museum collection contains some real rarities, including the
Lombard Log Hauler, a nineteen-ton behemoth invented in 1908 in
Waterville, Maine, and reported to be the first machine designed for
snow travel; a 1920s-era Model T Ford, outfitted with Virgil T. White's
patented "snowmobile" conversion kit; and the Arctic Cat that helped
driver Denis Boucher earn a spot in the *Guinness Book of World*

45

Records for traveling 10,252 miles on a snowmobile from Alaska to Nova Scotia over fifty-six frigid days in 1992. Perhaps the strangest snowmobile of the whole lot, though, is the 1973 Inovar Sno-Coupe, a snowmobile with a body designed to resemble a flashy 1970s-era car. (Of course, the *w* at the end of *Sno* didn't come standard.)

The New Hampshire Snowmobile Museum is just one of two great museums on the grounds of a Depression-era Civilian Conservation Corps camp located in Allenstown's Bear Brook State Park. The Museum of Family Camping, housed in an old CCC bunkhouse just across the dirt road from the snow-mobiles, is chock-full of

What about all those solo campers?

family camping gear (as opposed to singles camping gear?) from the mid-twentieth century. Out front you'll find a handful of vintage camper trailers, including an Airstream that's seen better days, and probably better campsites, and inside you'll find lots of old lanterns, stoves, and camp cutlery; a display of a "typical" twentieth-century campsite, complete with a union suit hanging on the clothesline and a "dingle stick" for, um, personal hygiene; and a Family Camping Hall of Fame boasting such family camping luminaries as Leon Leonwood Bean and Sheldon Coleman. Lombard Log Haulers and dingle sticks in one museum complex—what more could a family want?

The Museum of Family Camping and the New Hampshire Snowmobile Museum are located at 157 Deerfield Road in Allenstown's Bear Brook State Park. From the village of Suncook, take Route 28 north to Bear Brook Road, turn right, and continue for about 2 miles (the road will become Deerfield Road); the museum complex will be on your right. For information about the Museum of Family Camping, call (603) 485–9874. For information on the Snowmobile Museum, go to www.nhsnowmobilemuseum.com or call (603) 239–4768.

Mom's Bloody Revenge
Boscawen

There's nothing like attacking a woman's family, burning her house to the ground, and forcing her to march through dismal weather for over 100 miles to make her really, really mad. On March 15, 1697, a group of Abenaki Indians captured Hannah Dustin, along with her midwife, Mary Neff, and her brand-new baby, at her homestead in the town of Haverhill, Massachusetts. Her husband and six other children managed to escape, but Hannah must have presumed that they had either been captured, too, or killed. According to the account written by Cotton

Mather, the minister who made Hannah's story famous, the Dustin baby was killed not long after the group was taken captive, its head dashed against the trunk of a tree.

A seventeenth-century woman with an axe to grind.

Taking all that into consideration—especially the last part—you may not be surprised to learn that when Hannah Dustin managed to escape, she carried away with her not one, not three, not seven, but ten human scalps. Mary Neff and Samuel Leonardson, an adolescent boy from Worcester who'd been held captive for more than a year, helped Hannah with her bloody midnight work of killing and then scalping their sleeping captors, a group of two men, two women, and six children, on an island located at the mouth of the Contoocook River. The three then fled in a canoe down the Merrimack River all the way back to Haverhill. According to reports, Hannah did most of the killing and scalping herself, which explains why, when the group later took the bloody evidence of their deeds to Boston and petitioned the General Court for bounties, Mary and Samuel got twenty-five pounds to divide up between them, while Hannah got twenty-five pounds all to herself. It also explains why she's the one who ended up with a 35-foot-tall monument in her honor.

And what a monument it is. Erected in 1874 on the very island where Hannah Dustin got her revenge, it features a life-size statue of Hannah astride a massive stone pedestal, her right hand clutching a tomahawk and her left hand grasping a bunch of scalps. (Needless to say, she looks menacing and slightly mad.) According to some sources, Hannah's sister, Elizabeth Emerson, was executed just four years earlier, in 1693, for killing her twin babies. Murderous hearts must have run in the family.

The Hannah Dustin Memorial State Historic Site, with its dramatic statue, is located on an island at the mouth of the Contoocook River just off Route 4 in Boscawen. Take exit 17 off Interstate 93 and follow Route 4 west for about half a mile. The parking area for the memorial is a Park & Ride lot on the left-hand side. Follow the path down the hill and across a railroad trestle to the statue.

YOU DON'T WANT THIS MAN NOT TO KNOW YOU, AT LEAST NOT ANYTIME SOON

I don't mean to confuse you, but you probably don't want Eric Daniels not to know you anytime soon. Just to make things a little more confusing, if Eric Daniels didn't know you, and he happened to hear about you in a professional capacity, you'd probably want him to wish he'd known you. Wouldn't you?

Eric Daniels is a funeral director at Concord's Bennet Funeral Home who's written a book about his, um, clients titled *The Greatest People I Never Knew.* The book is filled with stories about amazing people who deeply touched the lives of those around them, but whom Daniels only came to know after their deaths, through the stories of family, friends, and loved ones. From a Loudon sawmill owner who was so honest he gave extra lumber to all his clients "just in case a piece or two weren't quite right," to a man from Bow who was a dead ringer for Santa Claus and who took a month off from work each December without pay to dress up as St. Nick and bring treats to children, the book is filled with ordinary folks who made an extraordinary difference in other people's lives, and made Daniels wish he'd known them when they were alive.

So he decided to write about them, collecting stories and letters from the friends and family members of thirteen people who struck him as particularly wonderful folks. According to Daniels, death doesn't turn us all into saints, but there are a lot more great people out there than you might think. Mark Twain, Daniels tells us, suggested that we all "endeavor so to live that when we come to die, even the undertaker will be sorry." If you'd like some pointers on exactly how to impress at least one local undertaker, I suggest you read the book.

Bennet Funeral Home is located at 209 North Main Street in Concord. Eric Daniels's book, *The Greatest People I Never Knew: A Funeral Director's Lessons About People He Came to Know Only in Death and How They Changed His Life,* is published by Authorhouse.

Do I Hear One Dollar, One Dollar for This Flattened Furbearer?

Concord

For years the New Hampshire State Road Kill Auction was the ultimate symbol of Yankee frugality to people the world over. Who else, folks wondered, except for those Yankee skinflints in New Hampshire would collect dead animals from their highways and byways, store them in a walk-in freezer for safekeeping until the end of the year, and then sell them to the highest bidder at auction? Meanwhile, we Granite Staters couldn't help but puzzle over the habits of flatlanders: Now why would they let their perfectly good roadkill go to waste?

Up until 1997, by state law the New Hampshire Fish and Game Department collected any and all furbearers killed by motorists over the course of the year (with the exception of moose and deer, which are often given to the motorists involved or butchered and donated to local shelters), from beavers, fishers, and otters to foxes, bobcats, coyotes, and black bears. In December the unfortunate, and now-frozen, critters were tagged (most through the nose), lined up in rows, and then auctioned off to the highest bidder at the state-owned White Farm in Concord to help raise funds for the Fish and Game Department and the state's trapper education program.

Not surprisingly, with auction items like slightly flattened opossum and mildly musty muskrat, the annual auction didn't ever raise a whole lot of money. The Fish and Game Department specifically advised against eating the auctioned roadkill for dinner, so no one was paying gourmet prices for wild game. Mostly, the buyers who came to the auction were beginner taxidermists and fur hobbyists looking for a cheap specimen: A decent-size coyote might go for $30, and a red fox in fair condition might fetch $10 or $15. When all the odiferous carcasses were carted away and the auction proceeds counted, some years so little money was raised, just a couple thousand dollars, that it was hard to tell if the Fish and Game Department had made anything at all, after organizers subtracted the cost of collecting and storing the roadkill. But it wasn't just about the money—it was the frugal principle behind turning accidental animal death by motor vehicle into greenbacks.

Unfortunately, the auction has been cancelled until further notice due to an outbreak of rabies in raccoons. Just immunizing the workers who handle the animals, experts say, would probably put the roadkill auction deep in the red. "We are frugal," wildlife biologist Eric Orff assured writer Jim Collins, "but at some point it's more frugal to not hold the auction." Even in its absence, the New Hampshire State Road Kill Auction represents the tightfistedness for which the state is famous. This kind of frugality, though, is just a whole lot less odoriferous, and a whole lot less colorful.

Egg-Shaped Stone a Mystery

Concord

Let me tell you something I've only recently discovered: Mystery is 99 percent presentation. And Doug Copeley, registrar at the Museum of New Hampshire History, knows how to present a mystery. Before he shows you the museum's so-called Mystery Stone, he'll take you to the bowels of the building, have you sign an official paper, and then let you peruse the multiple files packed with photographs and documents pertaining to the elaborately carved, greenish black stone that was, according to reports, discovered at the bottom of a post hole in Meredith in 1872. Only after you've had plenty of time to sift through the evidence will he emerge from what I can only imagine is a dark, wood-paneled, climate-controlled room filled with sundry treasures and then quietly, almost casually, set upon the table an old medium-size metal can. "I think this is the can it was originally in when it was donated," he might say, in an offhand way. Then he'll put on a pair of gleaming white cotton gloves, jimmy the lid off the can, and, after carefully parting the muslin where the stone is nestled, ever so gently lift the Mystery Stone from the can and hold it aloft for your inspection.

And what a beautiful Mystery Stone it is. About 4½ inches from top to bottom, smooth, egg-shaped, and covered with carvings that look like strange and ancient glyphs, the stone is unlike any I've ever seen. The largest carving is that of a face running the entire length of one side of the stone, which with its elongated profile, large nose, and wide bulging eyes, reminded me of those huge heads on Easter Island. There are also carvings of an ear of corn, a tepee, what appears to be a number of spears crossed over each other, and most mysterious of all, a group of three figures stacked inside a circle: what looks to be a small winged creature that might represent a hummingbird or a bee, beneath that a long slender figure that might be a hoofed animal leg, then a three-pointed, crown-shaped carving that might symbolize water.

Through the center of the stone, from top to bottom, runs a circular tapered hole, as if someone had drilled straight through the rock.

As befits a mystery stone, researchers don't know a whole lot about it. What they do know is that Seneca Ladd purportedly discovered it, encased in clay, in a post hole on a farm in Meredith in 1872. (Frances Ladd Coe donated it to the museum in 1927.) But the mysteries surrounding the stone are many. Who made it? When? Why? What do the symbols carved on its surface mean? We may never know—hence, the stone's name. For a true sense of the stone's mystery, though, it's best to have someone like Doug Copeley to present things just so.

The Museum of New Hampshire History is located in between North Main Street and Storrs Street at 6 Eagle Square in Concord. Admission is charged; free parking is located on Storrs Street. For more information or to set up an appointment to see the Mystery Stone, call (603) 228–6688.

Spoon Liberator Makes Trees Fork Over Their Cutlery

Contoocook

The afternoon I visited Dan Dustin, he was working on repairing a damaged tine on a hand-carved salad fork he'd sold a couple of years ago that had gotten chewed up a bit by the owner's dog. Repairs, he said, were free. "If someone buys one of my spoons and it cracks, they can send it back and I'll turn it into a fork." Now that, my friends, is a deal. I bought two Dustin spoons made from lilac wood for my morning cereal, and my mouth hasn't seen a stainless-steel spoon since.

Described by one commentator as a Yankee Zen master of wood, Dan Dustin handcrafts wooden spoons out of mountain laurel (known as spoonwood), lilac, apple, and blueberry wood, allowing the grain of the wood to dictate everything from the shape of the spoon's handle to the curve, depth, and angle of the spoon's bowl. He claims, in an admittedly Zen kind of way, that he doesn't so much carve a spoon out of wood as free the spoon that's trapped inside. (Who knew local trees had imprisoned so many defenseless utensils?) Needless to say, the spoons Dustin liberates are stunning to behold, their gleaming, beeswax-treated handles flowing with the graceful curves of the grain all the way down to the elegant tips of their scoops.

Dustin's roots go deep in the area, all the way back to an early nineteenth-century family farmstead, and when he returned to settle in Hopkinton with his wife and infant daughter, the young family lived in a tepee until they could build a house. Dustin still embodies that kind of Yankee independence and industriousness: Not only is he a famed spoon maker and now spoon-making teacher (at the Kimball-Jenkins School of Art in Concord), he's also an accomplished flutist, an innovative flute teacher—he gave me a free lesson in his living room using

Freeing spoons one tree branch at a time.

one of his Dustin-original "bound" flutes, with all holes taped shut with pipe thread tape—and, according to *This Old House Magazine*, the only crafter of custom hand-hewn beams in the country, from a single mantel piece to an entire timber-frame house.

Even with all his other projects, though, he finds time to "find" anywhere between 600 and 800 spoons a year. Any spoons he discovers beyond his set goals, he puts in a box for his retirement. "Someday I won't be able to make spoons anymore," he tells me, "and I'll have these for my retirement." The spoons in the box were gorgeous, each one a unique and functional work of art, and I couldn't help but envy him a little for his ISRA—Individual Spoon Retirement Account.

You can buy Dan Dustin's spoons at the League of New Hampshire Craftsmen's Sunapee Craft Fair, which begins the first Saturday in August and continues for a whole week. Or you're welcome to call him at home in Contoocook at (603) 746–5683 and arrange a time to drop by his workshop and pick out your favorite spoon.

Ahoy, There! May I Board Your Pumpkin?
Goffstown

Serious yachtsmen and yachtswomen might have serious questions about the legitimacy, safety, and even sanity of Goffstown's Giant Pumpkin Regatta, held each year on the Piscataquog River in the middle of town. For starters, a yachtsperson might ask, does a boat hull made from a 600-pound pumpkin meet even a single one of the U.S. Coast Guard's safety rules and regulations for recreational boats? What nautical nightmares await the unsuspecting captain of a personal watercraft hastily fashioned from a misshapen gourd of gargantuan girth? And lastly, will the damn things even float?

Well, of course they do. With a little help from forty or fifty pounds of sand ballast in the hollowed-out pumpkin hold, and with a small electric trolling motor attached to the back, the giant pumpkins and their costume-clad captains "race" down the river just about as well as you could hope. The only real problem is that a bottle of champagne probably bounces off the bow rind just about as often as it breaks.

While the Giant Pumpkin Regatta is the marquee event of the festival, Goffstown's annual Giant Pumpkin Weigh-Off and Regatta offers a lot more. First, there's the Giant Pumpkin Weigh-Off to determine exactly who has the heaviest pumpkin—in 2005 the prize went to festival organizer and New Hampshire Giant Pumpkin Growers' Association member Jim Beauchemin, who grew a 1,314.8-pound behemoth that went on to win the New England Giant Pumpkin title at the Topsfield Fair in Massachusetts. Then there's a Giant Pumpkin Parade, with trucks pulling trailers laden with giant golden-hued gourds and their proud growers from the high school to the town common; a Great Pumpkin Catapult Competition; a Giant Pumpkin Shopping Cart Race; a Pumpkin Cook-Off; and, of course, a Pumpkin Pie Eating Contest (no giant pumpkin pies allowed).

Goffstown, home to some of the founding members of the New Hampshire Giant Pumpkin Growers' Association, could very well be the giant pumpkin capital of the state, if anyone kept track of such things. Members share everything from pest control strategies to irrigation system designs to "Dill's Atlantic Giant" seed varieties, all in an effort to grow bigger and bigger, but not necessarily more river-worthy, pumpkins. At the peak of the growing season, these gourds can put on upwards of thirty pounds *per day*, and the results aren't always exactly symmetrical. But to the folks in Goffstown, a bigger pumpkin boat is always a more beautiful pumpkin boat, no matter how much it lists to starboard or to port.

Goffstown's Giant Pumpkin Weigh-Off and Regatta, hosted by the Goffstown Main Street Program, is held in the middle of October each

year. For information call (603) 497–9933. You can also visit the New
Hampshire Giant Pumpkin Growers' Association for some great pictures
of the regatta at www.nhgpg.org.

Politically Active Horse Put to Pasture
Gossville

You wouldn't know it by looking at him, but the wooden horse on
wheels on Route 4 in Gossville was a lot more political in his youth.
According to reports, he was originally built decades ago to protest the
United Nations, a body the horse's creators believed was detrimental to
freedom and democracy and the American way the
world over, maybe even in America. Scattered
on the lawn all around the U.N.,

A wooden horse who's lost his taste for politics.

"Trojan horse" were white crosses marked with the names of various communist countries, like Latvia and Lithuania. Rest in peace, you nations of the Baltic Republic, the U.N. Trojan horse seemed to say.

While the Gossville Trojan horse was a full-time protester for much of his youth, times change, and 10-foot-tall wooden horses on wheels change, too. New owners have purchased the property, and the horse with it, and the Gossville Trojan horse has become more conservative in his old age. He doesn't march in the Old Home Days parade like he used to, or indulge in tirades against the illegitimate authority of international bodies; he doesn't wear his mane long and complain about the Man; he doesn't even have a single mock grave marker at his wheels. Perestroika took the fun out of panicky cold war–inspired protests, and he hasn't been the same horse since.

Some say the Trojan horse has sold out and gone corporate, though there's no evidence he's ever tried to sell anything to anybody. As far as I can tell, he's just mellowed a bit with age. May Gossville's big wooden horse without a company or a cause continue to gaze down on passing motorists for many decades to come.

Gossville's Trojan horse is located on the north side of Route 4 right beside the old Sherwood Inn, less than a half mile east of Route 28.

Tall Tales Move Road

Henniker

Let the record show that my oddity inquiry in Henniker about the whereabouts of the Ocean Born Mary House is the only time a question I've asked about a curiosity has elicited a testy response from a local. "What do you wanna go see that for?" the woman said, eyeing me with suspicion. "You know it's a hoax, don't you?" Therefore, let the record also show that the house in Henniker known as the Ocean Born Mary

House is not, has never been, and shall never be the house of one Mary Wallace, more commonly known as Ocean Born Mary. And that, my friends, is a fact. But the story of how it came to be confused as such is a tale almost as strange as the legend of Ocean Born Mary herself.

If you haven't heard the legend of Henniker's Ocean Born Mary, I'll give you a quick lowdown: According to a story that is most certainly a mix of myth and fact, on July 28, 1720, a ship carrying Scottish and Irish immigrants bound for Boston was captured and held by pirates. Elizabeth Fulton Wilson, who that same day had given birth to a baby girl, and her husband James were among the passengers, and when the captain of the pirate vessel heard the newborn's cries, he sought the family out and told them he would spare the lives of the ship's passengers if they would name the child Mary,

The Ocean Born Mary House, where Ocean Born Mary never lived.

after his dear old mother. The Wilsons agreed, and in a spontaneous burst of baby-inspired generosity, the pirate returned to his ship, fetched a large bolt of sea-foam green silk, and offered it to the Wilsons, instructing them to use it one day for Mary's wedding dress. At the age of twenty-one, Mary married one James Wallace, and the dress she wore that day, so the story goes, was made of light green brocaded silk. You can even find what's claimed to be an admittedly sad-looking patch of that green silk in the Henniker Library today.

Now back to the so-called Ocean Born Mary House. The brown colonial with the hipped roof on the outskirts of Henniker was in fact owned by one of Mary Wallace's sons, Roger Wallace. But when the widowed Mrs. Wallace came to live in Henniker in 1798, at the age of seventy-eight, she took up residence with her son William, who lived a mile down the road from Roger. Various census records show that Mary lived with William, and *not*, I repeat *not*, in the so-called Ocean Born Mary House that belonged to Roger, until her death at the age of ninety-four, when she was buried in William's plot in the cemetery behind Henniker's town hall.

Now, over a hundred years later, enter one Louis Roy of Wisconsin and his elderly widowed mother. The pair moved to Henniker in 1917, bought the dilapidated old house that once belonged to Roger Wallace, renovated it, filled it with antiques, and then began promoting their new digs as the Ocean Born Mary House soon thereafter. And a hoax was born.

Roy spun fantastical tales about both Ocean Born Mary and her supposed house to paying visitors all the way up until his death in 1965. His mom helped, too, dressing up in colonial-era garb and impersonating an elderly Ocean Born Mary for tourists. Among the many whoppers Roy told, here's just a sampling: (1) The green silk–toting pirate "Don Pedro" came to Henniker to retire, built the house for Mary, and had her work as his housekeeper. (2) Said pirate buried his treasure in the apple orchard behind the house before he was killed, and the treasure has never been found. (3) Mary and/or the pirate Don Pedro were buried under the house's hearthstone. (4) Mary's ghost haunts the house.

The legends blossomed and spread, and subsequent owners of the home have been so plagued by ghost hunters and curiosity seekers alike that one couple eventually paid to move the road away from the house, just to have a buffer between the public right-of-way and their front windows. And that, my friends, explains the testiness.

The house that is erroneously known as the Ocean Born Mary House is a private home, and you should be ashamed of yourself if you're thinking of driving by and bothering the poor folks who live there. The patch of green silk from Mary's dress is in the Henniker Library, just off Route 114 on Western Avenue. Mary Wallace's grave is in the cemetery behind the town hall, about twelve rows back.

Heavyweight Ali Finds Home In Automotive Sales
Hooksett

After Stephen Singer, owner of Merchants Automotive Group in Hooksett, gave me a story-filled personal tour of his Muhammad Ali Museum, he left me with a parting gift: a personal-size bag of Muhammad Ali Popcorn with a cartoon picture of the Champ on the front and an expiration date marked April 1992. "It's fourteen-year-old popcorn," Singer told me with a smile, as if popcorn were like wine and improved with age.

Singer brought that same humorous sensibility to his collection of Muhammad Ali memorabilia, and the result is a truly one-of-a-kind museum. Displayed in a hallway leading to dealership offices (Singer's among them), the collection includes everything from a neon kinetic sculpture with a two-dimensional Ali rope-a-doping his way to victory, to a sculpture of the champ's hands made from plaster casts of his fists, to a life-size cartoonlike Ali sculpture getting ready to work an Ali punching bag inside a 4-foot-square ring. He's even got the original X-ray of Muhammad Ali's broken jaw from his fight with Ken Norton, signed not just by Ali but Norton as well. (Seems like a rather sporting way to handle a broken jaw, doesn't it?)

"I was a fan of Ali the boxer ever since I was a kid," Singer told me, "but his work as a humanitarian has inspired me most." His admiration for the Champ, whom Singer's been fortunate enough to meet on a couple of occasions, is palpable. "Sometimes when you meet a hero, you end up feeling a little let down. Well, meeting Muhammad Ali in person exceeded my expectations," Singer told me. His personal museum filled with one-of-a-kind pieces dedicated to the man and the legend does the same. The fourteen-year-old popcorn, though, is another matter entirely.

The Merchants Automotive Group dealership with the Ali Museum (there are two dealerships) is located at 1278 Hooksett Road in Hooksett. For information call (603) 669–4100 or (800) AUTO–999.

This is the GREATEST collection of Ali memorabilia.

One Heck of a Welding Job

Hopkinton

The pile of old horseshoes right in front of the offices of Sandy Heino & Associates Real Estate on Main Street in Hopkinton has certainly seen better days. In pictures taken over eighty years ago, the giant pile looks a bit like a horseshoe lighthouse, with a nice cylindrical tower about 7 or 8 feet tall and a narrower, rounded cylinder on top. At some point the horseshoes were welded together to prevent theft, but there seems little danger of anyone walking off with a horseshoe now.

They're badly rusted, and the whole pile has caved in on itself and fallen to one side as if the iron's melting away as surely as a snowbank in April. And I suppose it is. Someone's even wrapped a bit of chain-link fence around the pile to try to brace it up for a few more years.

The building where the real estate office is now located was once the home of J. E. Derry Horseshoeing— they've even got the gigantic old bellows used to keep the fire hot to prove it, hanging on the back wall inside the office. Legend has it that a boy who worked as an apprentice to Mr. Derry at his shop about a century ago threw any and all used horseshoes in a pile. Over the years the pile grew until the hulking mass of horseshoes took on the guise of one of those newfangled sculptures made out of recycled materials. And then, of course, it

A horseshoe pile that's seen better days.

didn't take long for the pile to start shrinking, first as a result of theft by souvenir seekers and then as a result of the abuse of Father Time and Mother Nature, negligent parents everyone loves to gripe about. May Hopkinton's pile of horseshoes rust in peace for many years to come.

Sandy Heino & Associates Real Estate is located at 185 Main Street just east of downtown Hopkinton. The old blacksmith shop turned real estate office is also haunted, according to one of the agents, and the ghost's most unique characteristic is that he smells of liquor. (I wonder if the ghost was a drinker before his passing, or if death drove him to drink?)

A Staring Contest with a Migrating Salmon
Manchester

Helen Dalbeck, the director of the Amoskeag Fishways Learning and Visitor's Center, admits that it's sometimes hard for kids to understand that the fish they're watching with rapt attention through the center's underwater viewing windows aren't in a tank. Instead, the American shad, Altlantic salmon, American eels, alewifes, and other fish swimming by are headed up a computer-controlled fish ladder, which allows them to bypass a hydroelectric dam at Amoskeag Falls and migrate farther upriver. Admittedly, the fish ladder pool does resemble an aquarium, with its Plexiglas, metal, and concrete walls, but those fish you see at the Fishways, they're wild ones, just passing through, rambling on, making their long and lonesome way home. And, unlike aquarium fish, they don't want any handouts.

In addition to the underwater viewing windows in the basement, the Amoskeag Fishways Center has some wonderful museum exhibits on everything from watershed threats to electricity generation to the life cycles of migratory fish. The center also offers special environmental

MAINE WOOING NEW HAMPSHIRE'S CURIOSITIES AWAY

Somebody write a letter to a congressman, somebody else start circulating a petition, let's get the legislature busy legislating, because we've got a problem. Maine, our Down East neighbor to the east, is stealing our curiosities. If the trend continues, by the middle of this century we won't have any oddball tourist attractions left: All our curiosities will have been dismantled, crated up, shipped to small towns in Maine, and then reassembled into new and improved tourist-friendly destinations.

Think I'm being just a touch paranoid? Well, for Exhibit A, I offer you the Lindbergh Crate Cottage. Did you know that Hopkinton was once home to a cottage made from the crate used to ship the fuselage of the *Spirit of Saint Louis* back home from Paris after Charles Lindbergh's historic, first-ever, solo transatlantic flight in 1927? According to reports, the man responsible for transporting the *Spirit of Saint Louis* back to the States on the USS *Memphis,* one Admiral Burrage, asked Lindbergh if he could have the crate for keeps. Lindbergh said yes, and the admiral shipped the crate to property he owned in Hopkinton, where he transformed it into a cozy little cottage nestled among pines on the banks of the Blackwater River, complete with gable roof, lots of windows, and not one but two porches.

Larry Ross, a schoolteacher in Canaan, Maine, bought the dilapidated Lindbergh Crate Cottage in 1990 for a mere $3,000, shipped it across the state line, and rebuilt it good as new in his backyard. Now it's the centerpiece of a wonderfully weird museum / theme park, complete with a miniature crane with a giant carrot hanging off it and a cannon that fires rolls of toilet paper. He uses the Crate Cottage to help teach schoolchildren about the value of having a vision, a plan, a team to back you up, and the focus to see your dream to fruition, just like Lindbergh.

For Exhibit B, I offer you the 32-foot-tall, 10-foot-wide wooden Moxie soda bottle. Moxie originally used the structure as a whimsical trade-show booth in the early 1900s, but for many years the three-story-tall soda bottle stood on the grounds of Pine Island Park in Manchester, where it housed a concession stand. In 2000 folks from the Matthews Museum of Maine Heritage in Union, Maine, bought the Moxie bottle, dismantled it, shipped it out of New Hampshire, and are now raising money to build a structure to house it, along with the rest of their large collection of Moxie memorabilia. I shudder to think what curiosity will be whisked away next.

The Moxie bottle isn't yet ready for viewing, but you can see the Lindbergh Crate Cottage (and a lot of other neat stuff) if you head to Larry Ross's backyard at 241 Easy Street in Canaan, Maine, home of the Lindbergh Crate Museum. To make an appointment to visit, call (207) 474–9841.

education programs, where kids can learn about things such as river wildlife, native crafts, and water-quality issues. And, of course, each spring the Fishways is flooded with visitors hoping to catch a rare glimpse of a ladder-climbing fish, a creature no one ever told you about in school. Where else can you look a wild American shad in the eye while she's migrating? Of course, she'll probably be too preoccupied to chat, but you'll just have to forgive her: She's in the grip of an overpowering biological imperative. Don't you sometimes wish you could have such a great excuse?

The Amoskeag Fishways Learning and Visitor's Center is located at 6 Fletcher Street in downtown Manchester. Take exit 6 off Interstate 293 in Manchester and follow Amoskeag Street east towards the Amoskeag Bridge. The Fishways will be on your right, behind the Ramada Inn, just before you reach the bridge. The center is open year-round, but fish viewing only happens when the

Stand back: Migrating fish at work.

fish are migrating, between mid-April and early June. The best time for fish viewing changes from year to year depending on variables like water temperature and river flow rates, so you might want to call ahead, (603) 626–FISH (3474). For more information go to www.amoskeag fishways.org.

They Don't Call Them Super Brownies for Nothing
Manchester

When asked what it was like to swim in a Manchester quarry all through the winter, Leona Sullivan Cousins offered the folks at *New Hampshire Crossroads* this interesting but highly dubious bit of physiological commentary: "No, it wasn't bad. See, we were circulatin' our blood. The people watching us, now they were cold 'cause they were just standing there. But we were circulatin' our blood." Theories about circulating blood aside, Mrs. Cousins must have been C-O-L-D, but I imagine she was also really T-O-U-G-H, just like the dozen or so other young men and women who garnered national attention in Manchester for swimming in an abandoned granite quarry known as the Ledge (now Derryfield Park) and breaking world high-diving records, with dives as high as 110 feet— all in the dead cold of winter.

I know what you're thinking: What about the ice? Throughout the 1920s the group, known as the Brownies, would cut holes in ice as much as 2 feet thick, turning a section of the old quarry pond into a veritable Olympic-size swimming pool and making it possible for members to dive and swim straight through the winter. Those Brownies who swam every day over the course of a year became known as Super Brownies. Old movie footage aired on *New Hampshire Crossroads* even shows a pair of Brownies playing chess, sitting on the ice in their bathing suits and dangling their feet in the water. True to Leona's theory, the chess players don't look the least bit cold, while the onlookers, bundled up in wool coats, hats, and scarves, look like they're ready for a warm fire and a hot cup of cocoa spiked with bathtub liquor. While most folks refer to that rollicking Prohibition-era decade as the Roaring Twenties, I've heard it said that some Manchester natives prefer to call it the Shivering Twenties.

At the height of the Brownies' fame, as many as 10,000 people came to watch them swim, dive from the cliffs at the Ledge, and generally frolic in the snow while wearing nothing but their bathing suits. I'm told only a few of the original Super Brownies are still alive, and the group itself died out long ago. Today, Polar Bear Clubs around the country make headlines for their once-a-year New Year's Day dips, but in front-page pictures those Polar Bears look a lot colder than you'd expect an Arctic mammal to be. Maybe Leona should offer them some tips about circulating their blood. Or about just grinning and polar bearing it.

The Ledge, or what used to be the Ledge, is located in Derryfield Park, just off Route 28A in Manchester. Take exit 8 off Interstate 93 and follow Wellington Road / Bridge Street a short distance west. After you cross Route 28A, take a right onto Oak Hill Road into the park. The Ledge, a granite quarry operated by the Amoskeag Manufacturing Company that flooded in the late 1800s, was located just north of the Weston Observatory on Oak Hill. After a number of deaths in the 1960s and '70s, the quarry was filled in sometime in the early '80s.

A Statue Whose Stature Has Fallen

Manchester

I'd be willing to bet that the long ceramic tongue hanging indecorously from the mouth of the Great Stone Face on the campus of St. Anselm College is a more recent addition, but otherwise he must look just as he did when he graced the top of the once-grand art deco State Theater in downtown Manchester. (Okay, he's probably had one or two paint jobs, too.) A representation of the Greek mask of comedy, the 5½-foot-tall concrete face was, like the circa 1929 State Theater itself, slated for the wrecking ball when a concerned citizen (and St. Anselm alum?) intervened. Now he sits, maniacally grinning (and tongue wagging) just outside the Dana Center, St. Anselm College's performing arts center.

The most striking thing about the Great Stone Face is that, to be brutally frank, he's not that great. In fact, as a sculpture he's kind of primitive and cheap looking, like a concrete party crasher on Easter Island. His less-than-winning appearance isn't his

In case you were wondering, the tongue isn't original.

fault, though. In my opinion, he's an innocent victim of a dramatic loss of statuary stature, from three stories up on the front of the State Theater to a place right on the ground, a precipitous decline that allows the viewing public (and sculpturally creative undergrads) to get way too up close and personal. Just like all of us, Mr. Face has an optimal distance from which to gaze upon his visage, and just like the more mature among us, a little bit of distance probably does wonders for his appearance. Still, most people on campus keep referring to him as the Great Stone Face, a sure sign the community has embraced him for who he is, rather than what he's not.

St. Anselm College is located at 100 St. Anselm Drive in Manchester. Take exit 5 off Interstate 293, then follow Granite Street west to South Main Street. From South Main, turn right onto Route 114A and follow it for about a mile until it intersects with College Street. Turn left on College and continue straight across Rockland Street onto St. Anselm Drive; the college will be on the left. Take the first main entrance on your left and follow the signs for the Dana Center. For information call (603) 641–7000.

You can also see the actual marquee from the old State Theater at the Manchester Historic Association's Millyard Museum. The museum is located at Mill #3 on the corner of Commercial and Pleasant Streets in Manchester. For more information visit www.manchesterhistoric.org or call (603) 622–7531.

A Hermit Whose Dance Card Was Always Full
Manchester

The Hermit of Mosquito Pond. Doesn't that have a lovely, romantic-sounding ring to it? Charles Alan Lambert was a nineteenth-century hermit who, after a severe disappointment in love in the 1840s, bought forty acres beside Mosquito Pond (now Crystal Lake) in south Manchester and lived there in solitude for the next seventy years. Of course, solitude is a relative term, especially when you've got a name with as much mystical mystique and rugged sex appeal as "The Hermit of Mosquito Pond." It probably wasn't very long before Lambert started receiving more visitors than was seemly for a hermit, and as his fame grew, reports say he entertained hundreds of guests over the course of a busy summer season. A teacher of mine once gave me this bit of sage advice, which I think is applicable here: "Get a reputation for being an early riser and you can sleep 'til noon."

When he wasn't receiving visitors, Charles Lambert the so-called hermit spent his time much the same way any saintlike hermit would, according to my *Encyclopedia of New England,* meditating on nature, tending his vegetables, selling plants and herbs to locals, and looking after his large flock of sheep. Like Henry David Thoreau, an even more famous hermit contemporary (who lived just one year, not seventy, alone in the woods), Lambert practiced a rugged self-sufficiency, building his own rather ramshackle house using logs and old lumber from his property and growing most of his own food. And like Thoreau, the Hermit of Mosquito Pond piqued the curiosity of a good many people by calling himself a recluse. Which leads me to wonder, when does a semi-famous recluse become a man about town?

The last two years of his long life, the Sisters of Mercy at the House of St. John For Aged Men cared for him. He died there in 1914 and was buried in St. Joseph Cemetery, his grave marked by a plain white tombstone inscribed with the words THE HERMIT.

Crystal Lake is located in south Manchester, off Bodwell Road. From Manchester, follow Route 28A (or South Mammoth Road) south to the Interstate 293/93 overpass. Just after you cross beneath the interchange, take a left onto Bodwell Road and continue until you reach the entrance for Crystal Lake Park. There's a public beach and a fieldstone bathhouse on nineteen acres at the north end of the lake. To visit St.

Joseph Cemetery on Donald Street in Manchester, take exit 3 off I–293 and head west on Route 101. Continue straight at the intersection with Route 114, then turn right onto Bedford Road. The first cemetery you come to (on your right) will be New St. Joseph Cemetery. Continue on Donald Street until you come to St. Joseph Cemetery on your left.

For Now, Scientists Concede Victory to Gravity

New Boston

Gravity's one of those laws of nature that's so everyday, so ordinary, you don't really start to work up a good strong resentment toward it until you stop and think about it. That fall your poor old grandmother took last year? Gravity. Your bad back? Gravity. Extremely poor gas mileage in your SUV? Gravity again.

Now that we've identified the problem and stoked our collective righteous indignation, what, oh what, can we do about gravity? For starters, we can head to New Boston and pay homage to a man who devoted his life to fighting gravity the way Smoky the Bear devoted his to fighting forest fires. It was here, in this quiet hamlet, that the business and investment guru Roger W. Babson, perhaps best known for founding Babson College, established the Gravity Research Foundation, an organization dedicated to beating gravity once and for all, or at least bringing it down a peg or two. On a traffic island in the center of town, you'll find a simple granite monument that pays tribute to the group's "active research for anti-gravity and a partial gravity insulator."

Roger Babson, who made millions and helped revolutionize the financial services industry by starting one of the first investment analysis services, established the Gravity Research Foundation in New Boston in 1948. The foundation, which occupied a number of buildings in town, held weeklong conferences on gravity (Igor Sikorsky, the gravity-defying inventor of the helicopter, once attended), sponsored a gravity essay contest, and collected statistics from hospitals regarding "the day and, if possible, the hour, of a fracture" in order to see if a relationship could be established between phases of the moon and rates of injury, and thereby implicate gravity in our orthopedic woes.

If you're starting to think Babson's beef against gravity was personal, you're right. In an essay titled "Gravity—Our Enemy No. 1," Babson discusses the drowning of his eldest sister in a river in his hometown of Gloucester, Massachusetts. "She was unable to fight gravity," he wrote, "which came up and seized her like a dragon and brought her to the bottom." In spite of Babson's millions and his powerful gravity vendetta, though, the foundation's conferences eventually ceased, the New Boston buildings were sold, and the Gravity Research Foundation seemed to disappear.

But the organization soldiers on, having switched its emphasis from beating gravity to understanding it—smart move. Now located in Massachusetts, they offer annual essay awards, with a top prize of $3,500, to physicists doing gravity-related research. A recent prize-winning

Gravity may not be Enemy No. 1, but it's certainly not our friend.

HERE AT NEW BOSTON, N. H.
ROGER W. BABSON
AND HIS ASSOCIATES
PIONEERED
IN ACTIVE RESEARCH
FOR ANTI-GRAVITY
AND A PARTIAL GRAVITY
INSULATOR

1959

paper boasted the heavy-hitting title "The Cosmological Constant Problem in Brane-Worlds and Gravitational Lorentz Violations," which, you have to admit, does make gravity sound like quite a problem.

The monument to Roger Babson and his Gravity Research Foundation is located in New Boston on the eastern side of the traffic island at the intersection of Routes 13 and 136. For more information on the Gravity Research Foundation, visit www.theinternetfoundation.org/grf or call (781) 431–1582.

Thanks for the Boulders

Nottingham

Just like a lot of geological oddities in the Granite State, the boulder field at the north end of Pawtuckaway State Forest owes its existence to ice. Glacial ice, that is, and lots of it. The last time a mile-thick sheet of ice skipped town for the Arctic about a dozen millennia ago, it left behind a rather stunning collection of house-size boulders on the eastern slopes of Mount Pawtuckaway. And the boulder field is easily accessible by car, so you don't even have to break a sweat to explore it.

In addition to the boulder field, the 5,500-acre Pawtuckaway State Park features the 803-acre Lake Pawtuckaway; the Pawtuckaway Mountains, a rare circular volcanic formation of mountains called a ring dike complex; and miles of hiking and mountain-biking trails. The highlight, though, is the boulder field, at least for natives who just can't seem to get enough face time with good-looking rocks. None are quite as big as the behemoth glacial erratic up in Madison, but the largest approach 30 feet in height and are plenty big enough to give you an appreciation for the unimaginable power of a glacier. And after spending a solid five months each year scraping it from our windshields, it's nice to be reminded of the fact that a lot of our state's natural wonders were a gift from good old ice. How cold would we be if we didn't at least offer a little thanks?

Pawtuckaway State Park is located in Nottingham between Route 156 and Route 107. The main entrance to the park is off Route 156, but the easiest way to access the boulder field is to take exit 5 off Route 101 into Raymond. Follow Route 107 north into Deerfield, then turn right onto Reservation Road and follow it for about 2 miles to Round Pond Road. Take a left at Round Pond Road and follow it up to the boulder fields. The road can be rough, depending on conditions. For information call the park at (603) 895–3031.

Now this is what I call rocky ground.

A Girl Who Lost Her Head
Pembroke

With the possible exception of the statue of Hannah Dustin up in Boscawen, shown clutching a tomahawk in one hand and a bunch of human scalps in the other, Pembroke's memorial to young Josie Lang-maid just may be the most grisly monument in the state. On the north side of Academy Road right across from the Three Rivers School, there's a granite obelisk marking the spot where Josie was brutally murdered and beheaded on her way to school at Pembroke Academy on October 4, 1875. The man accused of the crime was Joseph LaPage, an itinerant woodcutter who'd been charged with the rape of a young woman in Canada just four years earlier. He was eventually convicted and executed.

As if all that weren't horrible enough, the large monument is painfully specific when it comes to certain facts, including Josie's age at the time of her murder, a tragically young seventeen years, ten months, and twenty-seven days. But perhaps the most grisly details engraved on the wayside monument offer the visitor directions, first to the spot 90 feet due north of the memorial where Josie's body was found, and then to the spot 82 rods north, or a whole quarter mile distant, where poor Josie's head was found, both of which are marked with granite posts. According to reports, Josie's body was found on the evening of the day she was murdered, but it took searchers until the following morning to find her head. The monument doesn't say how it ended up so awfully far away.

When I went searching for the stone markers in the woods, I easily found the hitching post–like stone marking the spot where Josie's body was discovered, but the bramble got thicker and the ground swampier as I walked further north, and I eventually had to turn back. Besides, it was one of those gray winter days when something as utterly dispirit-ing as looking for a stone post marking the spot where a young girl's head was once found could really sour your mood if you weren't careful. I decided to let decapitated head posts lie and called it a day.

The monument to Josie Langmaid, the so-called Murdered Maiden of Pembroke Academy, is located on Academy Road in Pembroke. Follow Route 3 north out of the village of Suncook for about a mile, then take a right onto Academy Road. The monument is 0.75 mile east on the north side of Academy Road, just across from the Three Rivers School.

A monument that gives too much information.

America's Got a New Stonehenge
Salem

The folks at America's Stonehenge have done lots of homework on their thirty-acre hilltop maze of stone walls, man-made chambers, and ceremonial stones, said to be perhaps the oldest man-made construction in the United States. Maybe too much homework. The combination tour guide and map they give visitors is a total of four single-spaced pages, in a font small enough to bring out the reading glasses, filled with site maps, detailed drawings, and extensive descriptions of no less than thirty-two points of interest on your half-mile hike around the property. If you enjoy reading about exciting advances in carbon dating like the Bristle-Cone Pine Tree Correlations,

Four-thousand-year-old stone chambers! Read all about it!

though, this pamphlet is for you. Oh yeah, and there's a surprise quiz on this archeological mother lode of information when you get back to the visitor center, but of course they don't tell you that up front—it would ruin the surprise.

While it's said to have been constructed somewhere between 3,500 and 4,000 years ago, an estimate based on radiocarbon dating of charcoal fragments at the site, America's Stonehenge didn't open for business until 1958, when a well-developed roadway system and a burgeoning population of Americans with leisure time and disposable income made it possible for an American Stonehenge to turn a profit. Originally called the Mystery Hill Caves, the owners changed the name to America's Stonehenge when archeo-astronomers discovered that, like Stonehenge in England, the site functions as an ancient astronomical calendar, with stones marking the locations of various solar and lunar events. Researchers have also found tablets at the site that contain ancient inscriptions in Oghum, Phoenician, and Iberian Punic, none of which are taught at Harvard anymore, let alone public high schools. The inscriptions have led some to theorize that America's Stonehenge was built by Celts, Vikings, or Phoenicians who migrated to the North American continent, constructed megalithic sites throughout the region (with America's Stonehenge the largest and most elaborate among them), and then departed. Others postulate that Paleolithic Indians constructed the site and were merely taking correspondence courses in runic languages.

One gruesome highlight of the site is a four-and-a-half-ton granite slab with a carved channel running along its outside edges, presumably for blood, known as the "Sacrificial Table." Researchers believe it was once used for ritual sacrifices, animal or human the tour guide pamphlet doesn't say. Maybe there are some details even the America's Stonehenge researchers don't want to get into.

America's Stonehenge is located at 105 Haverhill Road in Salem. Take exit 3 east off Interstate 93 and follow Route 111 east for 5 miles to the junction of Island Pond Road and Haverhill Road. Turn right onto Haverhill Road and drive about a mile to the park entrance on the right. For information go to www.stonehengeusa.com or call (603) 893–8300.

My, What a Well-Dressed Zucchini You've Got
Windham

You planted your zucchinis in May, you watered them through June, and you weeded and watered and then weeded some more in July, longing for a taste of that mild and versatile vegetable. Then August rolled around, and it was like some B-grade horror movie: Invasion of the Zucchinis. Sure, you can slice, dice, and stuff, you can bake, grill, and fry, but the legions upon legions of zucchinis bursting from your garden will, one fine day at the tail end of summer, overwhelm you. What are you going to do with all those zucchinis?

Well, for starters, you can dress them up and enter them in a costume competition. For five years, the Nesmith Library in Windham hosted a weeklong Zucchini Festival in August, with the marquee event something called "Zucchinis on Parade," wherein folks took one of their surplus zucchinis; dressed it up to look like a popular figure from history, literature, sports, movies, and so forth; gave it a name; and displayed it in the library. Visitors to the library then voted on the best-dressed zucchini, and the winning vegetable and his or her proud grower went to Disneyland. (I made that last part up.) Notable zucchinis from years past include Moby Zuke, Monte Zuke, and Chia Zuke, but perhaps the most beautiful and enigmatic of them all was the framed and ever-so-slightly-smiling Zuka Lisa.

The Zucchini Festival also included more conventional contests like a competition to see who grew the biggest zucchini in Windham and a zucchini bake-off. The festival even inspired a song by local musician Ken Sheldon, "Ballad of the Homeless Zucchini"—I'm told it's a real tear-jerker. Unfortunately, Diane Mayr at the Nesmith Library has reported that the Zucchini Festival is on hold for 2006, due to lack of interest. Could it be that folks in Windham actually consume every last one of their zucchinis and so aren't interested in dressing up their vegetables and putting them on parade? If so, I'm sure lots of people want to know their secret to zucchini population control. For the sake of the rest of us, though, we hope Windham brings back the Zucchini Festival.

The Nesmith Library is located at 8 Fellows Road in Windham. You can find pictures of the Zuka Lisa and Chia Zuka, along with a host of other famous zucchinis, at www.nesmithlibrary.org under Event Photos.

MONADNOCK REGION

Who Needs Clothes When You've Got Fur?

Chesterfield

Want to be the favorite subject of idle gossip in a small New Hampshire town? Then just follow the lead of Madame Antoinette Sherri: Build a grand house on a secluded piece of property; throw lavish parties for paying out-of-town guests; spend lots of QT with a much, much younger man; and, for good measure, buy a pet monkey and perch him on your shoulder when you go riding in your chauffer-driven Packard. Oh, yes, and one last thing—when you head into town in summer to do a little shopping, be sure to wear a fur coat with absolutely nothing on underneath.

In 1929 Madame Sherri made the first of what would be many trips from New York City to the tiny town of Chesterfield as a guest of the Broadway actor Jack Henderson, who had a summer estate in town. A few years later, Madame used a portion of her generous inheritance from her recently deceased husband, an alcoholic Italian aristocrat thirteen years her junior, to build her own summer home in Chesterfield, hiring the obligatory crew of Italian stonemasons to do the job. And that's when the wild rumors began.

Even if she hadn't been a tad bizarre, Madame Sherri would have been easy fodder for Chesterfield gossips: She spoke French, wore lots of makeup, and worked as a costume designer for the Ziegfeld Follies,

Florenz Ziegfeld's musical revues that featured large casts of beautiful young women dressed in skimpy costumes in an era when female beachgoers showed about as much skin as asbestos-removal technicians. She threw lavish parties for acquaintances in, and patrons of, New York's theater and arts world, extravagant soirees where the young and the beautiful catered to an older, wealthier crowd. She spent most of her time with the much younger Charles LeMaire, also a costume designer for the Follies, whom she introduced to acquaintances as her "foster son" in order to feign propriety. And, of course, there was the whole business of what was rumored to be her summer ensemble of choice: a fur coat . . . and absolutely nothing else.

Cute place, but the second floor needs a little work.

Eventually her money ran out, her lover LeMaire left her (and went on to win multiple Oscars for his movie costume designs), she took ill, and the house was left abandoned. It burned to the ground on October 18, 1962, leaving behind only a stone foundation, a central hearth, and a huge curving stone staircase, which once led to a second-story porch but now leads, disconcertingly, nowhere. Madame Sherri died three years later, after donating the grounds of her vanished summer home for conservation. Today, you can visit Madame Sherri's Forest, a beautiful 488-acre park managed by the Society for the Protection of New Hampshire Forests, and walk among the ruins of what was once her grand home. Some locals claim that on moonlit nights, Madame Sherri's ghost appears at the top of the stone staircase, but whether the apparition wears a fur, or a monkey, or nothing at all, no one, not even the biggest town gossip, will venture to say.

Madame Sherri's Forest—and the ruins of her house, known locally as Madame Sherri's Castle—is located in West Chesterfield on Gulf Road. Take Route 9 west through Chesterfield. Just before the Chesterfield Bridge to Vermont, turn left at the state liquor store plaza onto Mountain Road, then take an immediate left onto Gulf Road. Travel a little more than 2 miles, and you'll find parking for Madame Sherri's Forest on the right.

What Would Jesus Do?
Dublin

If you're a philistine like me, then you watch PBS's *Antiques Roadshow* not for the graduate-level education on things like sixteenth-century Chinese printmaking or colonial-era pewter engraving, but for the delicious thrill of watching, say, a buttoned-up, middle-aged housewife from Peoria go daffy with joy when she's told that her great-great-grandmother's mantel clock is worth its weight in gold and then some. First the color might drain from her face. Then she might mouth the words "Oh dear" over and over again. Then slowly, slowly, a realization breaks like dawn across her face—I'm rich!—and she smiles the smile of the supremely, unexpectedly, unabashedly happy.

Rick O'Connor, Dawn Ward, and Roy Gandhi-Schwatlo probably had little if any idea of what they were getting when the three friends pooled their resources to buy a gold-and-tempera painting of the Madonna and Child at a Dublin Community Church auction for $3,200. It certainly didn't look like a lost treasure: At 12⅞ by 11 inches, the painting's just a little larger than your average piece of paper, and there were even chips of paint missing in places. So when the portrait of the serious-looking Madonna and Child on a throne flanked by Saints Peter and Paul and a handful of stern-looking angels turned out to be the missing panel of a fourteenth-century Sienese triptych on display at the Musée de Tess in Le Mans, France, they must have all behaved a bit like that woman from Peoria. Too bad the *Antiques Roadshow* wasn't around to catch it on tape. In January of 2004, just six months after the group bought it, the painting fetched $489,600 at Sotheby's Auction House in New York, a whopping 1,500 percent return on their original investment.

That's not quite the end of the story, though. When certain members of the Dublin Community Church, who shall remain nameless, found out by way of a local antiques dealer that Ward, O'Connor, and Gandhi-Schwatlo had made a killing on the painting, they felt a little, well, bad. Everybody seemed to acknowledge that nothing illegal had transpired, but for a while there was widespread debate in the town of Dublin about whether propriety (and maybe good old-fashioned neighborliness) dictated that the group donate a portion of their windfall to the Dublin Community Church, especially since the donation of the painting for auction by an unlucky local woman, Jessie Hale, was for the purpose of supporting said church.

No donations were forthcoming, but plenty of people in town thought that was just fine. "Would the church have given them their money back if the painting turned out to be worthless?" one crusty old Yankee asked me when I brought up the Dublin painting. Point taken. While some people read into the episode the decline of small-town New Hampshire values, I'd say it proves the continued vigor of what is, according to my wonderful *Encyclopedia of New England,* edited by David Watters and Burt Feintuch, the stereotypical Yankee character's most "enduring peculiarity . . . [a] bent for ingenious peddling and shrewd trades."

The Haunting of Haunted Lake

Francestown

In the golden glow of a late-summer afternoon, Haunted Lake doesn't look the least bit haunted. In fact, it looks beautiful in the way only a lake in New Hampshire can, with its clear, sun-dappled waters gently lapping sandy, white pine–flanked shores. Rest assured, though, that a body of water doesn't earn a name like Haunted Lake without good cause. On some moonless autumn evenings, when the wind sows through the trees and leaves scuttle the grass, some folks say you can hear along Haunted Lake's deserted shores the moans and howls of the unquiet dead.

Locals know it as Scobie Pond, but most maps, including my wonderful DeLorme *Atlas & Gazetteer,* call it by its spooky if somewhat less-than-subtle name: Haunted Lake. As for the origin of the name, there are a number of different stories, the most famous of which might be the legend of two settlers headed for Hillsborough who set up camp for the night by the lake's edge. During the evening, the two men argued—perhaps over who got the biggest baked potato for dinner, or perhaps over the covers they were supposed to share, we'll never know. After the argument, only one man was left alive (let that be a lesson to all you covers hogs), and it wasn't until years later that David Scobie, an early settler who built a home and a mill on the lake, discovered the skeletal remains of the other, less fortunate traveler by his mill site. The man's ghost is said to haunt the shores of the lake to this very day.

I prefer the story Francestown historian Veda O'Neill shared with me from the 1895 town history. Apparently, David Scobie's sons were fond of frightening "liquor laden loafers" as the men passed Haunted Lake on their way home from the tavern. The Scobie boys, according to the town history, "helped" belated travelers see all manner of dreadful ghosts, devilish visions, and fantastic apparitions.

Like the Scobie boys, you might find the idea of unquiet ghosts laughable in August, but on some dark November night when the summer folk have all gone south and the pines are wagging their heads in a disapproving way, you may not be so ready to dismiss the idea that at least one unlucky ghost who never made it to Hillsborough is howling in the wind.

Haunted Lake is located 2 miles east of Francestown on Route 136.

I'll Trade You My Rock If You'll Trade Me Yours
Gilsum

A Granite Stater who collects rocks is a bit like a Bedouin who collects sand. With so many samples underfoot, the collecting is easy—it's getting rid of the rocks that's the hard part.

That's where the Gilsum Rock Swap and Mineral Show comes in. At the end of each June for the last forty-plus years, around 8,000 rock fans, rock dealers, and rock swappers from all over the country come to this small village to buy, sell, and, of course, swap rocks of every size, shape, variety, and value. More than seventy dealers and swappers spread out their mineral wares on the grounds of the Gilsum Elementary School, and rock hounds from around the country buy and swap everything from quartz geodes to fossils to fancy jewelry. Samples range from the newly found and rough to cut and polished high-quality semiprecious stones.

In addition to loads of rocks and minerals, the Gilsum Rock Swap and Mineral Show also features lots of good eating, with a lemonade and bake sale, a chicken barbecue, and a Saturday-night ham and bean supper

Dr. Alan Russell shows off a fossil friend.

with all-you-can-eat homemade pie for dessert. And, if you're not too sugar-dazed after three helpings of pie to sit up and listen, there's after-supper entertainment in the form of an enlightening address on the subject of, you guessed it, rocks. A recent edge-of-your-seat talk (if you're a rock lover that is), was delivered by Jeff Fast and titled "Mineral Collecting Adventures in Mexico."

But why Gilsum you ask? The town has a rocky history, with over sixty defunct mines where locals made a living from minerals like feldspar, mica, and beryl up until the 1940s. At the rock swap, attendees receive a map showing the locations of many of the old mines so they can do some prospecting of their own, if they're so inclined and if they get permission from landowners first. But with all those rocks and minerals close at hand, and all that barbecue chicken and lemonade, it's more than tempting to stay right in town and rock swap 'til you drop.

The Gilsum Rock Swap and Mineral Show, hosted by the nonprofit Gilsum Recreation Committee, is held each year at the end of June on the grounds of the Gilsum Elementary School right on Route 10 in the village of Gilsum. Attendance and parking have always been free at the event, but donations to local children's recreation programs are encouraged. For information visit http://users.adelphia.net/~rmitchell60/ or call (603) 357–9636.

Wife Helps New Hampshire Carpenter Win Trapeze Artist Fans
Gilsum

Bill Whyte, founder and CEO of W.S. Badger Company, credits his wife, Katie, for inspiring him to invent a better balm. A former carpenter who suffered cracked hands and feet from working outdoors in harsh

New Hampshire winters, Bill turned to home remedies for self-healing after commercial products failed him. At his most chapped and desperate, he went to bed one cold winter's night wearing olive oil–soaked socks wrapped in plastic sandwich bags. His wife, needless to say, was not impressed. "That's really pathetic," she told him, as he gingerly slid his Baggie-bound feet under the covers. "I know you can do better than that."

In response to that bedtime matrimonial challenge, Bill got cooking and came up with a mean batch of olive oil and beeswax–based hand and foot balm, which he promptly rubbed all over his suffering tootsies. They healed so quickly, sans socks and Baggies, that Bill decided to package the balm in tins and sell it at hardware stores for miles around, and so the W.S. Badger Company was born. From that humble beginning, the fame of Badger Balm grew, eventually garnering glowing testimonials from the desperately chapped likes of everyone from trapeze artists to Antarctic researchers. (Rumor has it that there was even an Antarctic trapeze artist who ordered three cases . . .)

What began in a corner of Badger Bill's home is now a two-building, $3 million-a-year operation with thirty employees who turn out a variety of natural and organic healing body-care products in the so-called Badger Mines, from lip balm to massage oil to soap to baby lotion. There's a company chef, who fixes a delicious organic lunch every day, and a Wiffle ball and bat in the backyard for when the hard-working badgers need a break from mixing up balms. And just in case you were wondering if Bill's wife, Katie Schwerin, gets any credit for shaming her husband into founding a multimillion-dollar business, the proof is in the name: The *W* in W.S. Badger Company stands for Whyte, but the *S* stands for Schwerin.

The Badger Mines are located right in downtown Gilsum at 625 Route 10. You can find Badger Balm at natural-food stores around the country, or you can order on line at www.badgerbalm.com.

Pumpkin Ready! Aim! Fire!

Greenfield

While ripe pumpkins make great pie, they also make quite serviceable projectiles for laying siege to a mock castle. That's one of the lessons a guest might take away from a visit to Yankee Farmer, Steve Seigar's farm stand and medieval-style artillery range out on Forrest Road in Greenfield.

Every weekend in autumn, Seigar and the other folks at Yankee Farmer demonstrate their trebuchet—which is really just a fancy French word for "giant, scary flinging device"—by lobbing a few of their fifty-pound-plus pumpkins at a scale replica of a medieval castle that sits near the woods almost 600 yards away. And what a trebuchet it is: With its four 10-foot-diameter rust-covered steel wheels, its huge oak-beam supports, its 37-foot steel launching arm, and its 12,000-pound

A machine that turns a pumpkin's dreams of flight into reality.

counterweight, you won't need to be told twice to stand back for the demonstration.

Massachusetts tourists, Brownie troops, high school math and physics classes, and many, many others come to Yankee Farmer to witness the world's third-largest trebuchet in pumpkin-chucking action. The Yankee Siege, as it's called, currently holds the world record for trebuchet pumpkin tosses—a whopping 1,701.44 feet, close to a third of a mile—and is the reigning champion in the trebuchet category at the Millsboro, Delaware, annual World Championship Punkin Chunkin Contest. As the Yankee Siege's 12,000-pound counterweight drops, the whole contraption lurches, and then the orange ammo at the end of the long steel arm rises up, up, and up about 75 feet in the air, until at last the pumpkin sails free and flies in a beautiful arc across the autumn sky in the general direction of the minigolf-style castle way down at the other end of the field. Laser guided these gourds certainly are not: Direct hits are relatively rare, but no one seems to mind, especially not the kids.

If a world-champion pumpkin chucker isn't enough to get you out to Yankee Farmer, how about this pièce de résistance: an approximately 10,000-pound giant mace (a huge steel ball with long spikes sticking out of it) hanging from a crane, which Seigar occasionally drops on an old car with a terrific crunch for the amusement of others. "Everybody needs something frivolous, something stupid, in their lives," Seigar told the *Christian Science Monitor*. Now, whether he was talking about the trebuchet or the giant mace, you'll have to decide for yourself.

Yankee Farmer is located at 1301 Forrest Road in Greenfield, at the intersection of New Boston Road and Forrest. Trebuchet demonstrations take place about every half hour on autumn Saturday and Sunday afternoons through the end of October, weather permitting. For more information call Yankee Farmer at (603) 547–6421.

PLEASE RETURN COFFIN AFTER USE

New Hampshire folks are famous for knowing how to stretch a dollar and a dime, but sometimes Yankee frugality can get a little out of hand. As a case in point, I offer you the story of the Hancock town coffin. For many years, those who died and couldn't afford a coffin in Hancock were graciously offered the use of a nice pine box free of charge, whether they were tramp, pauper, or just plain poor. The only catch was, once the poor and deceased was resting in peace, the coffin had to be returned to storage in the town's tramp house so that it could be offered to the next poor stiff who came along.

Okay, I'm willing to admit it makes good frugal sense to recycle a coffin, especially since its temporary occupant wouldn't really miss it much. But when the Depression ended and the town of Hancock decided to sell their tramp house, and the coffin in it, to the highest bidder, things took a "fowl" turn. Guy Stover, a local poultry farmer looking to expand his operation, bought the tramp house and, setting it up with roosts and nests, turned it into hen housing. And what, you ask, did the thrifty farmer do with the coffin? Well, he filled it with grain, of course, and turned it into a feed box for his hens.

Ruth Johnson, for many years Hancock's town historian, heard that Stover's hens were feeding from the old town coffin, and, frugal reuse though it was, the whole situation didn't sit quite right with her. To rescue the coffin from its agribusiness fate, she had her husband, Willis, make a grain bin and traded Stover the new feed box for the old town coffin. She then presented the coffin to the Hancock Historical Society, where it was finally retired after many brushes with death and a brief stint in the food-service industry. Its third and, I can only hope, final incarnation as a museum display is one most anyone would approve.

The Hancock Historical Society Museum is located at 7 Main Street in Hancock. It's open throughout the summer on Wednesday and Saturday afternoons or by appointment. For information call (603) 525–9379.

A VCEB (Very Complex, Expensive, Big) Antenna

Hancock

I may not understand what the term Very Long Baseline Array (VLBA) means. I may not even have the faintest clue what a VLBA Radio-Telescope Antenna does, or how it can, working in concert with nine other antennas virtually identical to it spread across the Western Hemisphere, produce images of far-off celestial objects with hundreds of times more accuracy than the Hubble Space Telescope—even when all the Hubble's temperamental mirrors are actually working. But I do know this much: Very Long Baseline Array Radio-Telescope Antennas are very big, very futuristic-looking, and very impres-sive to have in your backyard. And Hancock's got one of their very own.

What do you think the edge of the universe sounds like?

According to their Web site, the National Science Foundation's VLBA is a system of ten identical radio-telescope antennas working together as a single instrument to produce images of celestial objects from radio signals received by each individual antenna. Though they are operated from the official and somewhat scary-sounding Array Operations Center (AOC) in Socorro, New Mexico, the ten antennas are located in far-flung places like St. Croix, U.S. Virgin Islands; North Liberty, Iowa; Pie Town, New Mexico (no, I didn't make that name up); Owens Valley, California; Mauna Kea, Hawaii; and, of course, Hancock, New Hampshire.

Construction on the project began in 1986, and the last observing station was completed in 1993, with the cost totaling some $85 million. And what did we get for those governmental millions? Ten very big, very powerful receivers that record radio waves from the farthest reaches of our galaxy and beyond. The antenna in Hancock (just like the other nine antennas) consists of a 240-ton dish that's a whopping 82 feet in diameter. In its stowed position, it's about as tall as a ten-story building, and when the dish moves in a slow and graceful arc in order to point at some spot in the heavens many light years away, it's as if a mountain is turning its head.

The VLBA Web site mentions that the system is capable of achieving a resolution so high, it's equivalent to standing in New York City and reading a newspaper in Los Angeles. My only question now is: Aren't there much easier—and much, much less expensive—ways to read the L.A. *Times* in New York?

Hancock's very own Very Long Baseline Array Radio-Telescope Antenna is located at 70 Windy Row. From the center of the village of Hancock, follow Route 137 south to Middle Road. Turn left onto Middle Road and then take the first right onto Vatcher Road, which turns into Windy Row. The gated road that leads to the antenna will be on your left about 100 yards past Boston University's Sargent Camp. For information go to www.vlba.nrao.edu or call (603) 525–4227.

Where an Old Mack Truck Can Rest Its Weary Engine

Hillsborough

Dick Kemp's property looks like one of those massive highway truck stops where great big diesel tractors line up mirror to mirror in long rows and idle in throaty unison through the night. The only difference is, none of Kemp's trucks probably turn over, let alone idle. They're all vintage trucks decades past their prime, Mack trucks and Internationals mostly, quite a few with rusting yellow and orange plows attached to the fronts, and many with Dick Kemp's name hand-painted on a sign above the cab. In other words, it's at once a young boy's and an old man's dream come true—a personal vintage truck museum.

You say junkyard, I say great big diesel truck museum.

There are old trucks lined up in rows on both sides of River Street, just a stone's throw from the center of Hillsborough along the banks of the Contoocook River. Even if Kemp's not around when you visit, you're welcome to have a look at the trucks, snap some photos, and reminisce about the trucks and plows of your childhood, or your father's childhood. He's got hand-lettered signs posted around the place, both to let you know the rules and to let off some steam about crooked politicians. ("The world will never run out of gas," one of Dick's many signs reads, "as long as politicians keep talking.")

Of course, children aren't allowed to wander among the trucks without adult supervision, and there's a firm warning against dirty words in the guest book that Kemp's kindly put out in an old wooden box for visitors to sign.One recent entry was particularly gracious and astute. "Thank you, Mr. Kemp," it reads, "for sharing this great collection of trucks." Then, just below that, the visitor wrote, "Thank you, Mrs. Kemp, for letting Mr. Kemp collect his trucks."

You'll find Dick Kemp's collection of vintage trucks on River Street, just a block downhill from Route 149 in downtown Hillsborough.

German Pretzels So Good They Inspire *Eifersucht* (Envy)
Hillsborough

"I make an Irish soda bread that I think is really good," Judy Schneider, the owner of German John's Bakery tells me, "but I don't guarantee it's authentic." Luckily, I have no qualms about eating delicious bread, no matter its authenticity. (A fake Irish accent in the movies, though, now that really bothers me.)

Her many German customers from all over New England and upstate New York, however, tend to hold her to a higher standard for her many German breads and baked goods, all of which have German names and none of which I can even come close to pronouncing properly. "I don't care how closely you follow a recipe," she told me. "If you don't know what a bread is supposed to taste like, then it won't be authentic. And I absolutely guarantee that all my German products are authentic." And her many German customers seem to agree.

That's because Judy knows whereof she bakes. Though she's originally from Henniker, she married a German, lived in Germany for twenty-two years, and speaks fluent German. When the couple moved to New Hampshire, Judy started her very authentic German bakery in downtown Hillsborough, which each year draws more and more German clients from around the region hungry for fresh baked goods from the old world. She says that now as many as 60 percent of her customers are German, an impressive percentage in a state not known for its German immigrant population.

You'll never be able to eat a Sterno-heated soft pretzel again.

Though German John's is probably most famous for its guaranteed authentic and indubitably delicious soft pretzels, you should try a sampling of goodies. Otherwise, how else will you know if the Germans are getting their baked goods right when you travel to Düsseldorf?

German John's Bakery is right on Route 9 in downtown Hillsborough. For store hours and other information call (603) 464–5079.

Did You Happen to Get the Plate Numbers on That Garage?
Hinsdale

Sometimes oddity is only a matter of scale. Who among us, for example, hasn't displayed, for aesthetic and/or nostalgic reasons, at least one old license plate in a bedroom, shop, or garage? Who among us hasn't chanced upon some old garage with five, ten, even twenty license plates nailed to the back wall, each one looking unfamiliar and strange and therefore a little more interesting than the plates screwed to our bumpers? And who among us hasn't driven past at least one garage completely covered on all four sides with hundreds of old license plates? Oh, you haven't? Well, then, I think I've made my point.

On Route 63 in Hinsdale there's a garage that's covered, every outside inch of it, with old license plates. The multicolored, multinumbered, multistate license plate siding produces a decidedly eye-catching and downright pretty effect, but it's hard to tell if that was the owner's primary intention. Maybe he just hated to throw away his old license plates. Or maybe, out of good old-fashioned New Hampshire frugality, the owner thought it best to use recycled aluminum to side his garage.

Even Alex Duso, the grandson of the man who covered the garage with license plates and who now lives on the property, doesn't know the reason why his gramps did it. What he could tell me, though, is that his grandfather ran a salvage business and simply liked to collect license plates. And, of course, once you've got a collection of anything, you need a place to showcase it.

A frugal way to side your garage.

Whatever the reason, Alex's grandfather took the practice of displaying license plates on garage walls to new heights, and for that he deserves some real credit. Maybe not as much as the guy with the really big ball of twine out in Minnesota, but still, he deserves some.

From downtown Hinsdale take Route 63 south toward Massachusetts a little less than 3 miles, and the license plate–covered garage will be on your right.

Man Helps Monadnock Battle Mount Fuji in Popularity Contest

Jaffrey

You may not have ever heard of this international mountain showdown, but Jaffrey's Mount Monadnock and Japan's Mount Fuji, located just outside Tokyo, have been in peak-to-peak competition for years over the distinction of being the most frequently climbed mountain in the world. Both are within a day's drive of tens of millions of potential hikers, both are beautiful peaks that tempt those potential hikers with stunning views, and both are relatively easy climbs. Unfortunately, most folks have long put Mount Monadnock in second place.

If more hikers took a cue from Jaffrey local Larry Davis, Mount Fuji wouldn't stand a chance. Davis climbed the mountain every single day between May 1, 1982, and February 18, 2000, a streak of 2,850 consecutive ascents of this bare-summit mountain with its 100-mile fair-weather views. In sickness and in health, sometimes richer and sometimes poorer, in bad weather and in worse weather and occasionally in good weather, Davis climbed to the 3,165-foot summit of Mount

Monadnock every single day for almost eight years. Once, when he gashed his knee in a fall and required stitches, he even climbed the mountain on crutches. "If I don't hike the mountain," he told Mark Arsenault of the *Providence Journal* in 2001, "I'm not Larry Davis."

In mid-February of 2000, Davis almost hiked himself to death. Unbeknownst to him, he was sick with pneumonia, but he kept climbing the mountain until one morning he had to use all of his energy just to crawl to his phone to call for medical help. Needless to say, there was no ambulance crew willing to make a quick stretcher dash up Monadnock, and his streak came to an end. Since then, Davis has climbed Monadnock hundreds more times, but he takes breaks now and then. And what, you might ask, does he do on days when he's not climbing his beloved hometown mountain? Climb other mountains, of course, like Mount Katahdin over in Maine.

Even without Davis's Sisyphean efforts, some argue that Monadnock is more oft-climbed than the 12,389-foot Mount Fuji. In their book *Grand Monadnock: Exploring the Most Popular Mountain In America,* Julia Older and Steve Sherman claim that, at least since 1990 when public transportation was established to the top of Mount Fuji, the 120,000 to 130,000 people who climb Grand Monadnock each year make it the single most climbed mountain in the world. Not to rub it in or anything but, Who's your daddy, Mount Fuji?

To get to Monadnock State Park, follow Route 124 west out of Jaffrey through Jaffrey Center, then follow the signs for the park. There are over 40 miles of trails on 5,000 acres of highlands in the park and at least five major routes to the peak, with the trailhead for the shortest and most popular White Dot Trail (hmm, wonder what the blazes on the trees will be?) just beyond the visitor center. For information go to www.nhstateparks.org or call (603) 532–8862.

WELL, WELL, WELL, IF IT ISN'T OLD WILLA

Some people you just don't expect to find buried in New Hampshire. Take Willa Cather, the great twentieth-century American novelist who was born in Virginia's Shenandoah Valley; raised in Red Cloud, Nebraska; and went on to write wonderful books set in the American West. But Willa Cather was so taken by Jaffrey Center and nearby Mount Monadnock upon her first visit here in the summer of 1917, that she returned for portions of nearly every summer until her death in 1947.

Even though the rest of her family is buried in Red Cloud—some say it even appears as if there's a space left open for her between two graves—she requested that she be buried in Jaffrey Center's Old Burying Ground, the graveyard behind the meetinghouse chock-full of the town's early settlers. Cather is said to have completed her novel *My Antonia* in Jaffrey, working in a small, third-floor room at the Shattuck Inn, so it's appropriate that on her gravestone in the far, far southwest corner of the Old Burying Ground are these words from the novel: ". . . that is happiness: to be dissolved into something complete and great."

Some folks have noted that her gravestone is on the very fringes of the cemetery, tucked away in a low and lonely corner. Could it be a sign, they wonder, that as an outsider to Jaffrey Center she never quite fit in? Actually, the truth is that she almost didn't fit in—fit in the Old Burying Ground that is. The graveyard was full when Cather died in 1947, but upon learning of her request, the townsfolk did their best to make a spot for her. They found room, of course. Where there's a Willa, there's a way.

To get to Jaffrey Center, take Route 147 west out of Jaffrey. When you hit Jaffrey Center, the beautiful old meetinghouse will be up a rise on your right, and behind it you'll find the Old Burying Ground. There's a long horse shed in between the meetinghouse and cemetery, and on the western end of the shed you'll find a graveyard map that will guide you to Willa. Her longtime friend and companion, Edith Lewis, is buried right beside her in a 2- or 3-foot gap between the ceme-tery wall and Willa's grave.

WILLA CATHER

December 7, 1876 – April 24, 1947

THE TRUTH AND CHARITY OF HER GREAT
SPIRIT WILL LIVE ON IN THE WORK
WHICH IS HER ENDURING GIFT TO HER
COUNTRY AND ALL ITS PEOPLE

"... that is happiness; to be dissolved
into something complete and great."
From My Ántonia

Willa found a way into a closed cemetery.

A Pumpkin (or Two) for Every Man, Woman, and Child
Keene

Keene's Pumpkin Festival, held each year in late October, is famous for churning out Guinness World Records. The category? Most jack-o'-lanterns lit at the same time in one place. To date, they've collected more world records than a track star on steroids, racking up a grand total of eight since the Pumpkin Festival began in 1991. Sounds impressive, right? And it is, especially when you take a gander at all those rows and rows of jack-o'-lanterns lighting up Main Street. But since Keene Pumpkin Festival organizers actually invented the Guinness category themselves, their early world records came a little easy. At the 1992 festival, for example, they set the first official world jack-o'-lantern record with a mere 1,628 pumpkins. In 2003, just over a decade later, 70,000 festival attendees/participants set the celebration's most recent world record by inundating downtown Keene with some 28,952 individually carved, hand-lit jack-o'-lanterns, which at the time worked out to about 5,000 more pumpkins than there were people living in Keene.

Ever since other New England towns took note of the record-setting fun Keene's been having, though, the competition has heated up. At the 2005 Keene Pumpkin Festival, the official pumpkin tally came to 22,157—no record, but a whole lot of pumpkin flesh—but an upstart pumpkin festival on Boston Common, a mere two-hour drive away, bested Keene with 24,541 jack-o'-lanterns. That's right—Massachusetts beat New Hampshire at their own pumpkin-carving game. It was reminiscent of that fateful day in 1972 when the Men's U.S. National Basketball Team suffered their first-ever Olympic loss to, of all countries, the Soviet Union. Only worse.

Okay, I'm being dramatic. And organizers like to say that Keene's Pumpkin Festival is *not* about the numbers just about as often as they rattle off pumpkin numbers. (Come on . . . we're Americans. It's all about the numbers!) Keene's consolation is that it still holds the world record, and I suspect they're going to pull out the big guns this year. If you go, be sure to bring a pumpkin or two or three (along with a 3-inch votive candle for each), register them at one of the pumpkin tally tables so that they'll count toward the total, and then enjoy the suspense as you wait for the official count, usually announced around 8:30 P.M. There's lots to do in the meantime, of course: a children's costume parade, a pumpkin-seed-spitting contest, a museum of pumpkin oddities, not one but two jack-o'-lantern scaffolding towers, live music, and lots of nonprofit food stands. Just remember, at the close of a beautiful, fun-filled day, when the last pumpkin has finally been counted and the finale fireworks are blooming across a darkened sky, it's not about anything so crass as numbers or world records. It's about making sure Massachusetts doesn't ever beat us again.

Keene's Pumpkin Festival is held each year on Main Street on a Saturday near the end of October. For information visit www.pumpkin festival.org or call (603) 358–5344.

Man's Fear of Fire Proves Well-Founded
Keene

The nice thing about phobias is that, statistically speaking, the events we most fear, obsess over, and have sheet-soaking nightmares about rarely come to pass: the bridge doesn't collapse, the elevator doesn't get stuck between floors, the 737 doesn't plummet to the ground. Even over the long haul of a lifetime, most phobic folks never get the grim satisfaction of having their so-called unreasonable and overblown fears justified by very bad luck.

Of course, the cloud inside this particular silver lining is that, statistically speaking, at least a handful of unlucky souls do end up falling victim to the very calamity they most dread. Fred Sharby of Keene was such a poor fellow. The owner of a chain of movie theaters who lost not one but two of his big buildings to fire, Sharby was so afraid of death by conflagration that he had a virtually fireproof home built for himself and his family on Roxbury Street. The wall and floor joists were steel, the walls themselves made of plaster and stucco. Contractors laid fireproof floor tiles, installed solid metal fire doors, and encased the furnace in a thick wall of cement.

Sharby, his wife, and their four children moved into their fireproof house in 1939. Just three years later, on November 28, 1942, Mr. and Mrs. Sharby accompanied one of their sons, Fred Jr., a star on the Keene High School football team, along with his girlfriend and her parents, to a college football game in Boston. After the game, they went to Boston's Cocoanut Grove Nightclub for dinner and dancing, but a fire broke out, and Mr. Sharby met the fate he so feared, dying along with 491 others in what is still the worst nightclub fire in the nation's history. Only two of the group from Keene survived—Mrs. Sharby and Fred Jr.'s girlfriend, Ann Gallagher.

Fred Sharby's house survives, too, a subtle reminder of the wicked twists fate sometimes takes. You'll find it on the north side of Roxbury Street in Keene. From downtown Keene, follow Roxbury Street east about 6 blocks; Sharby's old house, still a private residence, will be on your left. You can't miss it: It's the only one on the street covered in flame-retardant stucco.

You and Me, Buddy, in a Sap-Gathering Race, Right Now!
Keene

Sap gathering isn't yet an official (or even a trial) event at the Winter Olympics—in fact, as far as I know, it's not even on the Olympic Committee's radar screen. But as a late-winter sport, it's got a lot to recommend it: big well-trained horses, a beautiful woodland setting, and lots of golden grade-A maple syrup to pour on your pancakes at the finish line—that is, after all that sap gets boiled down. (Since it takes, on average, about forty gallons of sap to produce a gallon of syrup, the pancakes may have to wait a while.)

Until the Olympic Committee catches the sap wave, you can get your sap-gathering contest (and maple syrup) fix at Keene's Stonewall Farm, a nonprofit working farm and educational center. Each year in late March, the farm hosts a contest in which upwards of twenty two-horse teams and their sap-gathering drivers compete to see who can most quickly and skillfully collect forty buckets of sap from the woods. Each two-horse hitch is connected to a sled with a narrow sap tank affixed to it. Using voice commands, drivers direct their horses through the woods, all the while collecting sap buckets and emptying them into the tank on the sled. The horses and driver(s) with the best time and the best teamwork, as well as the fewest spills, are the winners. And what impressive teamwork there is between drivers and their draft horses, some of which literally weigh a ton, as they navigate the tight spaces between trees in the sugar bush: Some spectators have said it's as if the drivers have voice-activated remote controls for their sap sleds.

After the contest, you can check out the farm's sugar shack and indulge in a scoop or two of ice cream with as much maple sugar as you'd like on top. And when you're done, be sure to hug a draft horse for all his hard work.

Stonewall Farm is located north of Route 9 at 242 Chesterfield Road in Keene. Take Route 9 west out of Keene for about a mile, then take a right onto Chesterfield Road. Follow Chesterfield for approximately 1 mile until you reach a bend in the road, and Stonewall Farm will be on your right. For information visit www.stonewallfarm.org or call (603) 357–7278.

Marlow Looks to Raise Profile after Old Man's Downfall

Marlow

Okay, every region in New Hampshire's got to have at least one rock that bears a passing resemblance to a human face from certain carefully selected vantage points. The Marlow profile on Bald Hill in, of course, Marlow happens to be the Monadnock Region's main Rorschach man of stone. And even though folks around these parts have a soft spot for him and will claim, again and again, that you just can't miss him if you look up on the west side of Bald Hill, quite honestly, he's not that easy to spot. At least he wasn't that easy for me to spot. That might be one reason why, with the exception of locals, Marlow's not that well known in the great state of granite.

A stone profile that calls for a little imagination in the viewer.

MONADNOCK REGION

One might think that, since the fall of Franconia Notch's Old Man of the Mountain, a guy like Marlow might be able to catch a break—you know, start getting some real face time with the press in spite of his less-than-leading-man looks. Like a backup QB when the star quarterback goes down with a sprained ankle, Marlow must have felt bad that the Old Man ended up a pile of unrecognizable rubble, but his stony heart also probably skipped a few beats when he realized his chance had finally come. But, alas, with all the memorials and tributes and anniversaries of the Old Man's fall, no one's had much time to face the fact that we need a new granite mug to symbolize our state. And people like me who have come to terms with the Old Man's loss haven't been able to say with any degree of certainty that we've actually seen Marlow's profile.

So there Marlow waits on Bald Hill, a low profile watching what just might be his best chance for stardom pass him by. If you happen to be in Marlow and can spare the time, you might want to head on up to Bald Hill, look him right in the face (if you can locate it), and tell him to hang in there. His day in the sun (and the rain and the snow) will certainly come.

From the village of Marlow, take Route 123 west toward Alstead. The pullout for viewing the profile is on the right about a mile down Route 123, but you won't be able to see Marlow unless you drive partway up the road to the next intersection. If you turn around and look toward the left side of the rocky cliff, I'm pretty sure Marlow will be there, looking to the northwest.

GRANITE TERRAPIN RARELY COMES UP FOR AIR

Not a single soul has seen the Connecticut River's elusive Mud Turtle for the last thirty-seven years, but experts are virtually certain he still lurks somewhere beneath the river's swirling waters. It was in 1969 that the Mud Turtle was most recently spotted at the surface, when repair work on the Turners Falls Dam caused river levels to fall dramatically. When the dam went back online and the Connecticut River water levels rose once again, the Mud Turtle disappeared, and no one's seen him since.

The Mud Turtle isn't some extinct or even long-endangered species—it's a pyramid-shaped granite boundary marker, anchored in concrete at the western low-water edge of the Connecticut River right on the New Hampshire/Massachusetts/Vermont border. Built in 1895 to help mark the boundary between the three states, the Mud Turtle became important when, in 1936, the U.S. Supreme Court finally settled a long-running border dispute between New Hampshire and Vermont in the Granite State's favor. The ruling said that the state of New Hampshire would include the Connecticut River all the way to the low-water line on the Vermont side, and that the survey of said line should begin where the western low-water edge of the river crosses the Massachusetts border. That's precisely the spot where builders had set what came to be known as the Mud Turtle in 1895.

At the start of the twentieth century, the Mud Turtle was at least partially above water most of the year, and that's how it got its name: The waters would swirl around its upthrust granite nose, giving it a turtle-like appearance. With more dams, and more demand for power, the Connecticut's water levels rose and the Mud Turtle disappeared. Workers had to dig it out of the mud in 1969 to get a look at it when the Turners Falls Dam was being repaired. Curious onlookers came just to catch a glimpse of what had so long been hidden.

The Mud Turtle is submerged again, and there are few folks around who've ever laid eyes on him. He may reemerge someday if the Connecticut falls again, but I certainly don't recommend holding your breath. Unless, that is, you're going to take a dip in the river and have a look for yourself.

Uncle Sam Was Alive!

Mason

History, like politics, science, and sausage making, is a whole lot messier than we like to think. The simple story of Mason's claim to fame is that it's the boyhood hometown of one Samuel Wilson, the likely real-life progenitor of Uncle Sam, that striped-pants-and-top-hat-wearing embodiment of our nation. We know this much to be true about Samuel Wilson: From the time he was nine years old until the age of twenty-three, between 1780 and 1793, he lived in a small Cape on Village Road, now painted a beautiful colonial red. At the age of twenty-three, he and his brother walked to Troy, New York, and together started a slaughterhouse and meatpacking operation. Then, at the onset of the War of 1812, the brothers secured a contract with the U.S. Army to supply troops with beef and pork.

Now, here's where things get a little tricky. Each version of the story I've heard is slightly different, and no one seems to be able to say which, if any, is true. Common to the various permutations of the tale, though, is the "fact" that the Wilson brothers stamped the letters U.S. onto their crates and/or barrels that contained meat bound for U.S. government troops. According to one Plymouth State professor, the customary abbreviation for the United States around 1812 was *U. States,* and the newfangled *U.S.* abbreviation the Wilsons used caused one of their employees and/or a steamboat passenger and/or soldiers to misconstrue the abbreviation as the initials for *Uncle Sam,* since it was Samuel Wilson and his men who had slaughtered and packed the meat. But, you might quite reasonably point out, Samuel Wilson's initials would be S.W. not U.S. Well, *Uncle,* depending on whom you ask, was either Samuel Wilson's actual avuncular nickname or a common form of affectionate address for an older male authority figure. You get to pick which explanation you like best.

After that hazy beginning, Uncle Sam got a big boost from an illustrator known as the grandfather of political cartoonists, Thomas Nast, who first began drawing him in the mid-nineteenth century. In spite of all we don't know about Samuel Wilson, folks are pretty sure he didn't look anything like the gaunt fellow we know today as Uncle Sam. In fact, Nast's earliest drawings didn't even look like our Uncle Sam: In the 1860s he once drew Uncle Sam as a big-bellied, round-cheeked, jovial man carving up a turkey for immigrants gathered around a table. It wasn't until the 1870s that Nast's drawings of Uncle Sam started to bear a curious resemblance to the hollow-cheeked, bearded,

A national icon once lived here.

top-hot-wearing president Nast so admired, Abraham Lincoln. Of course, Lincoln was brave enough to go to war to save the union, but unlike Uncle Sam, he wasn't quite brave enough to wear white-and-red-striped pants.

Samuel Wilson's boyhood home is located just a quarter mile south of Mason on the west side of Route 123. There's a green historic marker out front that details one version of the story.

Murdering Baptists Get Multiple Life Sentences of Community Service
Milford

Let's face it, the epitaph on your headstone is the very last chance you'll have to speak, your last chance to say good-bye to this wonderful mixed-up world, to offer comfort and counsel to family, friends, and strangers still trying to make their way through this vale of tears. And, of course, it's your last chance to stick it to all your enemies.

The bizarre message on Caroline Cutter's 1838 headstone in the Elm Street Cemetery is a perfect example of this last, and perhaps most unusual, kind of epitaph. Not only does her gravestone report that she was murdered, it alleges the perpetrator of the evil deed to be none other than the Baptist Church. "Caroline H., wife of Calvin Cutter, M.D.," the stone begins, "murdered by the Baptist Ministry of the Baptist Church as follows . . . " And the tale of murder that covers the large face of the gravestone all the way down past the grass and into the dirt does not shy away from pointing fingers at respectable town citizens like the Reverend D. D. Bull, who apparently accused Caroline of lying at a church meeting.

Almost two centuries of weather has made the stone hard to read, but, in my opinion, juicy small-town gossip is made even juicier by having to work for it. Way down near the grass, the epitaph closes with this summary: "The intentional and malicious destruction of her character of happiness as above described destroyed her life. Her last words on the subject were, 'Tell the truth . . .'" I couldn't read what was written on the stone below that because the words disappear beneath the sod, and I didn't want to get caught digging in an old graveyard. I am under the impression that if Dr. Cutter could have afforded a larger stone, the story would have been a lot, lot longer.

Needless to say, the Baptist Ministry of the Baptist Church didn't do any time for the alleged crime. Instead, they were given what some considered a

This gravestone's too small for such a big grievance.

lenient sentence of community service in perpetuity, something they were planning on doing anyway.

From downtown Milford take Route 101A (or Elm Street) west a couple of blocks to Cottage Street, and the Elm Street Cemetery will be on your right. The Cutter plot is on the east side of the cemetery.

A Museum for Touchy-Feely Types

Peterborough

Peterborough's Mariposa Museum has the serious mission of educating people about cultures from around the world in order to promote peace and understanding, but the crushed aluminum can man on the first floor is a sign that the museum takes a refreshingly relaxed approach to that noble goal. In fact, the nicest thing to be said about this lovely new museum is that it's not really like a museum at all. It's more like your grandmother's attic, if your grandmother had done stints in the Foreign Service on six different continents and collected lots of folk art, textiles, dolls, puppets, clothes, and musical instruments along the way. And like your grandmother surely would, the Mariposa Museum lets you touch almost everything, as long as you play nice.

That's right, almost every item not labeled as off-limits is available for handling by curious, but careful, hands. Kids and adults alike can play the many musical instruments from around the world up on the third floor (now that's truly world music), dress up in kimonos from Japan and saris from India, and make the camel marionette hanging in the stairwell dance a little jig. After all, what better way to learn about a culture than to play with its toys and instruments and, of course, walk a mile in its kimono?

That camel marionette mentioned above isn't from some far-flung desert culture, though. It's actually one of the lone surviving cast members

What's a doll from Oaxaca doing in a place like this?

from the New England Marionette Opera, which once occupied the beautiful nineteenth-century brick building where the Mariposa now resides. A marionette opera, in case you don't know, is a real-life opera performed using recorded music and marionettes. Sadly, the New England Marionette Opera theater was destroyed by fire on January 1, 1999, along with 200 of the company's handcrafted puppets and all nine complete sets from their opera repertoire, including *Carmen, The Barber of Seville*, and

121

Madame Butterfly. Actually, Madame Butterfly was one of the few mari-onettes to survive the fire—at least, her head survived—and she's been restored to her original splendor and placed in a glass case on the second floor of the museum. The Madame is too delicate to play, of course, but she's surrounded by lots of new friends from around the world who'd be happy to oblige.

The Mariposa Museum is located at 26 Main Street in downtown Peterborough; admission is charged. For more information visit www.mariposamuseum.org or call (603) 924–4555. For information about the now-defunct New England Marionette Opera, go to www.marionettes.com.

The Red Coats Are Coming! (To Help You in Produce)
Peterborough

Roy's Market in downtown Peterborough is quite possibly the greatest grocery store in the state, maybe in all of New England. No bigger than a large convenience store, really, with narrow aisles, half-size shopping carts, and only one solitary checkout lane right up against the door, it certainly can't compete with the mega grocery stores in either selection, price, or speed of sale.

But, if you're a regular, the man in the red grocer's coat stocking the shelves will ask you about your day; and the butcher in the red grocer's coat at the meat counter might give you his finest cut; and the kid in the red grocer's coat at the cash register will probably know your name; and if you can't or just don't want to lug your groceries to the car, another kid in yet another red grocer's coat who doesn't look a day over fourteen will carry your bags for you, put them carefully in the trunk, and then wish you a good afternoon. (If you prefer to carry them yourself, he'll hold the door for you and say thanks.)

It's likely you've never even wondered what happened to all those red grocer's coats you remember from childhood. They disappeared so slowly, replaced by legions of corporate-looking white button-down shirts and name badges, you may not have even noticed that they had gone the way of the fedora and the poodle skirt. That's why it's surprisingly comforting to see a small grocery store full of employees wearing them, and offering their customers the kind of old-fashioned care and service that, at least to me, those lovely vanished red coats represent.

Roy's Market (603–924–3101) is located near the Mariposa Museum at 20 Main Street.

The butchers look dashing in red. (Plus it hides stains.)

Picnic Lunch Your Way to a Pulitzer

Peterborough

The MacDowell Colony's 5,500-plus fellows have won trunk-loads of the biggest awards in the arts since the year of the colony's inception in 1907, from Pulitzer Prizes to Rome Prizes to National Book Awards. And after thinking long and hard on the subject, I believe I've finally hit upon the secret to MacDowell's stunning success in inspiring talented artists from around the country and around the world. It's all about the picnic baskets.

Each year about 250 or so artists, including writers, photographers, composers, painters, architects, and filmmakers, spend about five weeks on average at this, the oldest artists' colony in the country. Besides the great joy of being chosen, MacDowell offers its artist fellows a room at a residence house, exclusive rights to the use of one of thirty-two artist studios scattered throughout the 450-acre wooded grounds, and, best of all, three delicious squares a day, including breakfast and dinner in the dining hall and, imagine this, lunch delivered daily in a picnic basket to the fellow's studio doorstep. Can you imagine all that you could accomplish without the distraction of having to figure out what to do for lunch every day? One of the first things on your to-do list, no doubt, would be collecting that Pulitzer you've always wanted but until now were too busy fixing up turkey sandwiches and veggie wraps to win.

The MacDowell Colony, founded by the American composer Edward MacDowell and his wife, Marian (with financial support from the likes of Andrew Carnegie and J. P. Morgan), is only fully open to the public one day a year, on Medal Day in August. That's when the MacDowell Medal is presented to an American creative artist whose work has made an outstanding contribution to the cultural life of the nation, like former recipients Georgia O'Keeffe and Robert Frost. The purpose of the day, of course, is to honor one of the country's great artists, and there's a presentation address to that end. But the highlight for many of the hundreds of visitors who come to MacDowell for the day might just be the afternoon visits to the studios of the artists-in-residence, where fellows show and/or talk about their work. And, since this is MacDowell, if you plan ahead you can even have your own box lunch waiting for you. As Peter Cameron, a former MacDowell fellow and author of *The City of Your Final Destination,* said, "One of the greatest luxuries an artist can have is a day in which nothing has to be done." And such a day feels pretty darn luxurious to the rest of us, too.

The MacDowell Colony is located at 100 High Street in Peterborough. From the intersection of Routes 101 and 202, proceed toward the downtown area on Grove Street. You'll pass

A tisket, a tasket, a magical daily lunch basket.

the town post office and the Peterborough Historical Society before you come to a stop sign at Main Street. Take a left onto Main, proceed uphill, and look for a sharp right onto High Street. The colony's office is just past the Monadnock Country Club on the left.

This Houseboat Never Leaves Port

Rindge

Lake Monomonac is one of just a handful of interstate lakes in the state—about a third of its 710 acres lie in Winchendon, Massachusetts—but it's probably the only lake in New England, as far as anyone can tell, with a house made to resemble the bow of a ship anchored upon its southern shore. Built as a vacation home in 1942 by Father Wilfred A. Tisdale, the SANTA MARIA, as the words above the cottage's wide bay windows read, looks just like a ship being launched into the lake. Only it hasn't budged for the last six decades.

The Santa Maria's large, gleaming white prow, made from concrete block and mortar and painted with black portholes on both sides for that extra touch of authenticity, sits grounded on sandy shore in late fall and winter, but by spring the lake level rises and she gets her nose wet again. That's when curious kayakers paddle close by the ship's deck— which, incidentally, does double-duty as a regular old deck—to get a good look at her beautiful lines. If you happen to be paddling by the Santa Maria, though, you should resist the temptation to board her, because she's a private residence and the owners might mistake you for a privateer.

Jeff Hide of the Winchendon Springs Lake Association told me that Father Tisdale once offered mass to lake residents in the Santa Maria's "captain's quarters" on summer Sundays—he recalled how painful it was as a kid to look out the windows during church and see people enjoying themselves on the lake. But Tisdale sold the cottage long ago, and since then the Santa Maria's had a number of owners, perhaps the most famous among them the singer Kenny Rogers, who, rumor has it, found his ship-cottage attracted far too much attention from curiosity seekers like you and me and quickly sold the place. (If all he wanted was a low-key place to enjoy some privacy, though, he should have looked into a lake house without a large concrete deck in the shape of a ship's bow.) Rumor has it that at least one owner was drawn to the house out of frugality: By buying a lake cottage shaped like a ship, the man figured he could avoid the expense and hassle of owning a boat.

The Santa Maria faces due north on the southern shore of Lake Monomonac in Rindge, just yards from the state line. Since it's a private residence, the cottage is best viewed from the lake. A boat launch is available to the public on Route 202 just north of the Massachusetts border at a place called, quite fittingly, North of the Border. It's located at 1207 Route 202 in Rindge, just across the street from Valley Marine. From the village of Jaffrey take Route 202 south a little over 7 miles and North of the Border will be on your left. For information and boat ramp fee, call (603) 899–3100.

Pagan War Heroes Finally Honored
Rindge

The Altar of the Nation, a national memorial to American war dead comprised of stones from all fifty states and containing soil from every country where American soldiers have fought, is clearly the focal point of the Cathedral of the Pines, an ecumenical outdoor place of worship and reflection in honor of the nation's heroes. In front of the altar are rows and rows of benches spread beneath the towering white pines, enough space for 2,000 worshippers to gather on a carpet of pine needles and pray to whatever god or gods they revere. Behind the altar you'll see a view of Mount Monadnock so beautiful, it will leave you primed and ready to give thanks.

Lieutenant Sanderson Sloane and his wife, Peggy, originally selected the site where the Cathedral of the Pines is now located as the place where they would build their home when "Sandy" returned from World War II. Dr. Douglas and Sibyl Sloane, Lieutenant Sloane's parents, transformed that same hillside overlooking Monadnock into a memorial after they learned that Sandy had died when his plane was shot down over German lines in 1944.

A church with rain cancellations.

The Cathedral of the Pines literature describes the site as "a place of spiritual fulfillment for people of all faiths," and if you explore the grounds you'll find a remarkable testament to the religious freedom and tolerance so many American soldiers, including Sandy Sloane, have fought for: a circle of stones in a small patch of woods where Wiccans, pagans, Druids, and other worshippers of so-called earth-centered religions can honor their god(s) and/or goddess(es) as they see fit. According to B. A. Robinson of the Ontario Consultants on Religious Tolerance, Diane DeRochers, a Wiccan high priestess from Groton, Massachusetts, was at first denied permission when she requested access to the Cathedral of the Pines site to perform a ceremony in honor of pagan, Druid, Wiccan, and other "earth-centered" religion veterans. After negotiations and some public debate and disagreement about the matter, the Cathedral of the Pines board decided to honor their commitment to religious tolerance and allow the witches onto the site. What's more, they even gave Wiccans and other neo-pagans a place to hold ceremonies. Just two circles of stones in a clearing with a statue of what looks like a winged pixie girl in the center, this ceremonial space for witches is quite possibly the most unique symbol in New England of the freedom and tolerance most Americans so value, and for which some even give their lives.

For more information and a schedule of services, go to www .cathedralpines.com or call (603) 899–3300 or (866) 229–4520.

LAKES REGION

War Veteran Horse Buried Beside Grandma

Alton

Should a beast of burden be given a town's best eternal digs? Is it fitting for a veteran who saw veterinarians to be buried right beside Grandma Mildred and Uncle Ed? That's the dilemma Alton townsfolk faced when Major George D. Savage expressed the desire to have his Civil War charger Old Tom buried in the town cemetery. A tough question, especially when the man making the request is an influential town citizen, not to mention a certified Civil War hero.

And as with many a small-town conundrum, Alton kept the peace through compromise. If Major Savage couldn't bury Old Tom *inside* the cemetery, well then, it wouldn't hurt to let him bury his trusty steed—who, after all, was like a minor member of the major's family—just outside the cemetery walls, now would it? The compromise was acceptable to Major Savage, according to Florence Davis, the part-time curator at Alton's local museum. He buried Old Tom right up next to, but not inside, the cemetery walls.

Graveyards, though, are like waistlines: They expand with age. And keep expanding in perpetuity. Fast forward over 150 years of funerals, and Old Tom now rests in peace deep inside the boundaries of the Alton Cemetery, so deep, in fact, that his grave sits on a little knoll in the dead center of the graveyard. If you go to pay your respects, you'll find Tom's small headstone and large burial plot—I can only imagine how big the coffin must have been—surrounded by a low white picket fence. Someone even posted a picture of Tom from his war days on the fence, and underneath the photo is a little information about his life, including the fact that he once saved Major Savage's life.

Whether intentionally or not, the town of Alton makes a clear case for greater equine equality in the funereal industry. Let's just hope that if the trend catches on, there'll be room for all of us in the graveyards, two legs and four. Alton's equal equine opportunity cemetery is just south of town on the west side of Route 11.

Do you bury a horse 6 feet or 4 feet under?

My Daughter Might Be a Vampire!

Barnstead

Poor twenty-one-year-old Janey Dennit of Barnstead wasn't dead long before her neighbors had what might seem to us the rather peculiar desire to dig her up and take another hard look at her. And dig her up they did, on September 5, 1810, with an out-of-town Freewill Baptist minister named Reverend Place observing the proceedings and noting them in his diary. It wasn't so much that her friends had a hankering to see her face again—all they wanted was to get a good look at her stomach, just to be sure nothing strange was growing on it. A perfectly normal desire, of course, considering the fact that the townsfolk suspected that Janey's body was harboring an evil spirit that was killing her dear father, sick with consumption (tuberculosis as we now know it), and that, if said evil spirit were left unchecked, it would go on to kill others. That's right: Family, friends, and neighbors thought young Janey Dennit was a vampire.

Ms. Dennit wasn't the only vampire that Michael Bell, author of *Food for the Dead: On the Trail of New England Vampires*, dug up in early New England lore. In fact, two or three centuries ago it may have been a relatively common practice for villagers in outlying areas to disinter the bodies of those who had died of consumption, a disease for which there was no scientifically known cause or cure, to look for unusual signs—anything from fresh blood in the heart to abnormal stomach growths—all evidence, they believed, the body was possessed by an evil spirit that was causing loved ones to sicken and die. And it gets even more ghoulish. If the townspeople found, say, fluid in the heart, they would typically remove the organ from the body, burn it on a rock nearby, mix the ashes with water to make a hearty broth, and then feed the potion to a sick family member believed to be in thrall to the evil spirit.

Call it extremely alternative health care or homeopathic medicine that's a little too close to home. In Janey's case, however, there was no such bitter, chalky pill for her father to swallow. When Barnstead citizens checked "to see if anything had grown upon her stomach," according to Reverend Place's journal, "[they] found nothing as they supposed they should." Janey's dad died anyway, but perhaps it was a source of consolation to him that his own child wasn't slowly draining the life from his body. Most parents can't be so definitively assured.

The Dennits are buried in the Hodgeton Cemetery in Barnstead. Take Route 107 north towards Laconia; after you pass the Pittsfield dump, it's a half mile to a dirt road on your left. The graveyard is a short way down the road, just beyond the trailer home. You'll find Moses Dennit's grave quite easily, but according to Stewart Merrel, town historian of Barnstead, no one knows for sure where Janey and the other children are buried, since a number of stones in the graveyard are unmarked.

Clubs from Yesteryear at Arlene's Caddy Shack

Barrington

Arlene of Arlene's Caddy Shack on Route 202 in West Barrington may have one of the most ingenious business plans ever devised: She doesn't pay rent, she doesn't advertise, and she's often just plain not around to peddle her varied stock of used golf club sets, bag included. (A sign says she also sells golf paraphernalia, like balls and tees, but used clubs seem to make up the majority of her inventory.) The sets, ranging from the fairly recent to the pretty darn ancient, are arranged in two long rows in Arlene's front yard, protected from the elements by small white party tents. I've stopped by three times now and haven't yet caught Arlene at home, or, you could say, at work. I envy her with a passion that's beginning to feel obsessive.

While it's hard to decide what to like best about Arlene's decidedly anticorporate Caddy Shack, my vote is for the handwritten marketing on the large red price tags tied to the golf bags with white string. As befits a purveyor of used sports equipment, Arlene has a knack for making older golf clubs sound appealing, as if age hasn't left them outdated so much as it's given them a patina of charm and good luck. "Semi-antique," reads one red tag that happens to be tied to a very old-looking set of clubs. "A lot of good rounds of golf have been played with a set like this." And though the subtext remains unspoken, we know what Arlene's getting at: If a lot of good rounds have already been played with that semi-antique set of clubs, well, then, it would stand to reason we could play many more good rounds of golf with those same clubs. "One of the great iron sets of yesteryear," reads another red tag. Doesn't "iron set of yesteryear" sound so much better than "really old golf clubs"? Give that woman a job writing ad copy on Madison Avenue. If you can sell semi-antique golf clubs, you can sell anything.

Arlene's Caddy Shack is located on the south side of Route 202 in Barrington, about midway between the Route 4 and Route 126 intersections. Hours are unpredictable, but the prices are right.

A Dinner Date with a Real Storyteller

Center Sandwich

It's not always such a rare treat to be told stories when you're on a dinner date. To put it as diplomatically as possible, some people are too confident that the tiniest details of their own lives will be as fascinating to others as they are to themselves. By the time the check comes, for example, you might feel as if you'd attended an in-depth CIA briefing on the strained interpersonal relations at your companion's place of employment. As my sister-in-law used to say when I'd reveal to her some less-than-tasteful nugget of experience from my own life: "Too much information."

The Corner House Inn's Storytelling Dinner Program aims to prevent such narrative narcissism by offering professional dinnertime story-telling that's captivating, absorbing, and downright entertaining. Held at the inn's restaurant every Thursday evening from late October through early May, the program boils down to this: The Corner House staff serves you and other participants a very reasonably priced and delicious meal, and then after dessert (mine was a scrumptious ice cream parfait) professional storytellers entertain you with their tales.

And what wonderful tales they are. Mary Ann Posner and Rebecca Flood told a total of three stories at the dinner we attended, including a whimsical yarn called "Alfie's Awesome Autumnal Adventures" and a charming story about nannies. The Corner House Inn hosts new story-tellers each week, so regulars get to hear a variety of stories and story-telling styles. And since the inn's dining room is cozy and intimate, listeners get fully absorbed in the tales, so absorbed that they might even feel comfortable enough to interject. At one point during our sto-rytelling dinner, Ms. Flood told us with genuine conviction that librari-ans come to be so smart not by reading the books in the stacks, but by absorbing information "like potatoes." "Like potatoes?" a proper-looking woman sitting near us called out. Yes, like potatoes. Profes-sional storytellers can pull off almost anything in a good story, even a simile comparing a librarian to a potato. In fact, just about the only thing they're not permitted to do is bore their listeners. If only that were the case with all our dinner dates . . .

Storytelling dinners begin each Thursday evening at 6:30 P.M. For more information and reservations, contact the Corner House Inn, which is located at 22 Main Street in Center Sandwich, at (603) 284–6219 or visit www.cornerhouseinn.com.

How Come Dad Always Gets to Be Mayor?

Effingham

"I don't go over *there*," Earl Taylor tells me, pointing across the street. Go where? "Over there, to New Hampshire." He's standing at a sharp curve on Route 153 in South Effingham, a corner known locally as Taylor City, made up of a handful of houses and two stores that sit quite literally on the New Hampshire–Maine state line. Earl's home and the general store he's run for the last six decades rest just barely in Parsonsfield, Maine, and *there*, a few short paces across the street in South Effingham, New Hampshire, his son Bill runs a wonderful gift shop called Ye Old Sale Shoppe. "I haven't seen him in a long time," Earl tells me, referring to his son. "Tell him I said hello."

You can't believe everything Earl Taylor, the self-proclaimed mayor of Taylor City, tells you. In fact, you might not be able to believe *anything* he tells you. Not only is he a local politician of sorts, he confesses to being a "dirty politician" who's tried everything from offering free ice cream to voters on election day, to blowing up the ballot box before

Who says the dead don't vote?

declaring himself victor (yet again), to writing out absentee ballots (in support of his own campaign, of course) for each one of his many dearly departed relatives in the graveyard up the hill. Dirty politicians rarely if ever come clean, though, the way Mayor Taylor so freely does, and that straightforward crookedness must make all the difference in the minds and hearts of voters. That and the free ice cream.

The annual Fourth of July parade and mayoral election in Taylor City died out a few years ago, but Earl, at age eighty-two, is still the mayor of Taylor City, and he wears a dusty baseball cap that says MAYOR OF TAYLOR CITY to prove it. More importantly for those who love authentic general stores, he still chews the fat behind the candy counter almost every day in the very same store his uncle built way back at the turn of the twentieth century. There's a black cat that sleeps in the sun-filled windows, a record-setting seventeen-point buck's head mounted on the back wall, and an eclectic collection of groceries, from canned marachino cherries to cornmeal to dried prunes, but no beer. "I won't sell it," Earl says matter-of-factly. "What if someone came in here, bought a pack of beer, and then had an accident? I guess I got a conscience."

Of course, the money from beer sales would help his bottom line, but Earl's not working for the money. "You know as well as I do that the big stores have taken over," he tells me, and this time I know for sure he's telling the truth. "I just do this because it helps keep me out of trouble." Apparently it keeps him out of New Hampshire, too, if we can take the mayor on his word.

To reach Taylor City go south on Route 107 from Center Effingham for about 4 miles. Bill's Ye Olde Sale Shoppe (603–539–7910), a store packed to the rafters with gift items, including dolls, toys, books, and antique glass, will be on the left, and Earl's store will be just across the street.

Big Mortar, No Pestle

Franklin

If you don't think a kitchen implement could make a fine tourist attraction, then you're sadly mistaken. On the northwest corner of the intersection of Central and Dearborn Streets in Franklin, there's a granite boulder with a hollow spot on top that was used first by Abenaki Indians and then by early settlers as a kind of natural mortar, a place where they could grind their corn into meal for making cakes and breads. For centuries upon centuries, native peoples and the settlers who followed them used this naturally occurring tool to perform the simple but crucial task of preparing the food that nurtured them. Okay, it may not be as exciting as Disneyland, but it still makes for a pretty fascinating detour.

But wait, there's more. Not only do you get the boulder with the natural hollow used for centuries to grind corn, but if you order now, you'll also receive, in this special one-time-only TV offer, a boulder with a shad carved on it. That's right, on the same corner where you'll find the granite boulder with the

I did, I did see a fish on that rock!

mortar on top, you'll also find a boulder carved with the faint outline of a fish, a fish that the state historical marker nearby tells me is a shad. If you're like me and you don't really know what a shad looks like, you've got a great excuse, since, as the marker tells us, "After the dams were built the fish disappeared." (The shad is making a bit of a comeback, though, now that they've built fish ladders up the dams in Lawrence, Massachusetts, and in Concord.)

The state historical marker also makes the harder-to-verify claim that the shad was the "red man's" favorite fish. As far as I know, the early settlers weren't conducting polls to determine the Abenakis' fish and game preferences, but maybe the proof is in the carving.

You can find the mortar and the shad at the northwest corner of Routes 3 and 11 in Franklin. The green state historical marker is clearly visible at the corner.

Fixer-Upper Castle w/Lake View
Gilford

If one fine summer morning, when the sun is just coming up over the Ossipees, you should be lucky enough to find yourself riding in a boat on the remarkably clear waters of Lake Winnipesaukee, New Hampshire's largest and most famous lake, look over to the western shore around Belknap Point, just southeast of Weirs Beach. If you raise your eyes to the top of Lockes Hill, you'll see a wide clearing in the northern hardwoods, and in that clearing you'll swear you spy an honest-to-goodness medieval castle, hovering above "the broads" of the lake like a vision from a dream. The towering gray granite walls, the castle's high battlements with their gap-toothed merlons and crenels, might even make you feel as if you'd been transported in an instant to the Scottish Highlands or the Rhine River Valley.

Of course, you haven't. However much the building might look like a medieval ruin, it's neither a ruin nor medieval. Benjamin Ames Kimball, a turn-of-the-twentieth-century entrepreneur in the Horatio Alger vein and president of the Concord and Montreal Railroad, built the castle—reportedly an exact replica of one he saw along the banks of Germany's Rhine River while on holiday in Europe—for the then quite lordly sum of $50,000. It took a hundred Italian stonemasons two years (1897–99) to build the castle, and during the months of construction Kimball housed them all on the *Lady of the Lake*, a tourist vessel he owned that once plied the waters of Winnipesaukee. To say Kimball spared no expense in the castle's construction may be an understatement: He even extended a railroad spur to the base of Lockes Hill so that he could commute to work in Concord by train—in his own private railcar, of course. It's good to be the guy who lives in the castle . . .

Kimball Castle stayed in the family's possession until the early 1960s, at which point it was bequeathed to a local nonprofit organization. Since that time, the property and the castle itself have limped along in a legal limbo that's included land conservation attempts, multiple ownership transfers, and other shenanigans complicated enough to make my head hurt. The end result is that, though the castle had fallen into serious disrepair, the current owners have made much-needed improvements and are now trying to sell it to hotel or resort developers with pockets deep enough to return Kimball Castle to its original splendor. With heating costs what they are these days, however, it seems developers are a little wary of drafty castles.

Kimball Castle is located at 59 Lockes Hill Road in Gilford. From Laconia, take Route 11 northeast past the airport. After Sawyers Ice Cream on the right, go approximately 1 mile. Just past the blinking yellow light, take a right onto Lockes Hill Road, go to the very top, and the castle will be up a rise on your right. It's privately owned, so be sure to ask permission before investigating.

AND YOU THOUGHT YOUR TOWN HALL WAS SCARY?

The ghost that Stephanie, the Alton town planner's secretary, saw one evening in the town hall's auditorium was dressed a lot like an L.L. Bean model in one of its late-fall catalogs: tan khaki pants, blue denim button-down shirt, and an orange fleece vest. And he looked like a model, too. Thin, tall, with salt-and-pepper hair, he had, according to Stephanie, the rugged look of an outdoorsman. But instead of slinging a backpack over his shoulder and striking a pose before a bucolic background of snowy peaks as a Bean model is wont to do, the apparition merely entered the room, paused for a moment as if to cast a glance at the town council gathered around a long table for its monthly meeting, and then quickly turned and vanished out the door.

Stephanie was recording the minutes of the town meeting that evening when she happened to glance toward the door. "I remember looking up and seeing him and not thinking much of it. I just figured he was looking for another meeting and had stepped into the wrong room." So how did she know she had seen a ghost? "No one else at the meeting saw him," Stephanie continued, "except for one woman seated at the table with me. And at the end of the meeting, she looked at me and said, 'Did you see what I saw?'"

After doing a little investigating, she discovered that no one else in the room had seen the apparition, including a few taxpayers seated in chairs across the room observing the proceedings. "He would have had to pass right in front of the people who were seated by the door, but not one of them saw him come into the room," Stephanie told me. I was convinced. There's at least one dapper, well-dressed ghost in the Alton Town Hall who's just not that into town politics.

Where do you think that ghost got his plain-front khakis?

Stephanie's sighting is certainly not the first at Alton's town hall. In fact, the turn-of-the-twentieth-century brick structure, with a spire that houses a chiming clock the building's caretakers still must wind by hand, has achieved minor fame for its ghouls. And though Stephanie isn't the only current town employee to have seen a ghost, she's the only one who would speak to me about it. Turns out they're a little protective of their ghosts down at the Alton Town Hall—perhaps they like the way their resident ghouls make the property tax assessor seem so much less scary.

Outdated Outboards Find Some Respect
Gilmanton

Outboard motors from the 1920s look like a cross between an industrial kitchen appliance and a Portuguese man-of-war. They're all-aluminum, burnished gray in color, with an uncovered lump of an engine on top and a thin shaft that leads down to a propeller at the bottom. Aluminum doesn't rust, of course, and since the outboards dating from that era weren't painted, there was nothing to chip, alligator, peel, or fade. They don't look old and antique so much as they look Spartan and useful.

I know this because I've seen at least thirty or forty of them, each clamped to its own alloy motor stand, lined up three deep in Larry Carpenter's

Wall-to-wall indoor outboards.

accordion addition between his 200-year-old Cape and his barn. The man-of-war-meets-kitchen-appliance models, though, are just one sub-set of Carpenter's large and surprisingly compelling collection of antique outboard engines. He's got Johnsons and Eltos; he's got Mercurys, Martins, and McGullochs; and, of course, he's got the ever-popular Evinrudes, all lined up in rows, shimmering in the glow of an old-fashioned outboard motor dealer's sign.

"Things have gotten so complicated," Carpenter told me, "that if your car breaks, even the dealer might not be able to figure out what's wrong with it. The great thing about these outboards is that they're simple." Of course, simple is a relative term. If you're like me and don't know a water pump from a prop, it's a little difficult to replace a couple of parts, which is all that most old outboards need, according to Carpenter, to be returned to perfect working order

More than just simple, though, the outboards are also quite beautiful. A 1955 Evinrude Big Twin and a 75-horsepower 1964 Scott McGulloch were two of my favorites: Both engines are fully restored, with sleek, crisp lines and covers that reminded me of the classic cars of the era. "I grew up on Lake Winnipesaukee," Carpenter told me, "and I didn't get my driver's license until I was eighteen. Until then, I could get everywhere I wanted to by boat—over to Laconia, up to Meredith, down to Alton Bay." And that's another thing these old outboards will do: bring the past rushing back for those of us who've spent any time on lakes over the last seven or eight decades, when inboards hadn't yet taken over the backs of most boats and American outboard manufacturers were still turning out light, powerful, well-made engines that an ordinary guy—someone smarter than me—could fix.

Carpenter's place is at 702 Province Road, just on the Belmont-Gilmanton line. He used to list his phone number in state tourist materials and be open to the public on some weekends and on a by-request basis, but he's scaled back his collection and no longer wants his number published. He's listed in the Belmont phone book, though, and he told me that those who are interested can look him up, give him a call, and pay him a visit.

20,000 Bikers Looking to Party in Your Town
Laconia

What's old, big, very loud, and runs the gamut from rowdy to raunchy to ridiculous? If you said your grandfather, you may or may not be right, I can't really say—after all, I don't know your grandfather. But if you said Motorcycle Week at Laconia, which at eighty-two years and counting is the oldest, one of the biggest, and certainly one of the best motorcycle rallies in the country, then you're most definitely correct.

The official events at this weeklong rally include a vintage motorcycle race through the streets of downtown Laconia, daily "gypsy tours" to the seacoast and the mountains and everywhere in between, races at the track in Loudon, hill climbs at Gunstock, and a gigantic motorcycle parade down the strip at Weirs Beach—some riders wear outrageous costumes, while others don't really wear much at all.

But it's probably the unofficial, unsponsored, and uncensored events in Laconia that have always been the most fun. For example, there was the time that . . . On second thought, I won't go into detail about that time here, since this book has been rated G for all audiences, but let's just say things used to get interesting when 30,000 to 40,000 leather-clad motorcyclists showed up in a town to have a good time. Nowadays, there are a whole lot more bankers and lawyers riding hogs, and things have gotten downright family friendly at Motorcycle Week.

Just a word of warning, though, about hanging at the Weirs with tens of thousands of Harleys: Loud pipes might save lives, like the bumper stickers say, but they certainly don't do your eardrums any favors. You might consider bringing some earplugs if you're sensitive to triple-digit decibels.

Laconia Motorcycle Week is held each year in early June. Most of the real bike and people-watching action happens at Weirs Beach, right on Route 3 in Laconia, but there are events scheduled throughout the area. For more information visit www.laconiamcweek.com.

Well, That's a Big Rock Alright

Madison

I once heard someone say about the Grand Canyon: "There's not much to see—it's just a big hole in the ground." Ouch. That's a sucker punch to one of our national natural wonders. Someone so darn insensible to the aesthetic and spiritual juju, for lack of a better term, of one of our most spectacular holes in the ground would certainly not be a good candidate for a visit to the Madison Boulder. The boulder may be less famous than the Grand Canyon—undeservedly so, of course—but it's a no less mind-blowing manifestation of the awe-inspiring forces at work in our natural world, if you just look at it in the right it's-so-much-more-than-just-a-big-rock kind of way.

First of all, any boulder visitant should know that the Madison Boulder holds a continental record. That's right—at 87 feet long and 37 feet high, it is the largest known "glacial erratic" on the continent of North America, a land area that must literally be littered with glacial erratics. Don't know what a glacial erratic is? Basically, it's a rock that ends up somewhere it doesn't belong as a result of being kidnapped by a glacier and dumped somewhere far away from home. Thus, through no fault of its own, it becomes labeled an "erratic" by the scientific community, an oddball, a geological freak—oh, the cruelty of labels. No matter, because this glacial erratic, as big as an average apartment building and weighing just shy of a million pounds, according to one estimate, was once picked up by a 5,000-foot-thick sheet of ice and carried miles and miles to where it now rests, in a fine patch of woods just off Route 113 in Madison. And you thought mountains couldn't be moved? Oh ye of little faith . . .

There are no T-shirts, coffee mugs, or key chains for sale (and no donkey rides to the top) at the Madison Boulder, making it a refreshingly natural wonder. From Conway follow Route 16 south to Route 113 south, then travel 3 miles and watch for the sign for the Madison Boulder Natural Area. Take a right onto Boulder Road, and follow it to the end. The Madison Boulder sits in the woods just beyond the parking area.

It just sits there for millennia and geologists still call this boulder erratic.

GOING POSTAL ON LAKE WINNIPESAUKEE

The 74-foot *Sophie C* may be the oldest floating post office in the country, but the kids on Bear Island don't run to greet it with such great gusto each day just to fetch the mail: In addition to delivering more than 25,000 letters and packages over the summer season to residents of a dozen islands on the north end of Lake Winnipesaukee, the vessel also happens to sell boatloads of ice cream to hungry kids and campers at select ports of call. And there's nothing like the promise of cold chocolate éclairs on a hot summer day to make the kids come running.

Owned and operated by the same folks who run the bigger and more famous tour boat, the M/S *Mount Washington,* the 125-passenger *Sophie C*—carrying on a tradition started in 1892—has been delivering Lake Winnipesaukee mail to Loon, Beaver, Three Mile, and Bear Islands, among others, since 1969. The U.S. government contracts the vessel as an independent rural route carrier for the town of Laconia, but by a special act of Congress in 1916 the *Sophie C* also has the right to cancel mail, making it the oldest official boat post office in the country. Jim Morash, the *Sophie C*'s captain, told me that stamp collectors come from all over the country for the rare red postage cancellation stamp that reads LAKE WINNIPESAUKEE.

You're welcome to accompany the captain and the mail clerk on their watery rounds Monday through Saturday, rain or shine. Two-hour trips depart from Weirs Beach twice a day, one at 11:00 A.M. and one at 2:00 P.M., with mail stops that include the private Beaver Island where Klondike the dog comes out to greet the mail boat, a couple of YMCA summer camps (the mail clerk says parents send loads of packages at the beginning of each two-week session), and, of course, Bear Island with its rush of dairy-starved kids. And if you're wondering what your fellow passengers on the mail run will be like, Captain Morash said that the *Sophie C* attracts "your PBS-type crowd, if you know what I mean." I think I know exactly what he means: geeks like me.

Reminding Churchgoers of the Ultimate Goal, Since 1872
Milton Mills

If you've ever seen people wave those gigantic foam hands at sporting events, the ones with an index finger pointing boldly skyward, then you've got a good idea of what the wooden carving that's perched atop the spire of the Milton Mills Congregational Church looks like. Of course, from a sociological perspective, those larger-than-life foam hands help fans both to celebrate and to mutually affirm their belief in the all-around greatness and outright supremacy of their home team and, by extension, themselves, though they've really done little more than buy a ticket and a foam hand, not the most arduous path to greatness to be sure. Waving of such foam hands is often accompanied by the chant, "We're number one! We're number one!" Trust me on all this: I read a paper on it once in college.

The message behind the hand with the raised index finger at the very top of the church in Milton Mills is, to be honest, a bit more obscure. Yes, it's possible that church founder and lead builder Aratus B. Shaw was acting as badly as a Boston sports fan when he carved the finger-wagging hand from a solid block of wood

Which way to the pearly gates?

and secured it to the very top of his newly constructed spire way back in the year 1872. Perhaps Mr. Shaw was shouting out his own congregation's praises from the rooftops, if you will, and taunting all the surrounding communities, from Sanbornville to Union to Laskey Corner, with the relative inferiority of their own measly churches.

But given the man's godliness—he's rumored to have single-handedly built the church pews—it's not likely he would have wanted to tell the whole world that he and his church were number one. More likely, he wished to remind his fellow worshippers to keep their eyes on the prize, the heavenly reward that awaited them if they did their work, loved their neighbors, and kept their pride in check. Or maybe, just maybe, he wanted people to look up more often and enjoy the star-filled New Hampshire sky.

The Milton Mills Congregational Church is on Highland Avenue just off Church Street. The easiest way to get there is to go straight on Church Street at the fork in the road where there's a sign for Milton Mills. Travel a few blocks, and Highland Avenue will be on your left.

Giant Petrified Frog Xing
Moultonborough

New Hampshire motorists know that when you're driving the back roads, you've got to keep one and a half eyes on the road and the remaining half eye on the woods. (I know it sounds difficult, but practice makes perfect.) Otherwise, you'll be totally unprepared when that white-tailed deer, or red fox, or black bear, or gray coyote, or black skunk, or half-ton brown moose comes bounding out of the trees and into the roadway, right into the path of your speeding vehicle. An eye attuned to wayside surprises could end up saving both you and a very big moose some splitting headaches, both the literal and the not-so-literal kind.

If you're traveling along the eastern shore of Lake Winnipesaukee on Route 109 between Tuftonboro and Moultonborough, keep a half eye out for a rare giant amphibian that lives in the area. As you cruise at 40 miles per hour down 109, it might first register in your field of vision as a bold flash of green. Then, if you turn your gaze upon it, you'll notice its girth, the sheer bulk of it, hunkered within a mere giant hop or two from the middle of the road. Take your foot off the accelerator, if you know what's good for you, and maybe even stop to check it out.

The giant frog is actually a green-painted boulder to which an enterprising local has affixed two round, painted eyes. While the shape of the boulder itself doesn't necessarily scream out frog, the green paint and the eyes and the tapered point at the front of the rock all conspire to make the boulder a fairly impressive giant frog imposter. All they need to do now is post one of those bright yellow road signs with a giant frog in profile, just to help prevent the terrible tragedy of an oversize-amphibian-meets-motor-vehicle collision.

One of New Hampshire's rarest species, the boulder frog.

The boulder frog is 2.1 miles south of Route 171 on the east side of Route 109 in Moultonborough. If you're heading south on 109, the frog will be on the left-hand side just after the sign for Ambrose Cove Marina.

The Castle That Shoes Built

Moultonborough

It wasn't until the 1960s that Thomas and Olive Plant's mountaintop estate, located on a promontory high above Lake Winnipesaukee, came to be known as "Castle in the Clouds," but it's certainly fitting that the name was changed from its original. The Plants, who built the estate between 1913 and 1914 on a world-class lake-view mountaintop parcel that would grow to include a whopping 6,300 acres, named their home "Lucknow," perhaps as a reminder of the great good fortune they had in possessing wealth enough, and then some, to build it. (It also happens to be the name of a town in India where Plant thought he might build his estate.)

But by the time of his death in 1941, this rags-to-riches French-Canadian entrepreneur from Bath, Maine—an industrialist, inventor, and former owner of what was reported to be the world's largest shoe company—was flat broke in the sixteen-room, eight-bath mansion he called "Lucknow," reduced to borrowing money from friends to get by. Plant had gone from brilliant industrialist to failed financier, investing heavily in Russian bonds just before the October Revolution in 1917, in sugar just before its post–World War I collapse, and in bad land deals throughout the 1920s. After he died, Olive had to watch creditors auction off everything she and her husband once owned. The Plants weren't so lucky now. Their castle, and everything else they had ever owned, vanished into the clouds.

Their loss is our gain, though, since 5,500 acres, seven mountains, miles of hiking trails, and the Plants' mansion itself are all at our disposal, thanks to the Lakes Region Conservation Trust, which now owns and manages the property. The acreage, part of an unusual circular arrangement of volcanic mountains called the Ossipee Mountain Ring Dike, remains surprisingly rugged and unspoiled, making for great nature hikes. But the true gem of the property is the house itself. An example of the Arts and Crafts style, it features simple and elegant materials, including granite quarried from surrounding mountains, massive wooden beams hand-hewn in Bath, a Spanish tile roof, and English lead doors. The list of amenities the Plants installed in the house would make any early twentieth-century real estate agent salivate, including a water-powered electric generator, a central vacuum system, a self-cleaning stove, and a brine-cooled refrigerator. And the view out the back door of Lake Winnipesaukee and the White Mountains is one of the most spectacular sights I've now had the good luck to see.

The mansion is open May through mid-October; admission is charged. From Moltonborough, take Route 109 south to Route 171 and proceed east toward Tuftonboro until you see the

When this Castle in the Clouds isn't in the clouds, the view is world-class.

sign for the main entrance to Castle in the Clouds. Trail parking is available on Route 171, just east of Severance Road. Trail use is free and access is year-round. Call (603) 476–2352 for more information.

This Arch Was Supposed to Be for Tilton

Northfield

Charles Tilton, nineteenth-century merchant and millionaire, had a thing about statues. It seems he couldn't stop building them all over town. The most famous among the five objets d'art that yet remain in the towns of Northfield and Tilton is called Tilton's Arch, a towering 55-foot vanity monument supposedly patterned after the Arch of Titus in Rome, dedicated to none other than Charles Tilton himself. And you thought your vanity plates were cool.

Of course, everyone should know by now that when you make a bold statement with statuary, you run the risk of looking a little foolish. Just remember that long-forgotten Egyptian king who wrote on his monument, now a crumbled ruin in the middle of the desert, something like: "Look upon all my great work, you pitiable little insignificant, sniveling worms, and see for

A monument to a man with a thing for bold statuary.

yourselves how great I am and how superterrific I'll always be, and then indulge me for a moment by thinking again about how powerless and tiny and unbelievably unimportant you are in comparison. Thank you."

Tilton's mishap wasn't quite as monumental, but it was still bad enough that some reportedly refer to the arch as "Tilton's Folly." Local lore has it that Tilton planned to be buried under the five-and-a-half-story-tall granite monument (who needs a gravestone that big?), but that when the section of the town of Tilton on which the monument rested became part of Northfield, Charles refused to be buried there. (Others claim that he also overlooked the fact that since the arch isn't located inside a cemetery, he couldn't have been buried there anyway. Details, details.)

The four other Charles Tilton–commissioned monuments around town are allegorical statues of America (depicted as an Indian princess), Europe, and Asia, as well as a zinc statue of Chief Squantum. None of these serve as gravestones for Charles either. He ended up being buried elbow to elbow with the rest of Tilton's nineteenth-century citizens, right in Park Cemetery, with a fairly sizable but certainly not colossal monument marking his eternal resting spot.

Park Cemetery is located on Route 3 about a half mile south of the center of Tilton; Charles's grave is to the back. The arch is in Northfield, just up the hill from Tilton. From downtown Tilton follow Bridge Street across the Winnipesaukee River, take a left onto Elm Street, and then a quick right onto Summer. The entrance to the park will be just up the hill on your right.

Cold, Cold Caves
Plymouth

New Hampshire has no shortage of rocks—it's known, after all, as the Granite State. Nor does it have a shortage of curious rocks, or odd rock groups, or (lest we digress into a discussion of the local music scene) unusual groups of rocks. In fact, there are so many curious rocks in the state, I had to impose a limit on the number I'd allow myself to include in the book, just to make sure I'd have space to write about a few non-granite rarities.

The Polar Caves in Plymouth, though, are too good to extrude, I mean, exclude. A series of boulder caves that were formed when huge chunks of rock cleaved from Raven's Cliff during an ice age over 50,000 years ago, the Polar Caves are a delight to explore. There's a visitor center, a gift shop, hiking trails, and an extended boardwalk that you can follow up into the caves. No need for your old spelunking clothes here—you can explore the caves easily on foot and without any shimmying on your belly through who-knows-what sliminess. There are, however, lots and lots of stairs, so be prepared for a little workout.

The Polar Caves are located in Plymouth a few miles west of town on Route 25, otherwise known as the Tenney Mountain Highway. The park is open daily May through October; admission is charged. For more information call (603) 536–1888 or (800) 273–1886.

Ye Olde Crutch Factory
Rumney

For decades and decades, your sprained ankle, twisted knee, or broken foot was Rumney's good news, since once you got done screaming, you'd be in dire need of something locals had lots and lots of: crutches. In fact, Rumney was for a while the largest manufacturer of wooden crutches in the world, with a handful of mills along Stinson Brook turning out thousands of pairs of crutches a week during World War I.

One might assume that since Rumney has long been the so-called wooden crutch capital of the world, the town might pay homage either to crutches themselves or to injuries of the lower extremities of every kind, all those minor mishaps that create a steady worldwide demand for mobility assistance. But in Rumney, you'll find no Crutch Memorial, no Avenue of the Overpronated Ankle, no form of homage whatsoever, really, to the invalid. You won't even find the town putting on a good Crutch Festival or hosting the International Crutch Olympics, with events that might include a crutch marathon, crutch gymnastics ("Look at the grimace on his face, Bob . . . He really stuck that landing."), or a crutch decathlon (who among us hasn't, at the end of a long convalescence, practiced the crutch toss?).

Maybe the town didn't want to attract too much attention for profiting from our pain. Or maybe they were too busy trying to keep pace with the world's clumsiness to worry much about dedicating monuments or putting on parades. Thankfully, the Rumney Historical Society Museum, located on Buffalo Road in the old town hall, displays a sizable sampling of Rumney-made wooden crutches and crutch memorabilia. And the president of the historical society, Roger Daniels, is more than happy to make disparaging comments about aluminum crutches, the competition that knocked the last remaining Rumney crutch factory (Kelly Manufacturing) off its feet back in 2002. "I wouldn't give two cents for those aluminum ones," Roger told me. "You know what I call them? Lightning rods."

The Rumney Historical Society Museum is open Saturday from 10:00 A.M. to 2:00 P.M., Memorial Day through Labor Day. For information call the society at (603) 764–9380 or Roger Daniels at (603) 786–9291. To see the old Kelly Manufacturing crutch factory, head north out of town on Stinson Lake Road for about 200 yards, then take the first right onto Water Street; the crutch factory, a red building with a couple of old crutches nailed to the siding, will be down a rise on your left.

Famous Summertime Resident Needs Bath after Cavorting with Locals
Silver Lake

You might suspect that there are days when the summer resident down the road, the one who bought the old farm with the leaning barn and a leaky roof, might rue the day he bought a piece of the Granite State. Well, for one famous summer resident, Edward Estlin Cummings, otherwise known as E. E. Cummings, one of the most famous American poets of the twentieth century, we have definitive proof of his New Hampshire ambivalence.

Cummings began visiting New Hampshire as a young child when his father, Dr. Edward Cummings, bought Silver Lake's Joy Farm from its previous owner, Ephraim Joy. After the tragic death of his father in an automobile collision with a train in Ossipee, he continued to return to the farm with a view of Mount Chocorua almost every summer for the rest of his life. Why he did so, however, isn't quite clear.

Yes, some of his most famous poems celebrate the beauty and joy to be found in the natural world—and there's plenty of that, of course, around Silver Lake—and he painted countless pictures of Mount Chocorua's bald peak. But he also wrote long, whiney letters to his mother about how many repairs the old Cape house needed and how tedious and never ending its upkeep was. "If only there were enough money to remodel this place completely so that human beings could live here," he complained to his mom, "instead of fighting leaks and drafts . . . [and] slaving like ditch diggers."

And he found even less joy in his New Hampshire neighbors than he did in Joy Farm. In fact, Cummings suspected that most of the locals he did business with were out to swindle him—of course, he may not have been too far off there. In one letter, he reports that after spending an evening dining with a couple of New Hampshire natives, whom he describes as "two of the stupidest people I've ever met in one room," he had to "take a bath to wash off the ennui." Cummings lived the rest of the year in Greenwich Village, where, we can hope, he found the company a bit more stimulating. Either that, or he took his postparty baths year-round.

E. E. Cummings's old farmhouse, now with a large new addition, is located on Salter Hill Road near Silver Lake in Madison. It's on the National Register of Historic Places, but it's a private residence, so there's no access to the public. There was an unusual two-story octagonal gazebo beneath some evergreen trees on the property where Cummings wrote and painted. You'll also find a small lighthouse dedicated to E. E. Cummings's father on the shore of Silver Lake in the village proper.

What's the Devil Doing Relaxing in New Hampshire?
Silver Lake

In New Hampshire, there really is no such thing as just a rock. On Route 113 near Silver Lake, there's a large boulder that, with the right amount of Rorschach-style imagination, looks like a chair for a giant. Known as Devil's Chair, the boulder's been a popular picnicking spot for generations. Families would park their carriages at the roadside, then clamber up to the rock's wide flat ledge, spread out their blankets thereon, and indulge.

But the rock has its darker, less picnicky side. According to local legends, horses frequently got spooked when they'd pass by Devil's Chair, particularly at night. Townsfolk too, it's rumored, preferred not to tarry at the rock on a dark fall evening, perhaps merely because of the rock's name, or perhaps because in those quieter, more desolate moments near Devil's Chair, they too could sense the very same ominous aura that so often spooked their horses. The size of the devil's chair suggests that he's a very, very large personage, and it's probably fair to say no one wished to be around if he should ever decide to take his seat.

Though no one in town with whom I spoke knew any more damning tales about the rock than its tendency to give horses and people the willies, everyone agrees that somewhere in the rock's hidden past must lie horrors enough to warrant the devilish name. The more important mystery is why Lucifer would want to spend any time at all in a place that looks so much like heaven.

Devil's Chair is located on the east side of Route 113 between Silver Lake and Madison.

Church in Your Bathing Suit

Squam Lake

We all know it's a little harder to make it to church when the weather's fine and you're spending time at the lake. Okay, it's a lot harder. But I've got a church recommendation that'll make the whole prospect of an hour spent in prayer on a heavenly summer Sunday seem a lot more appealing. Parking at the dock is limited, though, so be sure to get there early.

Once home to the nation's first boys' residential summer camp, Chocorua Island on Squam Lake now functions as an outdoor chapel and island devoted exclusively to worship and prayer. In 1903, over a decade after the camp closed down, former campers and others established the Chocorua Chapel Association for the purpose of holding summer religious services on the island. The island's owner eventually donated it to the association in 1928, and since that time the nonprofit

CROSS-COUNTRY SKIING FOR PET LOVERS

Sled and skijoring dog races aren't all that uncommon in the Granite State, but no sled dog race organization boasts as uncommon a history as that of the New England Sled Dog Club (NESDC). Founded by Wonalancet's Arthur Walden and wife Kate Sleeper Walden in 1924, the NESDC hosts numerous sled dog and skijoring races each winter in places like Tamworth, Hill Village, and Meredith, snow permitting and dogs willing, of course.

Arthur Walden, dog-sledding expert, Klondike gold rush adventurer, and Antarctic explorer, is probably most famous for establishing a new breed of sled dog, the Chinook, named after his hundred-pound, golden yellow, mastiff-looking wonder of a dog who—not to get too incestuous here—contributed more than his fair share of DNA to the new breed's gene pool. It was Chinook and his offspring who ran (and often won) the first sled dog races in New Hampshire; it was Chinook who led Walden's team on a first-ever dog sled ascent of Mount Washington in the early 1920s; and it was Chinook who accompanied Walden to Antarctica in 1929 as a spry twelve-year-old to run supplies in support of Admiral Richard

E. Byrd's bid to reach the pole. "Walden's team was the backbone of our transport," Byrd later wrote in his book *Little America.* "Had it not been for the dogs, our attempts to conquer the Antarctic by air must have ended in failure."

Midway through the expedition, though, Chinook went missing and was never found. It's said that newspapers around the country carried the tragic story of the dog's death. When Arthur returned to Wonalancet in 1930, he found his finances in shambles, his wife Kate ill, and half his Wonalancet Farm and kennels sold off. He soon got out of dog breeding entirely and spent most of his time and energy caring for Kate. Chinooks almost died out a couple of times over the last ninety years, but I'm happy to report the breed is currently alive and doing well, and still bearing a powerful resemblance to great-great-great grandpa Chinook.

For a schedule of the New England Sled Dog Club's events, go to www.nesdc.org. If you'd like to attend a particularly historic race, check out their late-January Tamworth sprint and skijor on Lake Chocorua, billed as the oldest continuous sled dog race in the Northeast. Lake Chocorua is on the west side of Route 16 in Tamworth, about a mile north of the intersection of Routes 16 and 113.

group has provided a unique place of worship and religious celebration for local residents and visitors alike.

Each Sunday at 10:30 A.M. from late June through the beginning of September, clergy of various Protestant denominations, many of whom are summer residents in the area, lead services at the island's outdoor chapel. Worshippers arrive by powerboat, by sail, by kayak, and by canoe, and then they gather in front of the stone altar, a large rough wooden crucifix behind it, to pray together under the open sky. If you want to park your boat at the dock, be sure to get there before 10:00 A.M.—if you arrive later, you'll have to anchor at a mooring offshore and get picked up by the association's water taxi. Canoers, kayakers, rowers, and other self-propellers, though, can just pull their boats up on shore.

Chocorua Island Chapel is located just west of the holy center of Big Squam Lake. For information about Sunday services, including which pastor (and which denomination) is on deck for the next service, call (603) 968–3313 or visit www.churchisland.org. To inquire about private services, including baptisms and weddings, call (603) 968–7931.

This Pulpit Rocks!

Tamworth

Tamworth is the next stop on our county-by-county tour of the state's 500 most important boulders. It's our mission to discover where the most important rocks are, to learn what exactly they're famous for, and to discern, if we can, their plans for what is likely to be for them a rocky future.

This particular rock, located just up the hill from the center of Tamworth, is a local landmark because it's the site where Reverend Samuel Hidden, Dartmouth College graduate and Revolutionary War veteran, was ordained as the first pastor of Tamworth's brand-new Congregational Church. On that day, September 12, 1792, both the town and the church itself were so new, in fact, that an actual church building didn't yet exist. No church, no problem, at least for a man like Samuel Hidden. He climbed to the top of what is now known as Ordination Rock and was ordained there before a small group of new church members.

At some point, granite steps were installed alongside Ordination Rock to allow for easy ascension, and a small marble obelisk was placed on top to commemorate the historic event. The boulder reportedly served as Hidden's pulpit until he and his congregants were able to finish construction of their church. Whether that's true or not doesn't really matter. The image of a flinty pastor delivering sermons to his flock from the top of a boulder is too rich an image to lose to pesky facts.

Each fall in early September, Tamworth holds a small service at Ordination Rock to commemorate Samuel Hidden's ordination. For informa-

A pulpit with a commanding view.

tion call the local historical society at (603) 323–2900 or Tamworth's Remick Country Doctor Museum and Farm at (603) 323–7591.

To get to the rock from the village of Tamworth, travel west past the Tamworth Inn and the Barnstormers Theater and up the hill on Cleveland Road for a little less than a mile. Ordination Rock will be on the right side of the road directly across from the cemetery.

Biggest Pines in These Parts
Tamworth

When settlers first came to the Lakes Region, they found vast tracts of virgin woodlands—mountains and valleys, hills and dales all covered in ancient spruce, fir, and pine. They proceeded to mow down most of those forests in order to scratch out a living on valley and hillside farms,

Go ahead, hug one of the biggest pines around these parts.

but in a few generations, as people left their farms for cities and the West in droves during the 1800s, those forests came back with a vengeance. Unfortunately for big and old tree lovers, there was a second round of clear-cutting around the turn of the century, but in some isolated and forgotten spots, older trees remained. And they just kept on growing.

In Tamworth's 1,958-acre Hemenway State Forest, a large stand of white pines escaped the turn-of-the-twentieth-century axes, and now you can hike among 150-year-old pines almost as big and tall as those early settlers must have felled. The whole stand, known as the Big Pines Natural Area, is just a short hike from the road, and an on-site map will guide you to the tallest pines—as if they aren't easy enough to spot as it is. Three of the trees on the 125-acre tract are over 140 feet tall, and the tallest specimen tops out at just a pine needle above 150 feet and growing, of course. If we're lucky, in another hundred or so years, 150-foot-tall pines will be as common as weeds. In the meantime, they're an eyeful to behold.

To visit the Big Pines Natural Area, head north on Route 113A out of Tamworth. In about 3 miles you'll see a sign for the natural area—if you cross the Swift River bridge on Route 113A, you've gone too far.

Words to Live By, or Scratch One's Head Over
Wakefield

If you're not scanning the roadside as you drive, ever alert, as I am, for the weird and wacky, then you'll probably drive right by the bizarre granite monument on Route 153 in the town of Wakefield, just beside Belleau (pronounced *Bell-oh*) Lake. The monument is big and tall, maybe 20 feet tall and 25 feet wide, with black marble accenting its top. And the message chiseled in the rock for generation upon future generation to read is enough to make you go . . . huh?

The most head-scratch-inducing section of the monument reads as follows:

> A dam connecting 5 small ponds into a beautiful lake. The bottom floated to the top causing a challenge that everyone thought could never be won. Thousands of ways were tried. With our faith we were finally blessed with success. And with the help of my guardian angel that sits on my shoulder and whispers to me what to do and how to do it. All of us have one. Listen to his whisper.

You can't tell me that paragraph wouldn't make your old English teacher shudder with indignation before sharpening her dreaded red pencil and going to work. "Fragment!" she'd scrawl in the monument's margins. "Unclear! What challenge? Give an example of one of the ways! Be specific!"

According to Marcy Kelly, a member of the private Belleau Lake Property Owners Association, the monument makes a somewhat oblique reference to the fact that after Ernie Belleau dammed a series of five ponds on his property in 1963 to create the 800-acre lake (and a whole bunch of valuable lake-

A monument reminding you of that angel on your shoulder you always seem to forget about.

BELLEAU LAKE
FOUNDED 1963

ERNEST R. BELLEAU Jr. HIS WIFE CATHERINE M BELLEAU

BEST TO REMEMBER TEST OF TIME AND SWEAT AND UNLAMENTED WORK
IT NEVER LET THE OTHER DOWN
THUS FROM US A GIFT OF SHORELINE AND FOREST TREES THESE
SEEM MEANT TO BE MEMORIAL AND TESTAMENT TO THE CEMENT IN
TRUE LOVE

A DAM CONNECTING 5 SMALL PONDS INTO A BEAUTIFUL LAKE THE
BOTTOM FLOATED TO THE TOP CAUSING A CHALLENGE THAT EVERYONE
THOUGHT COULD NEVER BE WON THOUSANDS OF WAYS WERE TRIED
WITH OUR FAITH WE WERE FINALLY BLESSED WITH SUCCESS AND WITH
THE HELP OF MY GUARDIAN ANGEL THAT SITS ON MY SHOULDER AND
WHISPERS TO ME WHAT TO DO AND HOW TO DO IT ALL OF US HAVE
ONE LISTEN TO HIS WHISPER

TRAVELED WORLD-WIDE
ALWAYS HAPPY RETURNING TO OUR FREE LIVING PEOPLE WHERE
FREEDOM RINGS THE LOUDEST PLUS OUR 100 YEAR OLD GIFT FROM
THE FRENCH THE STATUE OF LIBERTY THE WELCOME AND LOUD RINGING
SIGN OF FREEDOM KNOWN THROUGHOUT THE WORLD

NEW HAMPSHIRE — LIVE FREE OR D

COUNTRY DOCTOR
DR G BOZUWA
PRESIDENTS   GOVERNORS

THOSE WHO   FAMILY
HELPED CREATE
LLEAU LAKE

front lots), huge chunks of sodden land started breaking loose from the bedrock and floating around Belleau Lake. Many of these floating masses of soil and root systems have been towed to shore, chopped up, and hauled away in trucks over the years, but some larger land-masses, virtual floating islands with sizable trees and shrubs, drift around the lake to this day. As the monument proudly proclaims, the problem is pretty well taken care of, which gives residents plenty of time to sit on their docks, soak up some rays, and give thanks to Ernie's guardian angel.

From Sanbornville, take Route 153 north through Wakefield and East Wakefield villages (around 7 miles) and then watch for the monument on your left; there's a small circular pullout that takes you right up to it. If you hit Route 110, you've gone too far.

The Toys Have Taken Over
Wakefield

The Museum of Childhood of Wakefield has a doll overpopulation prob-lem: The small white Cape is literally stuffed to the rafters with over 5,000 of the smiling, glassy-eyed, immaculately dressed little munchkins, as well as nearly sixty furnished dollhouses for them to explore. But if you can squeeze your way past the nineteenth-century porcelain dolls, the Cabbage Patch Kids, and Barbie and Ken, you'll find lots of less-well-known childhood playthings tucked away in nooks and crannies throughout the house.

The place is chock-full of miniature trains, planes, and automobiles; push toys, pull toys, and wind-up toys; music boxes; and hobby horses; and a whole room full of bears (even the walls are covered with bears). My personal favorite, though, was the walnut-shell and acorn-head skier, with the pointy bottom of the acorn serving as her button nose and the acorn cap her dashing little hat. Was that the way Barbie looked 500 years ago? (Maybe back then she was making girls feel bad for not having heads shaped more like acorns.) There's even a fully appointed nineteenth-century one-room schoolhouse out back, no toys included, just to remind you that childhood has never been all fun and games.

The Museum of Childhood of Wakefield is located at 2784 Wakefield Road, just north of the village center. It's open from mid-June through Labor Day. For information call (603) 522–8073.

A house where the toy chest has exploded.

First Snowmobiles Slow and Old but Never Spin Their Wheels

West Ossipee

Virgil D. White of West Ossipee patented the term *snowmobile* way back in 1913, but the machines he assembled and sold at his Ford garage on Route 16 didn't bear much resemblance to today's high-octane, bullet-shaped, neon-accented sleds. They looked a lot more like cars on skis because that's in fact what they were: White invented and manufactured a snowmobile conversion kit for Model T Fords that consisted of two 5-foot-long skis for the front and dual 8-inch-wide caterpillar-style tracks on double rear wheels for the back. The end result was an odd-looking Model T that could travel at top speeds of 15 miles per hour over unplowed roads long off-limits to newfangled four-wheeled traffic.

Virgil sold both conversion kits and finished snowmobiles, but sales were slow until people started seeing the Model T snowmobiles in snow-churning action—eventually, some postal carriers even used them for winter delivery. By the late 1920s, when snowplows became standard equipment in almost every snowbelt town—effectively killing the Model T snowmobile market—White had manufactured and sold over 25,000 of his conversion kits.

In 2005 and 2006 the Model T Snowmobile Club of America gathered at the Whittier House Restaurant, just across the street from Virgil White's old West Ossipee garage (now Johnson's Gas & Appliance), giving the public a chance to see some of Virgil's now quite rare originals. The club won't be having their rally in West Ossipee in 2007, but the Greater Ossipee Area Chamber of Commerce and the Whittier House will be hosting a Winter Carnival in late February, with lots of great events throughout the week, including a chance to hitch a ride on one of a dozen or more Model T snowmobiles. Since these old-fashioned sleds don't travel much faster than a runner's sprint, though, you can leave your fancy crash helmet and goggles at home.

For information visit www.ossipeevalley.org or call the chamber of commerce at (603) 539–6201.

DARTMOUTH/SUNAPEE REGION

Wayside Pines Set Good Example with Protective Headgear
Bradford

While it's nice to stand out in a crowd, being big and tall does have its disadvantages beyond the ordinary apoplectic fits in the fitting room. If you happen to be a big and tall 200-year-old eastern white pine, for example, you're at increased risk for being struck by lightning and going up in towering (albeit pine-scented) flames. That's why state forestry workers outfitted the three tallest white pines in Bradford's Tall Pines Scenic Area with lightning rods. A metal pole and dangling wire may not be the most fashionable, or natural-looking, tree accent, but it sure beats becoming another smoking statistic. Burning trees can't stop, drop, and roll until it's way too late.

A five-acre tract of land owned by the New Hampshire Department of Forestry, the Bradford Tall Pines Scenic Area contains some of the oldest and largest white pines remaining in the state. And unlike other oldie-but-biggie trees in New Hampshire, these fourteen eastern white pines, all over 100 feet tall and still growing, aren't located in some remote mountain valley loggers simply couldn't reach, accessible only by backcountry expedition. In fact, these princely pines are growing right in downtown Bradford, just a short walk off Main Street. Over half a century ago, the Davis and Symonds Lumber Company had the foresight to give this prime real estate to the state in order to permanently protect the massive trees growing here along the banks of the West Branch of the Warner River. The three lightning rod–equipped pines, their wires dangling all the way to the ground, are all over 130 feet tall, with the largest specimen topping out at over 140 feet tall and 15 feet in circumference, making it one of the most impressive old pines in the Northeast. And that measurement doesn't even include the lightning rod on top.

Bradford's Tall Pines Scenic Area is located just southwest of the intersection of Main Street and Route 103 in Bradford. There's a small parking lot with a sign directing you 50 yards north to a quarter-mile trail through the woods. The main grove is located on the east bank of the West Branch of the Warner River, with footpaths leading to individual trees.

This is one tall pine that's well grounded.

I Like My Men Boiled
Charlestown

Even though James O'Neill didn't live in Charlestown long, just a few months shy of a year, he must have made quite an impression on the locals, because not long after he died and townspeople buried him in a pauper's grave, someone dug up his body and boiled it. That's right—someone in Charlestown dug up poor old James and boiled him. Who, why, and exactly how they boiled him—for example, whether they boiled him with or without spices and root vegetables—we don't know. But boil him they did.

O'Neill came to Charlestown in August of 1786, sick with an unnamed illness and in need of lodging but with no money to pay for his care. A tavern owner in town, Jonas Baker, agreed to house and feed the stranger after O'Neill promised to repay him in full with his labors once he recovered. But O'Neill's health only deteriorated over the course of the winter, and he eventually died in April and was buried in an unmarked grave.

If it weren't for the Charlestown town meeting held just a few months later on September 4, 1787, we wouldn't know a thing about the whole boiling incident. According to written records of that meeting, one pressing matter of business was to decide if the town should, "by a committee or otherwise," prosecute the persons who dug up and boiled James O'Neill. It's a credit to the good, anti-corpse-boiling citizens of Charlestown that they voted in favor (with one person dissenting) of forming a committee to file a complaint with the state's attorney against those who did the digging and boiling.

And that, unfortunately, is where the historical record ends. Town historian Barbara Jones has combed the archives and found no other mention of the incident to help answer tough questions like who boiled O'Neill and why. The most likely reason for the body boiling was fear of the illness that killed O'Neill, but the mystery remains unsolved. And we can only dream of finding the answer to an even tougher question: Why not roast?

Marge Reed oversees Charlestown's historical archives, located in the town hall. Her office is open Tuesdays from 9:00 A.M to noon or by appointment; call (603) 826–4478.

Local World-Record Wooden Bridge: Too Big for Its Own Trusses?

Cornish

The longest covered wooden bridge in the United States, and the longest double-span wooden bridge in the world, probably in the galaxy, stretches 460 feet from Cornish, New Hampshire, to Windsor, Vermont, across the Connecticut River. You might think that, by rights, only half the bridge belongs in this book since, presumably, only half the bridge rests in the state of New Hampshire and, ergo, only half qualifies as a bona fide New Hampshire curiosity. Not to worry, dear reader. New Hampshire had good lawyers in a neighborly border dispute with Vermont, and the boundary between the two states was established at the low-water mark on the Vermont side of the Connecticut River. Both the river and the world's longest double-span wooden bridge are ours. Mostly.

Built in 1866 by carpenter/engineers Bela Fletcher and James Tasker, the Cornish-Windsor Bridge, as it's somewhat accurately but none too creatively called, is composed of two spans measuring 208 feet apiece.

A long wooden bridge that's almost all ours.

To build it, Fletcher and Tasker employed something called the Towne Lattice truss, which means that the long sidewall supports, or trusses, from which the roadway is suspended look like giant lattices made of crisscrossed pine timbers fastened together. Operated as a toll bridge from the time it was built until June 1, 1943, and still open to interstate traffic, the bridge has undergone a number of repairs and renovations over the last 140 years including, most recently, a $4.5 million reconstruction in the late 1980s. I'm sure Vermont reminded us of the fact that the bridge is mostly in New Hampshire when that bill came due . . .

The bridge is well worth the money, though. When you see her from the banks of the Connecticut, she looks just like a covered bridge only longer—a stretch covered bridge, a slender reminder of another century vaulting between two states. Now if we can just change the name to more accurately reflect the fact that the Cornish-Windsor Bridge is almost all ours. Of course, we don't want to offend our eastern neighbors, but doesn't the Almost Wholly Cornish–Just a Little Bit of Windsor Bridge have a nice ring to it?

The Cornish-Windsor Bridge is located in Cornish, just across the Connecticut River from Windsor, Vermont, on Route 12A.

Exclusive Wildlife Don't Mind Mixing with Locals
Croydon

Never is it so obviously true that good fences make good neighbors than when your neighbor happens to be an exclusive, members-only, 24,000-acre wild game preserve, reportedly the largest private game preserve in the United States, whose well-fenced grounds were originally stocked with an ark-load of animals including bison, white-tailed deer, bighorn sheep, moose, antelope, elk, caribou, Himalayan mountain goats, German wild boars, and pheasants. The pheasants didn't pay much heed to the fences and flew away, and the more exotic species didn't survive, but the deer, bison, elk, and boars all flourished in the preserve at a time when large herbivores like deer and moose had been entirely eradicated from the state.

During the Hurricane of 1938, the preserve's fences were toppled and numerous animals escaped, including wild boars and elk that reportedly wreaked havoc on local farmers' crops. Needless to say, the literal fences were quickly mended, but the wild boars became such a nuisance that the state passed legislation in 1949 holding the Blue Mountain Forest Association, the nonprofit established to run the preserve, known as Corbin Park, responsible for any damages caused by escaped pigs. These days, according to reports, the association takes good care of the over 30 miles of wire fence encircling the preserve, and the neighbors most appreciate it.

Broken fence makes neighbors' boar sore.

Although privately owned, the park was open to the public for much of its early life at the begining of the twentieth century, with a key to the western gate available at the Cornish Flat store to anyone who asked. These days, access is restricted to members, their employees, and guests, with association bylaws dictating that membership remain between fifteen and thirty people. Just in case you're thinking of joining, you may want to reconsider: Members are required to own at least two but no more than four shares, which can be bought, rumor has it, for around $50,000 a share. And the yearly dues to keep the many miles of fences mended and all those wild boars fed sure ain't cheap either. Better to stick with the locals and hunt the wild boars that still roam the hills on the cheap side of the fence.

Corbin Park has no public access, but you can drive up to the park boundary in any one of at least four towns: Croydon, Cornish, Plainfield, and Grantham. Since Corbin Park comprises almost half the town of Croydon, though, you may want to take Route 10 north out of Newport to Croydon Flats, turn left, and then take a quick right onto Croydon Turnpike, which will bring you to one of the east gates near Croydon Corners.

There's Low-Grade Uranium Ore in That There Pit!
Grafton

If you're interested in starting a small uranium collection—strictly for household use, of course—the Ruggles Mine in Grafton could be your best local bet. While you won't be able to gather enough of the heavy element to fuel your own household nuclear reactor, if you're really lucky you might be able to find some very slightly radioactive, completely safe uranium-containing minerals, like gummite and autunite, that you can chisel carefully from the walls (watch for sparks) of this the oldest mica, feldspar, beryl, and uranium mine in the United States. What better way to impress your friends than with the uranium you mined on vacation?

Sam Ruggles discovered mica on what's now called Isinglass Mountain (isinglass is the name given to mica in the shape of thin semitransparent sheets) way back in 1803, and people have been blasting, digging, and tap, tap, tapping at the rocks there ever since, in search of mica for everything from heat resistant windows to nail polish; feldspar for fine china and other ceramics; beryl for space-age metals; uranium for all the glowing wonders that a radioactive element can offer; and, most recently, souvenirs for the kids.

A century and a half of mining has transformed the mountainside into a stunning and strangely beautiful landscape, a huge man-made canyon whose sheer walls of quartz and feldspar are riddled with towering arches, darkened passageways, and caves so perfectly shaped that they look straight out of the comic strip *B.C.* The best part is, visitors are encouraged to make the open pit a little bigger by mining for their own minerals, whether they be slightly radioactive or just plain pretty. An impressive informational video and a great big display of specimens of quartz, amethyst, mica, garnet, and a whole host of other minerals awaken the inner prospector in visitors before they pick a pick and set to work, hammering away at anything that glints a little in the sunlight. Was it just me, or do visitors get a strange look in their eyes when they enter the mine, perhaps indicative of a mild case of mineral fever? While it might be confusing to the kids, Ruggles is one historic site where the normal rules of Do Not Touch, Do Not Take, Do Not Break, and Do Not Smash This Support Column With a Hammer most certainly do not apply.

The Ruggles Mine is located in Grafton just off Route 4. Take Route 4 to Grafton Center, then at the sign for Ruggles Mine, turn left onto Riddle Hill Road and follow the signs. For information call (603) 523–4275 or visit www.rugglesmine.com. Admission is charged.

Sculpture Takes 12,000 Years and Creator Still Not Finished
Groton

A swimming hole is a swimming hole is a swimming hole, right? Well, not necessarily. How about a swimming hole at the bottom of a narrow canyon whose walls have been shaped and smoothed over thousands of years into elegant curves, half-arches, and hollows by a mix of glacial meltwater, rocks, silt, and sand? How about cool crystal-clear water, nice pools as deep as 15 feet in places, and some perfect rock ledges— not too high, not too low—to jump off? If you're still unimpressed, I suggest you head to the nearest water park and take a dip in the wave pool. For the rest of us, this is as good as swimming holes get.

The centerpiece of a 272-acre New Hampshire state park officially known as the Sculptured Rocks Geologic Site, this narrow gorge doubling as an outdoor art installation is nothing short of jaw-dropping. A footbridge over the Cockermouth River gives you a bird's-eye view of what Mother Nature can dream up with a little water, some sand, and eleven or twelve millenia, but the most impressive views of the sculptured rocks are to be had while you float on your back in the sparkling clear waters below. There, right inside a smooth granite hollow, you might get that fleeting but delicious sense of the immensity and mystery of creation and the smallness of your own single life. Or, you might just look up and say to yourself, "Now that's a great spot to jump."

From Route 4 in Canaan, head north on Route 118 to Bucks Corner and take a right onto Sculptured Rocks Road. Follow the road for 6 or 7 miles and watch for the sign directing you to the parking area. The sculptured rocks lie just north of the road. For those interested in checking out a natural waterslide, try Soup Bowl Glide on your way back to Canaan. Head west on Sculptured Rocks Road for about 1 mile to Orange Road (aka Atwell Brook Road), then take a left and follow the road for 0.8 mile to a logging clearing. Park and follow the footpath east toward Atwell Brook, where you'll find Soup Bowl Glide, a natural waterslide that, when the water level is adequate, gives you a nice easy ride.

A Mural to Mock a Cramming Coed
Hanover

While it's certainly quiet as a tomb, the reserve reading room in the basement of Dartmouth's Baker Library isn't the ideal study spot for the focus-deficient student. Yes, there's lots of room on the long study tables to spread out your hernia-inducing textbooks, and, yes, the high basement windows afford very little in the way of distracting views, and, yes, the chairs are sufficiently uncomfortable to discourage cat-naps. But, oh, those basement walls! Painted in fresco with not one but two 15-foot-tall depictions of human sacrifice, hordes of zombie school-children, the most frightening and severe-looking schoolmarm you'll ever see, and a towering Technicolor Jesus, to describe just a few pan-els, these library walls may be some of the most striking, and most dis-tracting, in the whole country.

Between 1932 and 1934, renowned Mexican muralist José Clemente Orozco painted one of his most ambitious masterworks, *The Epic of American Civilization*, right here in the basement of Dartmouth Col-lege's main library. Composed of twenty-four panels and covering a stunning 3,000 square feet of wall space, the mural traces the history of the Americas in two parts. The first, located in the east wing of the reserve room, tells the story of the development of pre-Columbian civi-lizations in America through the legend of the Toltec and Aztec god Quetzalcoatl (depicted as a white-robed, white-bearded, bright blue–eyed messiah), while the second part, located in the west wing, depicts the development of American civilization in the wake of European conquest and settlement. Painting in fresco, Orozco employed virtually the same techniques Michelangelo did in the sixteenth century, each day skimming a fresh coat of plaster onto a section of wall before applying his pigments, the colors penetrating the wet plaster in such a way that the towering and frequently downright menacing figures in Orozco's mural became a part of the wall itself.

Reportedly, the mural caused some controversy at Dartmouth, not necessarily because it distracted coeds from their studies, but, more likely, because it offered a striking critique of Anglo-American culture and the modern academy. In perhaps the most disturbing panel, located at the far end of the west wing and titled "Gods of the Modern World," a group of skeleton scholars, dressed in caps and gowns from universities throughout America and Europe, attend a

It must be hard to study with this guy looking over your shoulder.

ghoulish birth. Stretched painfully on a pile of ugly-looking tomes, a skeleton arches her back and strains to give birth to a few books through her pelvis, while a robed skeleton scholar-turned-gynecologist bends to grasp the "newborns" in his bony hands. Admittedly, it's not the ideal image to spur students on to ever-loftier academic heights, but it just might be the motivation some overworked physics major needs to take a little study break.

The Orozco mural in the basement of Baker Library can be viewed daily during normal library hours. Dartmouth College is in downtown Hanover, and Baker Library is the large building on the north end of the Quad.

Doom and Gloom Tomb Room
Hanover

So you can't find Dartmouth's old Alpha Delta Phi house, alum Chris Miller's real-life inspiration in writing National Lampoon's 1978 film *Animal House*? Just forget about those frat boys over on Webster Avenue and head to 9 School Street instead, where you'll discover a charmingly dilapidated 1835 columned mansion, once the Phi Sigma Psi fraternity house but now home to a coed undergraduate society called Panarchy. Though founded just over a decade ago on the sunny principles of inclusion, diversity, and mutual respect, the society hides a dark and disturbing secret in its darkened hall . . .

Okay, they don't really hide it: A Panarchy member named Ashley was friendly and welcoming and more than happy to guide me down the cellar stairs to the society's spooky claim to fame, their sinister-looking basement "Tomb Room." A large, windowless chamber lined on all four sides with concrete thrones, the Tomb Room could be one of the creepiest places I've ever been. Concrete floor. Concrete block walls. A few bare bulbs. Thrones (concrete, of course) built into long rows along the walls and etched with last names and dates ranging from 1897 to the 1940s. On a concrete altar at the far end of the room, in front of three larger thrones (presumably for the leaders of the unspeakable rituals that must have been performed here), someone had left a skeletal hand and forearm and what looked to be a plastic skull, but the props didn't look funny so much as appropriate and, well, disturbing.

Of course, the most likely explanation for the Tomb Room is that it was the site of the old fraternity's initiation rites and rituals, but why those rites required total darkness and a creepy concrete altar, we can only speculate. Whatever once transpired in the room, Panarchy members can't say. But it's ironic that one of the most liberal-minded and open social organizations on Dartmouth's campus has in its basement a physical reminder of the tribal initiations—possibly painful, probably terrifying, and most certainly secret—that once helped create the boundary line between insiders and outsiders, between those few who knew the dark secrets and everyone else left in the dark. Now, whose forearm do you think that was?

Panarchy is located at 9 School Street in Hanover, just a block and a half away from Dartmouth College's Quad. At the intersection of Routes 10 and 10a, head west on 10a about a block, then take a left onto School Street. Panarchy will be the large columned house on your right. The public is welcome at the society's weekly Wednesday-evening meetings, or you can simply drop by and ask to check out the Tomb Room.

SUPREME COURT SAYS YOU DON'T HAVE TO LIVE FREE OR DIE

New Hampshire's "Live Free or Die" slogan can at times seem downright uncompromising, especially when you put it beside other less-strident state slogans. Tennessee's, for example, is "Sounds Good To Me," which not only makes a nice rhyme when you say the state name and the slogan together, but it's also about as friendly and agreeable-seeming as a Labrador retriever. And someone mixed up their adjectives writing Idaho's rather food-obsessed slogan: "Great Potatoes. Tasty Destinations." (Do you think they use artificial flavorings to make destinations taste so good?)

For one George Maynard, formerly of Lebanon but now a resident of Connecticut (the "Full of Surprises" state), "Live Free or Die" was a little *too* uncompromising a slogan. In 1974, just four years after the somewhat macabre command started appearing on New Hampshire license plates, Maynard took the liberty of covering up the words "Live Free or Die" on his car's plates with red reflective tape. A devout Jehovah's Witness, he found the statement objectionable because according to his faith, *life* was in fact more sacred than freedom rather than the other way around. Kids in the neighborhood reportedly kept pulling off the reflective tape when George wasn't looking, so he eventually had to cut the words "or Die" off his license plate entirely.

Local police in Lebanon didn't take kindly to George getting artsy-craftsy with his car tags, though, and he was given numerous citations, small fines, and even a jail sentence of fifteen days. The irony of a man being jailed for covering up the words "Live Free or Die" was not lost on journalists, and the case attracted quite a bit of attention. After he got out of the pokey, the ACLU approached Maynard and offered to represent him in a federal lawsuit. He agreed, and in March of 1975, ACLU lawyers filed a suit against both Neal Wooley, Lebanon's chief of police, and the State of New Hampshire for violating Maynard's First Amendment rights to free speech. (Suing the chief of police in your New Hampshire hometown is probably one of the best reasons I've heard for moving to Connecticut.) In its 6–3 ruling in Maynard's favor, the Supreme Court wrote that "Whatever else may be said about the motto 'Live Free or Die,' it expresses philosophical and political ideas. Plaintiffs' desire not to be aligned with these ideas falls within the ambit of the First Amendment." Thanks to George Maynard, all us Granite Staters now have the freedom not to Live Free or Die.

Bread of the Day: Tombstone Loaf

New London

According to Marion Flaherty of Chadwick Funeral Home in New London, it's not every day that a local citizen is lowered by crane into a granite tomb that looks suspiciously like a loaf of bread. "I would say it's very unusual," she told me by phone, a comment that provided reason enough for me to count Emil Hanslin's tomb as yet another New Hampshire curiosity.

The word on the street was that a cemetery in New London was home to a baker's tombstone in the shape of a loaf of bread. Quirky, right? As it turns out, Mr. Hanslin was no professional baker but an award-winning real estate developer, his gravestone wasn't quite a gravestone but a casket-enclosing crypt, and said crypt wasn't sculpted to look like a loaf of bread but a . . . well, I'm not really sure what it's supposed to look like, and neither is Marion Flaherty. "It's not actually a loaf of bread," she explained, "but that's what a lot of people in town think it looks like."

Even though Emil Hanslin had no background in professional baking, his last resting place does resemble a delicious loaf of gray granite: rectangular in shape, flat on all four sides, with a gently rounded top. Admittedly, the six small granite pillars that flank the front of the sarcophagus, three on the left side and three on the right, don't add much to the yeasty theme, but they no doubt hold some other symbolic significance, albeit one unrelated to the food-service industry. If you walk around to the back of the tomb, you'll notice a small square brass door where, Flaherty told me, the ashes of Hanslin's widow will be placed when she dies.

Look even more closely at the tomb and you'll also see a couple of small openings covered in wire mesh, which presumably permit air to pass into the sepulchre. Could these air holes offer a clue as to why Hanslin chose a loaf-shaped tomb, a kind of granite casket holder, as his final resting place? After all, a room of one's own and a little fresh air is a more comforting prospect for a man than being buried 6 feet under, whether he be butcher, baker, or real estate deal maker.

Emil Hanslin's tomb shaped like a loaf of bread is located in New London's Old Main Street Cemetery. From Main Street in the village, take South Pleasant Street south to Old Main Street. Turn left and the cemetery will be immediately on your right. The tomb is large, easy to spot, and a bear to slice.

Give me a slice of that crypt.

Is That a Quaking Bog You're Standing On, or Are You Just Afraid of Me?

New London

The first thing you should know about the Philbrick-Cricenti Bog is that it isn't a true bog. An honest-to-goodness, 100 percent genuine bog should not, I repeat, should not have an outlet. My friends, I'm here to tell you that the Philbrick-Cricenti Bog most definitely has an outlet. And, after having slipped a little on the outlet's footbridge, I've got one muddy shoe to prove it.

Still, Philbrick-Cricenti is an ecological wonder thousands of years in the making, so it deserves some grudging respect, even if it got my foot wet. Home to such botanical curiosities as the insect-eating pitcher plant, bogs were once stagnant glacial ponds whose waters turned highly acidic over thousands of years. Arctic plants uniquely suited to the nutrient-poor, low-pH environment, including sphagnum moss, sedge, and leather leaf, grow slowly around the edges of the pond and then, century by century, creep across its surface, forming a mat of tangled mossy growth that can one day cover the pond entirely.

Danger: This bog has been known to swallow horses and not even burp.

At this point a bog, even a less-than-true one, gets treacherous. At the Philbrick-Cricenti Bog, deer, cows, and even a horse have reportedly wandered out onto the mat of vegetation and fallen through, never to be hunted, milked, or ridden again. More troubling still, the animals' remains are probably well-preserved under the sphagnum, since the water's high acidity inhibits the growth of bacteria and other microorganisms that aid in decomposition. That's why bog mats eventually thicken enough to support spruce trees and even people—as the moss, sedge, and other plants die, they don't decompose entirely but instead form layer upon layer of peat.

Visitors should take care to stay on the wooden boardwalks at Philbrick-Cricenti, though, since the bog mat varies in age and thickness, with some boardwalk loops taking visitors through areas that were open water only 150 years ago. On the appropriately named Quaking Loop, which passes over a relatively young portion of the mat, the boardwalk quivers beneath your footsteps as if it were a living thing, which I guess it is. And if even the idea of walking the Bog Peril Loop, where at least one horse is known to have perished, starts your knees knocking, you can always blame it on the bog.

The Philbrick-Cricenti Bog is located on Newport Road just a couple of miles outside of New London. Take exit 12 off Interstate 89 and head toward New London on Newport Road. The pull-off area will be on the south side of the road about a half mile before the hospital road. Maps and guide sheets are available at the trailhead.

Blue Lips, Back Hair, and Pink Chiffon
Newbury

If you're not up for seeing burly men in back-hair-revealing tutus, then you should just skip Mount Sunapee's Annual Slush Cup. A pink, size

So you can't wait until summer to water-ski?

XXL ballerina outfit may not be mandatory attire for all male Slush Cup participants over 250 pounds, but it certainly seems to be a popular event-day ensemble with the husky and hairy set. The outfits are nothing less than stunning, but what's truly shocking is how poised and, well, natural some of these guys look in their pink chiffon and ski boots. How, I wonder, do the judges award Best Costume honors when so many burly ballerinas look like they've just pirouetted off the stage at their very first recital?

So exactly what do all these scantily clad cross-dressers and other crazily costumed skiers and snowboarders do at the Slush Cup? Each participant gets a chance to speed straight down the slope and attempt to cross an 84-foot-long, 40-foot-wide artificial pond, constructed over a period of two days just for the event. As you can probably imagine, reaching the snowbank on the other side ain't easy. Participants use poles outfitted with mini-skis for extra balance (the same devices used by wheelchair skiers), but beyond that it's just them, their boards, and a wide-open stretch of ice-cold water. Oh yeah, and a tutu.

The swift and the lucky reach the farther shore, but other Slush Cuppers take late-winter dunkings that'll send sympathetic goose bumps down your back. For safety Mount Sunapee stocks the pond with four dry-suit-clad staff members, who swiftly offer a helping, neoprene-covered hand to those who crash and burn, or more precisely, crash and freeze. And though it might sound absurd, it's actually quite heart-warming to see a cold man in a sopping wet pink dress being helped to safety by two rescuers in scuba gear. In fact, if a sight like that doesn't bring a tear to your eye, I don't know what will.

Mount Sunapee's Slush Cup is held each year at the end of March. From Newbury Village, take Route 103 west to the Mount Sunapee traffic circle; the resort entrance will be on your left. For more information call (603) 763–2356 or visit www.mountsunapee.com.

My Chairlift for a Horse!
Newport

For all you skiers tired of brutal mountain winds, snaking lift lines, and hordes of six-year-old hotshots who make your snowplow turns look a little less than flattering, the North East Ski Joring Association offers the chairlift-free sport of equestrian ski joring. Good-bye artificial snow. Good-bye $8.00 hamburgers. Good-bye way-too-steep vertical drops. Hello Mr. Ed.

While ski joring has a history that dates back hundreds of years to Arctic locales like Finland and Norway, where Lapps tied ropes to reindeer to carve turns on the tundra, it was only in 1999 that equestrian ski joring became an officially sanctioned sport in the United States. Inspired by ski joring events in places like Wyoming and Montana, Geoff and Brooke Smith of New London's Never Done Farm founded the North East Ski Joring Association and, in the winter of 2004–5, hosted New England's first official equestrian ski joring competitions.

From the point of view of an uninformed spectator like myself, equestrian ski joring looks like a frozen mix of waterskiing, horse racing, and ski jumping. A rider on a horse uses a 30-foot rope to pull a skier or

Do these lifts close at 4:00 P.M. too?

snowboarder down and around a J-shaped, 1,100-foot-long course at speeds of up to 40 miles per hour.

Besides holding on for dear life, the skier is charged with navigating a series of cones, sailing off a few jumps, and snagging some jousting rings as quickly as possible in order to earn maximum points. Of course, the skiers are impressive (one competitor I saw even raced on telemark skis) and the riders can make sprinting a horse on snow look easy, but the animals themselves steal the show, galloping at breakneck speeds down the length of the course, nostrils flaring, snow flying high from all four hooves.

In case you're ready to give up alpine skiing for good to pursue an equestrian ski joring championship, though, you may want to consider this: As expensive as lift tickets are these days, they're a bargain compared to the price of a good horse. And a good Finnish reindeer probably isn't much cheaper.

Each year the North East Ski Joring Association hosts three equestrian ski joring events at Newport's Parlin Field Airport, just off Route 10. From Newport take Route 10 north to Corbin Road. Turn left, drive just a half mile or so down the road, and the parking lot and ski joring course will be on your left. For a schedule of events, visit www.nesja.com.

Good Old Good Humor Man
Newport

Spend a few hours on Newport's uncommonly long stretch of common one sunny summer afternoon, and you're almost sure to see Randy Bragdon and his ice-cream truck. At first, you'll think you're in the grips of a dairy-craving-induced hallucination or a nostalgic flashback from summers of yore, but then, when the kids start hyperventilating and haranguing you for petty cash, you'll realize that both Randy and his truck are the real McCoy.

An old-fashioned Good Humor man and his "helper."

Known locally as the "Good Humor Man," Randy's developed a devoted following in Newport simply by being the most authentic old-fashioned Good Humor Man he could be. Of course, he wears the genuine Good Humor Man summer ensemble: white pants with black suspenders, white shirt, and white cap. Customers have even given him more specific wardrobe tips (trade the straight tie for a bow tie, one customer advised), and now Randy looks like he drove his ice-cream truck right out of a Norman Rockwell painting to sell ice-cream bars in a new millennium. His antique 1966 Ford Good Humor Ice Cream truck is the same one you remember from your childhood—that is, if you were lucky enough to have a genuine Good Humor Ice Cream truck in your hometown—with an open-air cab, an ice-cream cooler right beside the driver, and a square white box in back painted with the classic Good Humor Ice Cream logo: a mouth-watering chocolate-covered ice-cream bar on a stick with one bite already vanished into some lucky mouth.

Ice cream is a family affair for Randy, his wife Tracy, and their seven-year-old daughter Janine, who either helps dad out on the common or stays home with mom at the ice-cream stand the Bragdons operate from their Brick Farm in Unity. Her parents may be extra busy during the summer months, but Janine can't really complain: Her mom's constantly dishing up ice cream, and her dad's always in a good humor.

Randy the Good Humor Man makes regular Tuesday and Thursday evening passes through various Newport neighborhoods. Look for him also at the Newport Common, especially during Sunday night Concerts on the Common. The Bragdons' Brick Farm Ice Cream stand is located at 434 Lear Hill Road in Unity. From the center of Newport, follow Route 10 south for 4.3 miles and turn right onto Lear Hill Road. Travel 1 mile and Brick Farm Ice Cream will be on your right.

Make Ice When the Sun Shines (Hopefully)
North Sutton

Before refrigerators and ice makers, a cold summer cocktail must have tasted a little sweeter, if for no other reason than the fact that the tippler knew what hard and hazardous work went into chilling his glass. First, winter workers would scrape lake or river ice using a team of horses and an 8-foot blade, sometimes numerous times, just to keep it clear of snow. Once the ice was a foot thick, sawyers cut hundreds of 350-pound cakes, loaded them onto horse-drawn sleighs, and drove the 3,000-pound loads over frozen hill and dale to icehouses, where they unloaded the blocks, stacked them neatly in rows, and covered them with 6 inches or more of sawdust. Delivering the ice during the summer months was, of course, more work, but at least the ice blocks had shed some major winter pounds. In the nineteenth century, ice from New Hampshire even traveled the world, moving from Wolfeboro to Boston and onward to places like New Orleans and Cairo.

If you'd like to gain a hands-on appreciation for the miracle of modern refrigeration, you should attend Muster Field Farm Museum's annual Natural Ice Harvest Day. Held at the end of January, Ice Day features local sawyers cutting ice using both crosscut handsaws and a gas-powered machine that looks a bit like a miniature Zamboni with an attitude. You can try your hand at the handsaw, or just sit back and watch as volunteers use a fulcrum to wrangle ice blocks onto wagons and trucks for the trip to Muster Field Farm's circa-1890 icehouse, where the ice will be stacked, covered in sawdust, and stored for summer use. At Muster Field Farm, a museum that features working gardens, a homestead, and over a dozen restored buildings moved to the site for preservation, staff and volunteers offer free Ice Day hayrides and serve up cocoa, homemade soups, and goodies at the museum's Ryder Corner School House. But the sweetest reward for all that hard,

AN ELECTRIFYING PERSONALITY

This shocking tale comes from Orford, where an unfortunate woman became charged with electricity and, for more than three months in the winter of 1837, shot bright sparks out her fingertips at family, friends, and neighbors. According to William Hosford, the local physician who examined her over many weeks and reported his findings in the *American Journal of Science and Arts,* the subject, a "lady of great respectability" about thirty years of age, rarely got close to anyone or anything without discharging a visible, audible, and moderately painful electrical spark. Her brother was shocked. Her sister was shocked. Even the doctor was shocked—a brilliant spark a little less than an inch long flew from her knuckle to his nose. And after getting shocked a few times, they all gave the poor unnamed woman who became known as Orford's "Electric Lady" a wide berth.

It seems the Electric Lady sparked a great deal of scientific curiosity in Dr. Hosford, since he filled pages and pages of his notebook with detailed observations about her condition before even attempting a cure. Among his many discoveries was the fact that the woman seemed most charged after "moderate exercise . . . and social enjoyment" when the temperature was around 80 degrees Fahrenheit. What's more, "the excitement," as the good doctor called it, diminished as the temperature fell, vanishing altogether before reaching 0 degrees. At her most shocking, say, after a nice game of bridge and with the woodstove really cooking, the woman could deliver a 1½-inch spark every fifteen seconds or so from her fingertip to the ornamental ball on top of her stove. Now that's what I call a great parlor trick.

According to Dr. Hosford, the woman suffered "severe mental perturbation" as a result of her condition, never knowing when she was about to shock a family member or shoot a spark at an innocent metal kitchen implement. When he finally got around to seeking a remedy, the doctor suggested she change her silk clothes to cotton and flannel, imagining friction was the culprit. The shocks, however, continued, and nothing the doctor did improved the poor woman's situation in the least. The Electric Lady's charge diminished gradually over the course of the winter on its own, and by the middle of May her affliction had vanished entirely, never to return. The only other shock came, I imagine, when the family got the bill for Dr. Hosford's weeks-long house call.

hand-numbing work won't come until the following summer, when staff use Kezar Lake ice blocks to make ice cream the old-fashioned way—by earning it.

Muster Field Farm Museum's Natural Ice Harvest Day is held at North Sutton's Kezar Lake at the end of January. The Muster Field Farm Museum is located on Harvey Road in North Sutton just off exit 10 of Interstate 89. For information call (603) 927–4276 or visit www.muster fieldfarm.com.

Parrish Drops Backdrop in Small Town
Plainfield

In his early sixties artist Maxfield Parrish said, "I'm done with girls on rocks." At his age, maybe girls on rocks were also done with him? Parrish, the most popular American illustrator of the early twentieth century, designed and possibly painted a stunning stage backdrop in Plainfield's town hall that can still be seen today. True to his word, with this work at least, Parrish's Plainfield set design contains not a single girl on a rock.

Maxfield Parrish moved from Philadelphia to Plainfield in 1898, where he became a member of the Cornish Art Colony that grew up around the home and studios of famed sculptor Augustus Saint-Gaudens. A student of classical and Renaissance art and architecture who was strongly influenced by the mountainous landscape of the American West, Parrish became famous for fantastical, dramatically colored paintings and illustrations combining things like Renaissance gardens, Rocky Mountain peaks, Greek columns, and nubile girls dressed in what appear to be chic togas. Parrish's 1922 painting *Daybreak*, probably his most famous, brings together columns, mountains, gardens, and two beautiful reclining girls (sans rocks) under an ethereal blue sky. In the 1920s, you could find reproductions of it hanging on thousands of parlor walls throughout the country.

The backdrop and wings for the 1916 rear stage addition to the Plainfield Town Hall, largely funded by Cornish Colony artist William Howard Hart, was one of only three sets Parrish designed in his sixty-eight-year career. This New England pastoral scene presaged Parrish's turn in the 1930s from otherworldly paintings of garden nymphs and Greek vases to straight-up, locally inspired landscapes. While Parrish certainly designed the backdrop and wings (the study he painted for the Plainfield Town Hall set still exists), there's no solid proof that he painted them; some suggest that stage painters did the work of transferring his design to the backdrop's linen, but no one knows for sure.

What is certain, however, is that the backdrop is magnificent. It features an idealized Mount Ascutney bathed in a heavenly blue that the artist used so often, it became known as "Parrish Blue." According to reports, Parrish designed the set so that changes in stage lighting would produce the appearance of either sunrise, midday, or sunset. The wings complete the woodland scene, with trees and large rocks flanking both sides of the mountain vista. And upon those rocks, you'll find not a single reclining girl. "There are always pretty girls on every street," Parrish said in 1931, "but a man can't step out of the subway and watch the clouds playing with the top of Mt. Ascutney." The artist must have lived in Plainfield so he wouldn't be forced to choose between the two.

The Plainfield Town Hall is on Route 12A. You can view Maxfield Parrish's backdrop on summer Sundays from 1:00 to 5:00 P.M. or by appointment. For information call Plainfield librarian Nancy Norwalk at (603) 675–6866.

Tickling Tithing Man
South Sutton

If you plan to attend the Sunday church service during South Sutton's Old Home Days celebration, be sure to wear the oldest clothes you can find. No, not your ratty Carhartt overalls and that oily sweatshirt—go and put those right back in the closet. Might I, in a motherly way, suggest something much more appropriate and much, much older, say a suit and tie from the late nineteenth century? South Sutton's Old Home Days Sunday service is a strictly period-costume affair. You certainly wouldn't want to be the only twenty-first-century boy in the pews, would you? Now march right back up those stairs and change into your great, great, great grandfather's Sunday best.

As long as I'm telling you what to do, might I also recommend that you make a generous donation when the Tithing Man comes around. Trust me on this one—mother knows best. If you try to get away with slipping a single crumpled dollar bill, or worse, just a few measly coins into the collection basket, then you'll be held to account. The Tithing Man might even interrupt the holy serenity of the service by holding up your single, sweat-wrinkled bill and calling the whole congregation's attention to the fact that you are the somewhat less-than-generous donor of said sorry-looking bill. Or worse, the Tithing Man might tickle you until you dig into your pockets and fork over more dough. Really. They don't call him the Tickling Tithing Man for nothing.

Watching your fellow congregants get tickled makes for a more entertaining Sunday service, and those tight collars and that itchy nineteenth-century homespun sure do make it a lot easier to stay awake. Sutton's Old Home Days Sunday service is held in the Old Meeting House just off the town green in South Sutton village. For more information call Gloria Meyer of the Sutton Historical Society at (603) 938–5126.

It Takes Two to Lock Antlers

Springfield

To find hidden treasure that's really ripe for discovery, sometimes all you've got to do is follow your nose. When Ray Deragon, an outdoorsman and hunter, noticed a distinct odor while out scouting a remote tract of woodlands in Springfield's Gile State Forest, he did just that. The secret treasure he discovered? Two rotting moose carcasses scavenged by ravens and coyotes and emitting the unmistakable scent of death. I don't even want to mention the maggots . . .

But wait, it gets better. Really. Because those two moose Ray got wind of on October 9, 2003, just happened to be bulls who, only weeks before, had come together in what we can only imagine was a furious battle over the privilege of wooing some local cow (no disrespect intended). Sometime around the end of September they had met, sized each other up, exchanged fairly elaborate signals with their antlers to indicate that they were ready to rumble, and then rushed headlong at each other, probably more than once, their racks colliding each time with a terrific crash that, if anyone had been around to hear it, probably sounded like a jumble of hockey sticks being slammed in a heap on the ice.

After one of those collisions, the two bulls tried to back away from each other and found that they couldn't. Their racks had become permanently locked. They must have shaken their heads from side to side. They must have pushed and shoved and glared at each other across the few inches of space between their locked heads until chests heaved and eyes glazed over with exhaustion. And then they must have spent the next four or five days learning to live with each other as they died.

Ray knew he'd found something quite rare, so he contacted New Hampshire Fish and Game conservation officer John Wimsatt, who joined Ray at the site to examine the carcasses and remove the heads for transport out of the woods. Fast forward now to the fall of 2005, right past the brainstorming (what to do with a rare set of locked antlers?), late-night planning (how about a museum quality taxidermy display of the two bulls locked in mortal combat?), hours upon hours of fund-raising, months of work by Maine taxidermist Mark Dufresne, and the all-around Herculean efforts of Conservation Officer Wimsatt. On a beautiful September day, at a picnic area just a couple of miles from the place where Ray had found his treasure, the nonprofit New Hampshire Locked Moose Antler Project unveiled a magnificent taxidermy display featuring the two bull moose (with skins thankfully donated from other, less odiferous animals) in midcollision, their antlers locked together, not even after death do they part. The hundreds of people gathered around for the unveiling absolutely loved them. And after such bad luck, isn't it nice to see two big lugs get a second chance at love?

The "Forever Locked" taxidermy exhibit is mobile (it has its own trailer) and available for display at sports shows, state fairs, and festivals. To request the static duo for an event, contact John Wimsatt of the New Hampshire Locked Moose Antler Project at (603) 271–3361.

Carve a Pumpkin with a Grave Digger
Warner

Plenty of farmers do something special at Halloween—from building a house of hay to chucking pumpkins with a giant catapult—in order to draw as large a crowd as possible to the pumpkin patch. None can match Courser Farm in Warner, though, for sheer Halloween authenticity, since the outfit is owned and operated by honest-to-goodness grave diggers. Doesn't it make your pumpkin seem more festive to know that it was plucked by hands calloused not just from tilling the soil but from burying the dead as well?

Like most farmers in the state, the Coursers keep their oxen fed and their 700-plus-acre working family farm afloat by taking on second and third jobs. Gerry and brother Timothy's side work digging graves in area cemeteries seems peculiarly appropriate for men who do a brisk business around Halloween. Since the spring of 1971, when a local undertaker called Gerry for help putting in a backlog of winter business, the two brothers have been taking pickax and shovel to the rocky soil in cemeteries all over the area, from Sunapee to Henniker, Contoocook to Salisbury. And when they hit a granite ledge, as you're bound sometimes to do in these parts, they're not afraid to do a little blasting.

Every year on the Sunday before Halloween, Gerry and Timothy Courser take a break from digging graves and offer up as many as 600 free pumpkin "seconds"—pumpkins that are green or blemished—for family, friends, and guests to carve into an almost infinite variety of jack-o'-lanterns. Most years at least a hundred people show up for the event, which is held rain, snow, or shine; some carve just for fun while others, outfitted with pumpkin stands, templates, and specialty tools, carve for serious fun. Then, two days before Halloween, the jack-o'-lanterns, arranged in rows in the fields along Schoodac Road, are lit up, every last one. The result is breathtaking, especially if you visit the farm late at night when most folks have gone to bed and the quiet stubbled fields are ablaze with ghoulish faces. Of course, grave diggers would know how to do Halloween up right.

From downtown Warner take West Main Street (Route 103) east about 1.5 miles to Schoodac Road. Take a left and follow Schoodac Road past the intersection with Poverty Plains Road; Courser Farm will be on your right. Call (603) 456–3521 for information.

You Mean, They Didn't Have Cell Phones in 1932?
Warner

If you still don't believe old-timers had it a whole lot tougher, then consider the telephone. For decades, callers had to hand-crank their phones, like the 1907 Western Electric Model 317, just to generate a signal to raise the operator on the other end of the line. In some New Hampshire towns, as many as a dozen or more businesses and homes piggybacked on the same party line, with each and every phone ringing whenever one of the subscribers happened to receive a call. (Different ring combinations signaled to subscribers who should pick up.) Of course, if another party was already on your party line, you could eavesdrop—a nice little side-benefit—but you certainly couldn't make that urgent call. And the town operator, well, she knew more secrets (yours included) than the local priest.

If such communication hardships pique your interest in the early days of telephony, you should pay a visit to the New Hampshire Telephone Museum, a brand-new collection of phones, telephone equipment, and line repair tools located in downtown Warner. The creation of Dick and Paul Violette, former chairman and president/CEO, respectively, of the Merrimack County Telephone Company, the museum includes hundreds of telephones dating from the earliest nineteenth-century models to the cell phone; a replica of the phone Alexander Graham Bell first used on March 10, 1876, to boss around his assistant, poor Mr. Watson ("Mr. Watson," Bell is reported to have said, "Come here—I want to see you."); a working antique switchboard; samples of telephone cable, some as thick as a man's wrist and containing an ingeniously organized jumble of 600-plus individual color-coded lines; and a working 9-foot-tall stepping switch.

What's a 9-foot-tall stepping switch you ask? I think I'll let Dick Violette, the man who literally climbed his way from lineman all the way up to chairman of the local phone company, do the explaining here. If you're lucky, as I was, Dick will be around to give you a personal tour of the phones and equipment he's not only collected, but also operated, repaired, and installed over a lifetime of work in the rural telephone business. "I tell people if they want the all-day tour," the woman work-ing the desk said, "then they should go with Dick." She's exaggerating, of course, but Dick knows a lifetime's worth and more of telephone technology, and he's a generous and enthusiastic teacher. After the tour, I still didn't know exactly how the 600 color-coded wires were organized in a telephone line, as Dick patiently tried to show me, but I sure had a whole new appreciation for my single-party cell phone.

The New Hampshire Telephone Museum is located at 22 East Main Street in Warner. Take exit 8 or 9 off Interstate 89 and follow Main Street (Route 103) into downtown Warner. For infor-mation including hours, call (603) 456–2234 or go to www.nhtelephone museum.com.

Introduce your cell phone to his great-great-great-great grandparents.

DEARLY DEPARTED THIGH

It's clear that Captain Samuel Jones was pretty attached to his leg, and probably vice versa. Otherwise, why would the good captain have gone to all the trouble and expense of buying a plot in the Washington town cemetery and giving his beloved amputated leg (left or right, we're not sure) a decent, Christian burial? That's right—Captain Jones buried one of his legs in the Washington cemetery. And no, I'm not pulling your leg.

Captain Jones chose an unassuming, classic headstone for his dearly departed limb—with a simple eight-pointed star as its only adornment, the stone reads, "Capt. Samuel Jones Leg which was amputated July 7, 1804." What's curious is that the stone bears no epitaph, no tribute from the captain for the leg that he gladly leaned upon for support and balance for so many years until that fateful summer day when their connection was painfully severed. Perhaps Captain Jones said all he wanted to say at the funeral service? (I'm sure he must have remarked upon the fact that his leg was always there for him.)

The captain's brother, it's rumored, gave a nice little speech about the leg. When he was done, legend has it, there wasn't a dry eye in the church. "They went everywhere together, my brother and

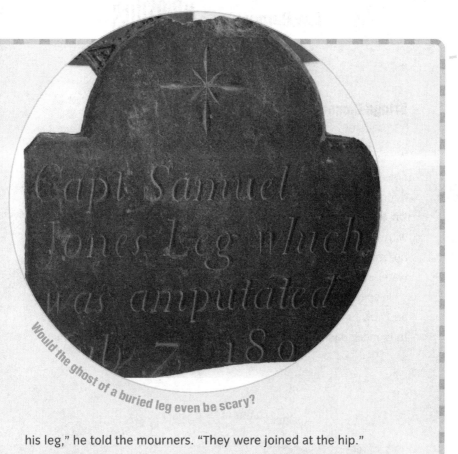

Would the ghost of a buried leg even be scary?

his leg," he told the mourners. "They were joined at the hip."

From Route 31 in Washington, head west on Faxen Hill Road. Before the intersection with Millen Pond Road, you'll pass two cemeteries, one on the left and the other on the right side of the road. The cemetery on the left-hand side is where you'll find the grave of Captain Samuel Jones's leg. Also, be sure to look for the large communist gravestone marking the burial site of Fred and Elba Chase. It's the only Soviet-style hammer-and-sickle statuary you're likely to find in the live-free-or-die state.

Bridge Closed to Traffic . . . Indefinitely
Webster

When Jon Pearson first moved into his great aunt's covered bridge, the cracks between the wallboards were so big, he never had to open the door to let the dogs out. Okay, I'm exaggerating just a bit, but Jon did say the cracks in the walls were big enough for him to see outside. Even with all the windows closed, the bridge supposedly had a gentle breeze. "The place wasn't winterized at all," he told me. "If you left water in a glass, it would freeze."

In spite of all his early sufferings, Pearson clearly loves his renovated and now fully winterized house, a nineteenth-century wooden bridge that once spanned the Blackwater River a couple of miles from the hill-

Be sure to ask the owner before passing through this bridge.

side where it stands today. The covered bridge was condemned in 1909, but Jon's great aunt Jessie Pearson purchased it in 1910 and hired workmen to disassemble, transport, and reconstruct the bridge as a summer guesthouse on her property just north of Lake Winnepocket. "She was thinking about going with more of a Swiss chalet look," Pearson said, "but she decided to keep the bridge pretty much the way it was." She added a large fieldstone fireplace on one wall, a couple of lofts, and a lake-facing balcony with beautiful paper birch railings that you can still see today.

Jon's dad inherited the house from Aunt Jessie but later sold it, and it was decades before Jon was able to buy it back. He's done a great job with his renovations, and he's proud of the bridge in the way a person might be proud of a special family member—he's even got an old picture of the covered bridge up on the fridge. If you happen to stop by for a look, it's easy to spot the bridge the house once was: Most obviously, both side walls are angled outwards and look just like the vestibule entrances so common to covered bridges. As authentic as it looks, though, just remember that the Pearson Bridge is permanently closed to through traffic unless you're on foot, knock first, and say please.

From Contoocook Village, follow Route 127 north for about 8 miles to Swetts Mills, then take a left onto White Plains Road. Follow White Plains for a little less than a mile, and Bridge House Road will be on your right; the bridge house will be just up a rise on your left.

WHITE MOUNTAINS

Three Feet of Snow? What Better Excuse for That Slice?
Bartlett

Ah, spring in New Hampshire! Time for the snow to thaw and then freeze up as hard as asphalt before another nor'easter blows into town. Time to pack away your expedition-weight long underwear for the season and break out your less bunchy medium-weight long underwear. And time once again to dust off those old irons and play a round of golf in the snow.

Each year at the end of March, Attitash Mountain hosts their annual On-Snow Golf Tournament for all those golf fanatics who just can't wait until the snow clears. Attitash's groomers design a nine-hole course on Whitehorse Trail, and then teams of four players each—dressed in costumes and strapped to skis or snowboards, of course—chip, putt, and slalom their way down this black diamond trail, competing for prizes donated by local businesses.

Golfing on skis on the snow on a mountainside while dressed in a costume naturally poses a number of challenges. Most ordinary golfers never have to worry about the possibility of exposed skin sticking to the shaft of a nine-iron, for instance, and if you think it's hard finding a shanked ball in the rough, just try tracking down that Titleist off-trail in 3 feet of powder. But there are certain advantages to playing on snow, including the fact that there aren't any sand traps, the water hazards are all frozen, and you never have to replace a divot. And it's always nice to have a whole mountain of excuses to explain away your whiffs, missed putts, and miserably misplaced shots.

If snow golf doesn't satisfy your craving for late-winter madness, Attitash also hosts the Red Parka Yacht Club Regatta in late March. Instead of on-snow golf, this event is an on-snow yacht race, with the term *yacht* so broadly defined as to be able to include almost anything, from canoes to couches, bathtubs to Barcaloungers. Individuals or teams design their boats, get gussied up in costumes, and then do whatever they can to get down the slopes as quickly as possible. The White Mountains in March may not be the time or the place for the Masters or the America's Cup, but after a long cold winter, we're entitled to dream a little, aren't we?

Attitash is located on Route 302 in Bartlett, about 3 miles east of the intersection of Routes 16 and 302. For information about events call (603) 374–2368.

There's No Business Like an Old Business
Bath

Dating way back to 1790 when the very first President George was still in office, the Brick Store in Bath is said to be America's oldest continually operating general store. If you want proof the place is old, you need look no further than the counters: Their slanted fronts gave female customers in hoop skirts enough room to sashay up and make their purchases, thank you very much. You'll even find a few nineteenth-century mailboxes from when the store did double duty as the town post office.

The building is made of brick, of course, and there's a portico out front with a porch above, both fronted by four very tall Doric columns that run from the ground all the way up to the roofline—the whole effect is trés colonial. But inside, instead of encountering barrels of dry goods and great big tins of bag balm to rub on your cows' udders (as nineteenth-century patrons surely did), you'll find loads of cheese, fudge, maple syrup, honey, and meats smoked right on the premises. And take it from someone who knows: Nancy's homemade fudge smells so much better than bag balm.

All the sweets and treats are delicious, of course, but if you want a truly unique foodstuff, purchase one of singer Patti Page's Pure Maple products. That's right, Oklahoma native Patti Page, who sold over a hundred million albums over the course of her career and had a whole slew of top ten hits in the 1940s and '50s, including "Doggie in the Window" and "Tennessee Waltz" (still the best-selling record by a female artist in history with ten million copies sold), has a line of maple syrups and pancake mixes. She and her husband, Jerry Filiciotto, live half the year in Bath on a farm just down the road from the Brick Store and have been making syrup and pancake mix products since 1995. In between overseeing tap lines and sap boiling, Patti, who's pushing eighty, still finds the time to perform all around the country, sometimes twice a day. The Brick Store is an oldie filled with goodies, and Patti Page sings the oldies but still finds time to make the goodies.

The Brick Store is located at 21 Lisbon Road (Route 302) in Bath. Call (603) 747–2074 or (800) 964–2074 for information.

Dollhouse Scenes for Children of the Damned
Bethlehem

If dollhouses received ratings the way movies do, the ratings board would certainly slap Frances Glessner Lee's dollhouse scenes with an R, maybe even an NC-17, rating. Just to give you a representatively gory example, in one scene a 5-inch woman lies in a bed on her side, the bedclothes pulled up to her waist, her face obscured by copious amounts of dried blood. On the floor beside the bed, a 6-inch man in blood-soaked little blue-striped pajamas lies face down, limbs akimbo, on what looks to be a blood-stained comforter. Rose-colored stains bloom on the carpet at the foot of the bed, a large pool of blood darkens the white bedsheet beside the woman (the poor little doll), and there, just above the 2½-inch bedside table, tiny drops of blood fleck the wallpaper. And you were afraid little old Barbie might be a bad influence on your child.

A Chicago heiress who moved to her family's thousand-acre summer estate in Bethlehem after her divorce in 1914, Frances Glessner Lee developed an interest in forensic science, and in miniature macabre bedrooms, after her brother introduced her to his friend George Burgess Magrath, a Harvard-trained medical examiner. Magrath's seedy casework, which included murdered prostitutes, homicidal husbands, and suicidal housewives, fascinated the well-to-do Lee, and

What evil deeds transpired in this dollhouse basement?

over the years she became both a patroness of forensic science at Harvard, funding a new Department of Legal Medicine there in 1936, and a crime scene expert in her own right.

Concerned that poorly trained police were botching investigations, she developed an educational curriculum for homicide investigators consisting of her own obsessively detailed dollhouse re-creations of real-life murders, suicides, and accidental deaths. Lee referred to these eighteen diabolical dioramas, lovingly handcrafted at her home workshop in Bethlehem throughout the 1940s and '50s, as the Nutshell Studies of Unexplained Death. With stunning details like miniature potato peelings in the kitchen sink and half-inch pencils that actually write, they were intended to train investigators to look and look again for the smallest clues—the headline on a mini newspaper, a window shade left askew, an outdated wall calendar—that would help them, according to the police saying, "Convict the guilty, clear the innocent, and find the truth in a nutshell."

Most of the Nutshell Studies are now housed in Maryland's Chief Medical Examiner's Office, where they're still used in forensics seminars twice a year. The Glessner estate, known as the Rocks Estate and now owned by the Society for the Protection of New Hampshire Forests, also houses a couple of Nutshell Studies that were never completed in a small outbuilding behind the horse barn. It's open to the public for hiking and guided tours. But remember, parental dollhouse guidance is suggested.

For information on the Rocks Estate, call (603) 444–6228. To get to the Rocks, located at 113 Glessner Road in Bethlehem, take Interstate 93 to exit 40 and follow Route 302 east for a half mile. Turn right opposite the Exxon station, and follow the signs to the parking area and program center.

A TISKET, A TASKET, A FOURTH-GENERATION INDIAN BASKET

The more polished, primped, and Disneyfied a tourist destination is, the less likely you'll find it in the pages of this book. If you'll permit me to generalize here, the unusual and the out-of-the-ordinary are ordinarily a tad rough around the edges. While Newt Washburn's beautiful handmade ash baskets are masterful works of art that have garnered him national acclaim and a prestigious National Heritage Fellowship from the National Endowment for the Arts, his shop is decidedly downscale. The white building on his property is small, not much more than one room really, and the red hand-painted sign that says HAND MADE BASKETS above the door is a little faded. Still, you can't miss the shop, as Newt assured me when I talked to him on the phone—just take Route 142 north out of Bethlehem for about 2 miles until, at the bottom of a steep hill, you come upon a medley of rusted vehicles and dilapidated heavy equipment that would make any junkyard owner feel at home. Newt's basket shop is right there in the middle of it all.

Washburn, a fourth-generation Abenaki Indian basket maker, has been making brown ash baskets in the Sweetser family tradition since he was a young buck. "If we wanted to eat in the winter," he told me, "we had to make baskets." And fear of hunger must have been a powerful teacher for the young Newt, since at age eighty-three he's still making the most beautiful baskets you're likely ever to see, and in every conceivable shape and size.

Making brown ash (sometimes called black ash) baskets, though, is a labor-intensive process that includes harvesting ash trees from swampy lowlands, pounding the skinned logs with a mallet to separate growth layers, carefully peeling each year's growth from the log, and then dividing those layers into as many as eight strips each (and we haven't even gotten to the weaving yet!). Washburn's slowed down some, of course, but as of winter 2006 he was still making baskets with the help of an apprentice. And do you still sell baskets? I asked him. "If I make one, then I'll put it up for sale in the shop," he told me, sounding a little surprised at my question. After all, he seemed to imply, everyone's gotta eat.

Newt Washburn can be reached at (603) 869–5894.

A Giant Train Set for a Very Big Kid
Bethlehem

"Parents, do yourself and the kids a favor," the Crossroads of America Exhibitorium Web site exclaims, "and go see a complete record of history in miniature!" Such a grandiose claim of historical completeness, even if it is in miniature, might be a touch hyperbolic—I saw nothing, for example, concerning the oceangoing vessels of the Phoenicians and not one bit about Elizabethan drama—but I can assure you that Crossroads of America contains loads and loads of stuff, most of it miniature and much of it historical. No matter how complete a record of history it offers, though, you'd still be doing yourself and your offspring a favor by checking it out.

The museum, located in an old boardinghouse, contains whole rooms full of model airplanes and boats, a collection of miniature cars from the 1950s and '60s, a fair number of guitars, and as many as forty antique outboard motors. The crown jewel of the collection, though, is Roger Hinds's ³⁄₁₆-scale (or ³⁄₁₆ inch to the foot) model railroad layout, a train set that's reported to be the largest and most elaborate of its kind on public display in the entire history of the full-scale world. And that's no overstatement.

A whole big collection of collections.

Stretching throughout most of the third floor, the train set is electronically controlled to simulate a full twenty-four hours of activity: lights brighten and dim to indicate the rising and setting of the sun, steam billows from a little engine, a mail car stops at a depot platform to eject a tiny pouch of mail, a cow even wanders onto the tracks before startling at an oncoming locomotive. (Don't worry, there's no train-versus-bovine collision.) When I visited him in the winter of 2006, Roger had taken apart much of his beloved train set and was in the midst of handcrafting in mind-boggling detail a historically accurate reproduction of the railroad line that runs through Crawford Notch. Dozens of archival photographs of the rail line lay scattered around the room to help Roger get everything just right, from the shape of cliff faces to the spacing of girders on the Frankenstein Trestle, all the way down to the configuration of granite blocks in the tiniest drainage culvert. In the face of such a profound labor of love, who could quibble over a little advertising overstatement?

Crossroads of America, located just a mile east of downtown Bethlehem on Route 302, is open June 1 through mid-October from 9:00 A.M. to 5:00 P.M.; closed Mondays. Tours are offered every half hour. Admission is charged. For more information call Roger Hinds at (603) 869–3919.

Antiques on the Odd Side
Bethlehem

Calling the Mt. Agassiz Trading Company in downtown Bethlehem an antiques shop is a bit like calling Ozzy Osbourne an entertainer or referring to Eddie the Eagle, Britain's construction worker–cum–ski jumper, as an Olympic athlete: All are technically true statements, but they manage to miss the point entirely. Better to think of Mt. Agassiz Trading

Company as an antiques odditorium, a shop of the most curious collectibles, the overstuffed love child of *Antiques Roadshow* and Ripley's Believe It or Not. In other words, this is definitely not your grandma's antiques shop.

Just to give you an idea of how eclectic a collection of the rare, odd, and bizarre owner Roland Shick has assembled, I offer a partial list of recent items up for sale: a set of exquisite hand-painted ostrich eggs from an artist in Romania; an antique bear trap, a deer antler carving of two human skeletons; an early twentieth-century New York City hot dog cart, in fine wiener-selling condition; a taxidermy alligator head, with teeth bared, of course; a rat's skeleton, fully assembled, nose to tail; a collection of vintage embalming fluid bottles; a fish fossil; a Shredded Wheat box from 1939; and a lamp made entirely out of seashells and tiny Christmas lights. And the list goes on . . .

Shick has so much at his shop, in fact, that his out-of-the-ordinary antiques fill the store, crowd the wraparound porch, and spill out toward the sidewalk on a small patch of lawn. If you can't find something bizarre at Mt. Agassiz that fills you with awe and wonder, or at least makes you go "hmm, now would you look at that . . . an electroshock therapy machine from 1854," well then you may not have a pulse. In which case, Roland probably would be happy to include you in his collection if he's able to find the shelf space.

Interspersed among the items for sale are selections from Roland's own collection of antique oddities, including a 1924 Model T Ford moving truck, a 1920s dentist's chair—believe me, it ain't pretty—and the above-mentioned nineteenth-century Patent Magneto-Electric Machine "for the treatment of nervous conditions." The pinnacle of peculiarity in the collection, though, has to be Roland's X-Ray Shoe Fitter, a machine that created an X-ray image of a child's feet in his or her prospective new pair of shoes. Thousands of the machines were in use in shoe stores throughout the country from the 1930s through the 1950s before they were banned due to concerns about irradiated tootsies. "It was a total gimmick," Roland told me. "It showed the kid's toe bones and where the end of the shoe would be, but, of course, you just can't beat the thumb-on-the-toe method to see if the shoe fits." Some technological advances, clearly, were never meant to be. And that, my friends, is where Roland and the Mt. Agassiz Trading Company come in.

The Mt. Agassiz Trading Company, located at 2056 Main Street in downtown Bethlehem, is open June through December. Call Roland at (603) 869–5568 for store hours and information.

That Ski Train's A-Rollin'
Bretton Woods

Mount Washington, the tallest mountain in the Northeast at 6,288 feet, seems the conflicted center of the state's natural world: All roads, and all tourist brochures, seem to lead to its cloud-snagging, tourist-tempting peaks. With nearly year-round snows, a yearly average temperature of 27 degrees Fahrenheit, and a world-record land wind speed of 231 miles per hour, the summit is at once both forbidding and eminently accessible, with an 8-mile auto road switchbacking up the eastern slope and a 2.8-mile cog railway line ascending the western slope, not to mention the miles and miles of hiking trails snaking their way to Washington's more-than-mile-high parking lot, weather station, museum, and restaurant.

Let the record show, however, that the most extraordinary way of ascending this unusual mountain is by coal-fired steam engine on the Mount Washington Cog Railway. Started in 1866 and completed in 1869, the Mount Washington Cog Railway was the first and is now the oldest cog railway in the world. What's a cog railway, you innocently ask? Quite simply, it's an elegant engineering solution to the problem of pushing a passenger railway car up a mountainside with grades as steep as 37.41 percent, just to get a little exact on you. Built entirely on wooden trestles, the track consists of two light steel rails spaced about 4½ feet apart with a heavy-gauge cog rack running directly between them. A large-toothed cogwheel connected to the driveshaft of the steam engine engages the cog rack, allowing the engine to climb, cog tooth by cog tooth, and push a railway car loaded with seventy passengers all the way up the side of Mount Washington. Staffed by both an engineer and a fireman shoveling up to a ton of bituminous coal into the firebox each trip, the steam engine stays on the downslope side of the passenger car for ascent as well as descent to maximize safety.

Next stop, the Bunny Slope!

WHITE MOUNTAINS

In the winter of 2004–5, the Mount Washington Cog Railway began running Cog Ski Trains throughout the season, offering skiers a heated fifteen-minute train ride up the mountain with their choice of two stops—the first for beginner runs and the second, higher stop for inter-mediate runs. It's the only ski train of its kind in the country, and the only steam-powered ski train in the entire world. And did I mention that the passenger car is heated? High-speed quad chairs with their high-speed winds don't sound quite so appealing anymore, do they?

The Mount Washington Cog Railway, located on Base Road off Route 302 in Bretton Woods, is open year-round. The Cog Ski Trains run December through March. For a schedule and rates, call (603) 846–5404 or (800) 922–8825 or visit www.thecog.com.

A Princess Who Went Out of Her Way to Avoid Peas
Bretton Woods

Famous for hosting the 1944 Bretton Woods International Monetary Conference, which established the World Bank and the International Monetary Fund, the Mount Washington Hotel sets the gold standard for grand hotels in the state.

Joseph Stickney, a Concord native who made his fortune in coal min-ing and railroads, hired a crew of 250 Italian craftsmen to build the Mount Washington, a majestic red-roofed, Spanish Renaissance–style hotel outfitted with electric lights, a pool, and a private bath in every room. They completed it in 1902, but Stickney only got to enjoy his grand new property for a brief season before dying in December of 1903. Upon his death, his young widow, Carolyn Foster Stickney, became sole proprietor of the hotel. In 1908 she married a French nobleman she met during travels to Europe, thereby acquiring the title of Princess Clarigny de Lucinge.

Is it kosher for a princess to have a queen-size bed?

Maybe it was the fancy new title, maybe it was all the royal treatment said title brought her, or maybe the Princess formerly known as Carolyn just really, really loved her own bed. Whatever the case, each year when the Prince and Princess returned from Paris to spend the summer at the Mount Washington Hotel, the Princess's wonderful bed was disassembled, crated up, and shipped across the Atlantic to New Hampshire. And each time she returned to France, the process was repeated in reverse, with the bed disassembled, crated up, shipped across the pond, and then reassembled in France. (She probably could have bought five or six new beds for the cost of shipping—remember, they didn't have UPS in those days.) Princess Clarigny de Lucinge may have been as refined and as sensitive about her bedding as that fairy-tale princess who, though she lay atop forty mattresses and twenty feather beds, couldn't sleep a wink because of three little peas.

You can sleep on the Princess's bed, now upgraded to a Queen, in room 314 at the hotel. Also, be sure to check out Babe Ruth's golf locker. The Mount Washington Hotel is located on Route 302 in Bretton Woods. For rates (which include full breakfast and dinner), information and reservations, call (603) 278–1000 or (800) 314–1752 or visit www.mtwashington.com.

Baldy Knows Snowshoes

Conway

You might be savvy enough to guess that, with a name like Treffle Bolduc, the eighty-seven-year-old snowshoe maker, snowshoe seller, and snowshoe renter Conway locals call "Baldy" is of Franco-American stock. But what you probably wouldn't guess, unless you're a little psychic, is that Bolduc once dreamed of being a concert violinist and, at the age of eighteen, headed south to study at the Boston Conservatory of Music. "Things didn't work out," Baldy said. "If it's not meant to be, you can practice awfully hard and not get anywhere." (I wish I could have fed that nugget of wisdom to my old algebra teacher.)

Baldy's snowshoes are made for winter walking.

Lucky for us, though, Baldy's failure in music led to his great success in yet another characteristically Franco-American endeavor—snowshoeing. After stints as a factory worker, ship's welder, and carpenter, Bolduc made a trip to Quebec, where he met Native American craftsmen who helped him learn to build some of the finest white ash snowshoes you're likely ever to strap on your feet. Not long after—apparently he didn't need much practice—Baldy opened the Kancamagus Snowshoe Center, his small snowshoe shop and museum at the eastern terminus of the Kancamagus Highway.

Not much seems to have changed at Baldy's place over the years, and that's a big part of its appeal. Visiting the shop is kind of like rummaging through your grandmother's attic, if said grandmother happened to have a powerful obsession with subarctic Indians and their snowshoes, moccasins, and beaded mukluks. There's a small museum located in the back, where you'll find everything from birch bark vessels to bird decoys made of reeds to a replica of an Indian lodge with an electric fire pit, along with lots and lots of snowshoes. Rent a pair for a day's tramp in the Whites, or place an order with Baldy for a pair of your very own. And if you've never tried the sport, don't worry—it's a whole lot easier than algebra and a whole lot more fun.

Baldy's Kancamagus Snowshoe Center is located on the Kancamagus Highway, just a few hundred yards from the intersection of Route 16. For information or to place an order, call (603) 447–5287 or 356–8402.

The Old Man of the Mountain Lives! (On a Cow)

Franconia

I first heard about the Holstein with the white marking on her side that supposedly bears a striking resemblance to the Old Man of the Mountain when I was interviewing a woman in Littleton. "You're looking for oddities, huh?" she said. "Well, there's a woman from Sugar Hill who marches her cow in the Fourth of July parade because she says it's got the Old Man of the Mountain on its side." The woman seemed distinctly unimpressed—maybe barnyard animals marked with 12,000-year-old rock profiles are a dime a dozen in the North Country?—but I scribbled notes and thought to myself, "Jackpot!"

While I haven't yet had the good fortune of meeting Bossie the cow in person, I have seen pictures on the Web. And if the opinion of an agricultural ignoramus means anything to you, I can says she's a fine-looking Holstein with a thick, shimmering black coat and a scant few white markings, including the one just above her left shoulder that, from pictures anyway, does bear a cloud-in-the-sky kind of resemblance to the Old Man of the Mountain. Rumor has it that she was headed for the slaughterhouse when Mickey de Rham, founder of the White Mountain Animal League, rescued Bossie and started her on the road to stardom by putting her to work for a good cause.

Since the Old Man's fall, Bossie's become a bit of a local celebrity, and like lots of celebrities, she now devotes a fair amount of her time to helping her less-fortunate brethren. As the new "spokescow" for the White Mountain Animal League, Bossie continues to make appearances at parades, festivals, and local events, but she's no longer just another cow with a famous face in her fur: Now she's on a mission to remind people to get their pets spayed or neutered. I'm told she's committed to her work and makes a rather moo-ving presentation.

The White Mountain Animal League and its bovine PR director are based in Franconia. For questions or upcoming Bossie appearances, contact Mickey de Rham at mderham@adelphia.net. Mickey has also written a children's book about Bossie titled *Hey Bossie: You're a Spokescow,* available at local and online bookstores.

THE GRANDADDY OF NEW HAMPSHIRE CURIOSITIES

It wasn't much to look at, just a small, clapboard-sided, two-story house 6 miles from its nearest neighbor at the base of what would come to be called Mount Willey in Crawford Notch. But a peculiar tragedy brought the Willey house national fame, investing it with an aura of the uncanny that drew first hundreds and then thousands of visitors and making it one of the first, and one of the more bizarre, tourist attractions in the country.

In October 1825, the Willey family of North Conway moved to a house in Crawford Notch and opened a travelers' hostel. Less than a year later, torrential rainstorms caused severe flooding and extensive landslides. At some point during the evening of August 28, 1826, with the flooded Saco River raging below and the terrifying sounds of landslides echoing throughout the Notch, Samuel and Polly, their five young children, and two hired men fled the Willey house, presumably for the greater safety of a nearby shelter. As the party made their break, they were overwhelmed by a wall of earth, rock, and trees that had originated on the mountain directly above the house.

Not a single one of them survived; in fact, three of the children's bodies were never even recovered. Certainly a terrible tragedy, but the irony that helped to generate both nationwide fascination in the fate of the Willey family and loads of White Mountain tourism was the fact that their house remained perfectly intact. According to reports, a ridge of land and a couple of boulders on the hillside behind the Willey place divided the landslide in two, causing tons of debris to pass on either side of the house without harming it in the least.

The first truly weird tourist attraction in the United States.

It was mere weeks before the first visitors came to see the Willey house, with the contents of its rooms just as the family had left them, a kind of macabre freeze-frame of domesticity just before natural disaster came to call. Intellectuals and writers mined the tragedy for meaning (including Nathaniel Hawthorne, whose story "The Ambitious Guest" is based on the Willey tragedy), presenting to readers an image of the White Mountains as a wild, primeval place. By 1845 a large hotel directly abutted the Willey house, and tourists paid twelve and a half cents apiece to take a tour.

The site of the Willey house is on Route 302 between Hart's Location and Bretton Woods. The house and hotel burned down in the late nineteenth century, but the Crawford Notch State Park headquarters is located here, as well as a gift shop and restaurant. A boulder marks the site of the house. For information call (603) 374–2272.

Skiing in Style (and to Save the World)

Franconia Notch

As kids, my three brothers and I would laugh until our stomachs hurt whenever we saw old photographs, taken before we were born, of our mother sporting a beehive hairdo. Ever since then I've understood that one of history's most important functions is to give us inside informa-tion on our forebears, so that we youngsters can share a laugh and feel a subtle but delicious sense of superiority to those who came before. And, of course, after we've enjoyed our feel-ings of superiority, we then can learn-from-so-as-not-to-repeat-the-past and thereby avoid becoming laughingstocks for the merriment of our own children and grandchildren.

At Franconia Notch's New England Ski Museum, a large collection of ski clothing, equipment, accessories, and memorabilia that traces the evolution of ski-ing in New England, you'll find some comedic history in the section on the devel-opment of ski clothing. From a pair of pleated gabardine wool knickers to the body-hug-ging Spandex suit worn by

Who knew a WWII combat skier would look so stylish?

World Championships medalist A. J. Kitt, the display highlights historical advances in ski clothing material, like Blizzard Cloth and Adirondack Poplin, Gore-Tex and Polartec, as well as fluctuations in fashion and failures of good sense.

Kids, if you want to feel sartorially superior in your black Patagucci parka, just take a look, if you can bear it, at the hot pink and Day-Glo pastels from the 1980s, when fashion meant big hair, bright colors, and an accessory called leg warmers. What, you might wonder, were they thinking? How could they even look at each other in the bright sunlight of a spring ski day, without damaging their corneas or retinas or pupils or whatever it is you risk damaging if you stare directly into the sun? I have no answers for you. My only hope is that my descendants never find that photograph of me in parachute pants and a Members Only jacket with spiky mousse-filled hair.

Among all the old skis and ski memorabilia, you'll also find an exhibit on C. Minot Dole, the Connecticut man who, at the start of World War II, convinced the government to form the 10th Mountain Division, a specialized ski infantry unit that would later be credited with breaking the German front in northern Italy after a 1,500-foot vertical nighttime ascent of an icy rock face in the Italian Alps. The museum displays the 122 pounds—no joke—of equipment, arms, and supplies each ski trooper carried. And that, my friends, is history's other function: to give us a sense of how god-awful hard it would be to live up to the free-world-saving folks who came before us.

The New England Ski Museum is located in a renovated highway garage at the base of the Cannon Mountain tramway. Take exit 2 off the Franconia Notch Parkway (Interstate 93). It's open daily December through March. For more information call (603) 823–7177.

The Tragic Tale of a Loss of Face (or, The Old Man of Rubble)
Franconia Notch

By now, everyone's heard the awful news: Sometime during the night of May 3, 2003, the Old Man of the Mountain, our world-famous granite profile that once loomed 1,200 feet above Profile Lake in Franconia Notch, broke from his promontory and plummeted, unseen, to the valley below. Our great Granite State symbol, the Neanderthal-browed, John Kerry–chinned mug that graces everything from the state quarter to state road signs to state license plates, lies fallen, unrecognizable, just another heap of broken rocks. Without him and his chiseled good looks, we are bereft, lost, utterly symbol-less in this great big symbol-demanding world. We miss our Old Man.

The powers that be have responded heroically to the tragedy, their upper lips almost as stiff as the Old Man's used to be, calling for committees, memorials, tributes, honorary statuettes. They've set up special viewers just north of Profile Lake so that visitors to the Notch can gaze up at the cliff where the profile used to be and see an Old Man of the Mountain mirage. While I appreciate the effort, the end result feels a bit like having your dearly departed dog stuffed: On the one hand, it's nice to have a visible reminder to gaze upon, but on the other hand, a stuffed pet reminds you that Fido's gone forever and all you have left is a lifeless fake who won't ever run or fetch or, in this case, gaze down upon you in a grim but protective way as you pilot your car through Franconia Notch some summer evening on your way back home. There's even been talk of creating a life-size replica, but so far it's all just talk.

None of these solutions satisfy me, of course: I want my Old Man back. So, I'd like to take this opportunity to suggest a treatment that, though increasingly common for baby boomers, hasn't been mentioned yet as a feasible remedy for our hero's loss of face: a facelift. At a whopping 40 feet 5 inches from top of forehead to tip of chin, his face was about sixty-six times larger than that of the average patient, a difference in scale that will no doubt make the procedure prohibitively expensive. Plus, since he lived on the edge, the Old Man didn't have insurance. But I'm willing to argue before the legislature that cost should be no object when it comes to saving one of our own.

To those who say the Old Man was always au naturel and should stay that way, I say that's hooey. Though he looked old-fashioned, he was never opposed to a little artificial enhancement. As long ago as 1916, in fact, a man named Edward Geddes installed three giant turnbuckles that functioned like metal stitches across dangerously deep wrinkles on his 300-ton forehead. And for the last four decades, first Nils Nielsen and later his son David (who joined his dad on the Old Man for the first time at age eleven) performed yearly facials on the Old Man of the Mountain. They cleared brush around his brow, scoured some trouble spots, epoxied smile lines and crow's feet, and even covered his face with a special chemical mask to fight acid rain. But an Old Man reaches a point when he needs far more than just a day or two of spa treatments each year to keep his 12,000-year-old good looks. Let's all pony up and call the best cosmetic surgeons for bids on a facelift. You know he's worth it.

The Old Man of the Mountain Museum is located in Franconia Notch State Park at the southbound Old Man viewing area just north of Profile Lake off Interstate 93. For information call (603) 823–5563.

New Hampshire's Gorgeous Flume
Franconia Notch

The second stop on our tour of geological curiosities in Franconia Notch State Park is the Flume Gorge. If you enjoy your visit to this, one of the more wondrous of the state's natural wonders, you can just thank "Aunt Jess" Guernsey. In 1808, at the spry age of ninety-three,

Aunt Jess happened to be doing a little bushwhacking in Franconia Notch in hopes of finding some new fishing holes, as the story goes, when she came upon a stunning 800-foot-long natural gorge at the base of Mount Liberty. At the time Guernsey discovered it, a huge egg-shaped boulder hung suspended between the gorge walls, like a giant stone stopper in a bottleneck, but in 1883 torrential rains caused a small landslide that swept it away.

If Aunt Jess were to return today, I think she might accuse us all of going a little soft. Now there's a visitor center, bus service to the footpath, guided tours, and a boardwalk that follows the course of Flume Brook through the gorge, just to help those of us less agile than Aunt Jess find our way into the deliciously cool, moss-fragrant shadows of the Flume. Its sheer granite walls, separated by as little as 10 feet in places, rise as high as eight stories above the boardwalk, and sometimes, on clear days when the light is just so, the mist rising from the water creates a rainbow of colors above visitors' heads.

If you're inspired by Aunt Jess's explorations, you can climb a set of stairs at the north end of the Flume and follow the 1-mile trail loop, first down into old-growth forest and then across Sentinel Pine Covered

Good old Jess sure didn't need no stinkin' boardwalks.

Bridge, which spans the Pemigewasset River and was reportedly built from a single pine tree. Look down from the bridge and you'll see a deep, glacier-carved basin called The Pool, Aunt Jess's other discovery that fine June day almost 200 years ago. Some nineteenth-century writers suggested that Aunt Jess was going senile—"a second childhood" they called it—when she made her wondrous discoveries, and that locals doubted her tale of a great chasm hidden in the woods. If that's true, then Aunt Jess had just the kind of second childhood I'd wish for, one marked by bushwhacking, discoveries, and a little sticking it to the neighbors.

The Flume is open May through October; admission is charged. For information call the Flume Gorge & Visitor Center at (603) 745–8391.

And You Thought Our Weather Was Bad?
Haverhill

Admittedly, New England weather is worse than it has a right to be. Even though Portsmouth sits at about the same latitude as the French Riviera, we have no Riviera, no turquoise sea the temperature of a baby's bathwater, and certainly no Cannes Film Festival. The many reasons behind our miserable weather run the gamut from our mountainous terrain (and who would want to give that up for a few more days of sunshine?) to the fact that the continent's mercurial Polar Jet Stream runs, more often than not, right through our living room. One weather-related source I read claimed that New England's all-time high temperature of 107 degrees Fahrenheit is actually higher than the record highs for both Miami, Florida, and Atlanta, Georgia, while our all-time low of 50 below zero is colder than the record low for International Falls, Minnesota, an unfortunate city that's often the coldest place in the Lower 48. How's that for unfair?

But in devoting a whole museum to four cataclysmic weather events in New England's history, the Museum of American Weather just might give the local climate an even worse rap than it deserves. With exhibits devoted to monstrously bad weather—like the Blizzard of 1888, when a massive nor'easter stalled over Block Island and dumped over 4 feet of snow in places like Middletown, Connecticut, killing hundreds; the Vermont Flood on November 3–4, 1927, when over 9 inches of rain fell in twenty-four hours, causing severe flash flooding and killing eighty-four; and the Great Hurricane of 1938, a probable Category 3 hurricane that packed 121-mile-per-hour winds, downed 275 million trees, and caused almost $2 billion in damage in today's dollars—the Museum of American Weather is a showcase of the most dramatic meteorological miseries New Englanders have had to endure over the last 200 years.

Even though I can't argue with the fact that these cataclysmic events are worthy of inclusion in a New England weather museum, I'd like to see a little more balance in the exhibits. How about a display, for example, about that brief climatic window in early fall, when the black flies and the mosquitoes have finally dispersed, and the skies are clear and the air is warm, and we're able to enjoy our New England weather for a few heavenly moments before the leaves fly and the snows begin to fall. But we wouldn't want to give the wrong weather impression, now would we?

The Museum of American Weather is located on Haverhill's South Common. For information call (603) 989–3167.

Snow Sculptures Leave Critics Cold (Fans, Too)
Jackson

The difference between snow sculpting and sand sculpting is not unlike the difference between ice fishing and just plain old fishing: The basics are all the same, but one's just a heck of a lot more painful than the other. When the sand sculptor competes, she enjoys warm sun on her skin, perhaps a cool ocean breeze, the crash and soothing hiss of wave meeting sand. But pity, oh pity the poor snow sculptor, who stands for hours and hours in subfreezing temperatures, his toes losing all feeling, his breath riming his eyelashes until they stick when he blinks, his poor ungloved hands returning again and again to a bucket of icy water. Talk about suffering for one's art.

Each year at the end of January, Jackson hosts the New Hampshire Snow Sculpting Competition, a three-day regional championship, with the winner going on to the U.S. Nationals Snow Sculpting Competition in Lake Geneva, Wisconsin. (What, you didn't know there was a national snow-sculpting competition? And you call yourself a northerner . . .) The field is composed of three-member teams of artsy gluttons for punishment from all walks of life, from MFA students and architects to social workers and set designers. Each team creates their masterpiece over the course of two long, cold winter days (and perhaps even a long winter's Saturday night) from identical cylinders of compacted snow—each measuring 8 feet in height and 4 feet in diameter—using only simple hand tools, snow, ice, and water. Judging is weighted toward creativity and originality instead of perfection of execution, so the designs tend to be wonderfully fanciful, with sculptures ranging from a climber scrambling up a surprisingly realistic-looking rock face to a whole school of fish and other random sea life inhabiting a coral reef. But competitors be forewarned: The judges, I'm told, take snow-sculpting safety seriously and won't hesitate to deduct points if any team member loses more than one digit to frostbite.

The New Hampshire Snow Sculpting Competition takes place at the Jackson Town Park in the center of the village. For information contact the Jackson Area Chamber of Commerce at (603) 383–9356.

A Lost Virgin Is Hard to Find
Jefferson Notch (near Randolph)

Perhaps one of the worst places to lose a virgin is deep in the White Mountains when you're lost, starving, and being hunted by Abenaki Indians whose village you razed just a couple of weeks ago. And that, according to a story that is part history and part legend, is when Robert Rogers and his small band of rangers, returning from their raid on the Abenaki village of St. Francis, deep in French-controlled territory in present-day Quebec, lost their solid silver statue of the Virgin Mary and Child. And she hasn't been seen since.

During a colonial-era skirmish between England and France that would come to be called the Last French War, Rogers was in charge of a 600-man group of green-clad scouts and frontiersmen who, with a nice bit of consonance, came to be known as Rogers' Rangers. While he didn't dream up the wilderness warfare tactics he popularized—a number of which were borrowed from the Native American warriors he was intent on killing—he did systematize the tactics into a teachable set of twenty-eight so-called Rogers' Ranging Rules. His men were intensively trained, highly mobile, and pretty darn lethal, in part due to the fact that they pulled MacGyver-style stunts like wearing their snowshoes backwards to confuse trackers.

On October 4, 1759, Rogers and a group of about 200 of his rangers attacked St. Francis, a Catholic missionary village whose Abenaki inhabitants, according to reports, had sacked numerous New Hampshire settlements. While executing their nighttime raid, Rogers' Rangers plundered both the town and the church of its riches, carrying away with them, according to accounts, silver plate, gold coins, a ruby ring, a pair of gold candlesticks, and an eight-pound silver statue of a seated Virgin Mary with the Christ Child upon her knees, modeled, supposedly, after a statue at the Chartres Cathedral in France.

Rogers' Rangers were hotly pursued by survivors, and, after sustaining casualties, they decided to split into smaller parties and take overland routes through country that was still uncharted wilderness. Suffering from Abenaki attacks, starvation, and exposure, many of the rangers died before reaching home, and as the remaining men fought for survival, they abandoned their treasures in the wilderness. Rogers' group, who reportedly carried the statue as well as other goodies, lost their Virgin in the treacherous wilds north of Mount Washington before as many as eight of them perished. (It's rumored that some of the survivors even fed off the remains of the dead.)

In the nineteenth century scads of treasure seekers searched the area, and even today the Lancaster Historical Society receives requests for maps and information from metal-detector-wielding tourists. But the silver Virgin remains lost in the woods, as she has been for almost 250 years. If any of you happen to find her, though, you might consider giving me a cut of the profits.

For information about trails and conditions in the northern Presidential Range, where the Virgin was supposedly lost, you can call the Appalachian Mountain Club at (603) 466–2721 or the USDA Forest Service at (603) 466–2713.

Black Bears' Exotic Dance for Dairy
Lincoln

"Bears! Bears! Bears! Real Live Black Bears, Unmuzzled and Unleashed!" Okay, now that I've got your attention, let me tell you about the trained North American black bears performing all summer long at Clark's Trading Post in Lincoln. The main attraction at Clark's for almost fifty years, the bears perform half-hour shows, bicycling, climbing into barrels, swinging on a big swing, and eating lots of vanilla ice cream in front of sold-out crowds two or three times a day throughout the summer and on weekends through the first week of October. The union has done a great job at the bargaining table, too, so the bears get six months off each year to hibernate.

What do these live, unmuzzled, and potentially ferocious black bears do during their performances? First and foremost, their trainers, Maureen and Murray Clark, reward the bears handsomely with local dairy products each time they perform a trick, so they eat significant amounts of ice cream and drink lots of milk and honey from "bear cans." (Luckily, none of the bears are lactose intolerant.) According to the Clarks, there's many a wild bear who would love a job working the crowd at the Trading Post, not only for the great health insurance and the 401K, but because of the steady supply of performance-enhancing treats. A young bear balances atop a large ball and slowly walks it down an incline? How about some vanilla ice cream! A small bear rides a bicycle around the ring? How about some milk and honey! A 250-pound-plus bear grasps a

Clark's Trading Post's re-creation of the old Old Man.

"bearskatball" between his paws and then wows the crowd by putting it through a hoop? How about a little more vanilla ice cream!

Clark's has been around since 1928, when it was known as Ed Clark's Eskimo Dog Ranch, and since then four generations of Clarks have built the business into a full-scale tourist destination, with attractions like a half-hour steam-engine train ride into the territory of one Mr. Wolfman, a hirsute gentleman dressed in Neanderthal casual who doesn't take kindly to trespassers, at least not at first; a climbing wall in the form of a ¼-scale replica of the Old Man of the Mountain; and a museum containing, among other things, a stuffed calf with two heads that lived only three minutes—in this case, two heads were worse than one. The bears, though, take top billing at Clark's Trading Post, and deservedly so. I'm going to make a prediction: You'll love the performance, but at show's end you'll be overcome with a powerful craving for dairy.

Clark's Trading Post in Lincoln is open from the end of May through the beginning of October. Special events include a Wolfman Weekend in the middle of June, featuring a Wolfman look-alike contest and a growling contest. Take exit 33 off Interstate 93 and head 1 mile south on Route 3. For information and bear show schedules, call (603) 745–8913.

If It's Not Scottish, It's . . . Not at This Festival
Lincoln

It's probably no accident that men in the habit of wearing skirts came up with the übermanly idea of seeing who could throw a tree the farthest. (It can't be definitively proven, but I'm pretty sure the guy who gave the first caber a toss was named John Q. McHernia, of the once-but-no-longer-proud McHernia Clan.) If you've never seen men in kilts toss cabers, hurl hammers, and put shot (can you even say that?), you won't want to miss the Scottish Heavy Athletics at the New Hampshire Highland Games, the largest Scottish cultural festival in the Northeast.

At the Scottish Heavy Athletics you'll see lots and lots of men dressed in kilts, but I guarantee you won't feel the least bit tempted to crack a joke about hairy legs, since all the Scottish heavy athletes are, well, heavy, and bear a striking resemblance to NFL linemen in tartan drag. Only instead of tossing each other around, these heavyweights toss hammers for distance and weights for height and cabers for the coveted 270 degrees of rotation insiders call "twelve o'clock." To successfully toss one of the eighty- or ninety-pound poles, a heavy athlete must lift it straight up to his chest, run a little ways down the field with his tree sticking straight up in the air, plant his feet firmly, and then give the tree a terrific heave to try to "turn" it, or flip it once end over end. And then he proceeds to the medical tent for treatment.

Other highlights of the three-day event include Celtic concerts and a ceremonial Gathering of the Scottish Clans and Massed Pipe Bands, as well as workshops on whisky tasting, Scottish history, and Scottish Country and Cape Breton dance. Visitors can also enjoy the Sheep Dog Trials, as well as Highland dance, fiddle, bagpipe, drumming, and harp competitions.

The New Hampshire Highland Games are held in September each year at Loon Mountain Resort in Lincoln. For information and, if you're up for a little tree tossing, to download contest registration forms, go to www.nhscot.org. To inquire by phone call (603) 745–8111.

More Candy Than You Can Count(er)

Littleton

The Guinness-certified longest candy counter in the world at Chutters in Littleton is, according to the experts, just a touch shy of 112 feet. Ask Chutters' candy buyer Rodney "The Candy Man" Bengtson how

Heaven is not being able to see the end of the candy counter.

long the candy counter is, though, and you just might detect in his voice a hint of resentment toward the yardstick sticklers at the *Guinness Book of World Records*. "The candy counter is 111 feet and ¾ inches," Rodney told me. "They wouldn't give us the last ¼ inch because of the molding."

Ah well, no use crying over a lost quarter inch of counter, especially if you've got the world record, not to mention one of the most extensive selections of candies in the entire world staring you in the face. With three tiers of candy counter stretching from the very front to the way back of the store, the Candy Man's charged with filling somewhere between 600 and 700 glass jars with just about every kind of confection you could imagine, and some you probably couldn't imagine. You've probably heard of gummi worms and gummi bears, but what about gummi sharks, gummi lobsters, gummi frogs, and gummi turtles? If it's edible accessories you're looking for, Chutters has necklaces, watches, rings, and bracelets—all candy, of course—but no candy earrings, at least none that I saw. According to my quick calculations, Chutters also has around thirty jars of penny candy, about twenty-five kinds of licorice, lollipops ranging from a three-pound sucker to the venerable Tootsie Roll pop, and virtually every traditional candy bar known to mankind in rows of jars toward the back. If you can't find the candy you're craving at Chutters, they probably haven't invented it yet.

For more grown-up tastebuds, Chutters also houses over 12 feet of specialty chocolates, about thirty varieties of homemade fudge, and shelves and shelves full of specialty gourmet foods, from hot sauces to salad dressings to blueberry jams. But on busy midsummer days, the candy counter is where the action is, with youngsters gravitating toward the gummis and the more "mature" crowd lingering around the licorice. If you want to see real talent, watch one of the girls at the register speed-count a bag of 200 or so penny candies. Come to think of it, they should probably invite the folks from Guinness back, since Chutters could very well have the fastest candy counter in the world, as well as the longest.

Chutters General Store is at 41 Main Street in downtown Littleton. For information or orders call (603) 444–5787.

How to Bury a Horse without Heavy Lifting
Littleton

The marker at Littleton's Eli Wallace Horse Cemetery, a small fenced-in enclosure that contains stones for three Wallace family horses, does a little whitewashing of the facts. Yes, Maud and Molly, the matched pair of bay Morgan horses Eli bought as a gift for his bride, Myra, on her twenty-ninth birthday—"the only children . . . [the couple] would have," the marker says—both died thirty long years later in 1919. And yes, the horses were buried in their roomy graves like Egyptians, surrounded by all their earthly effects: their harnesses, bridles, blankets, and feed-boxes. But what that little marker on a post at the front of the cemetery doesn't say is *how* Maud and Molly and their barn-load of accessories were laid to rest.

It turns out that Maud and Molly, old and infirm, were laid away, or put down, or put to sleep, depending on the euphemism you're used to. Eli Wallace dug two deep holes with earthen ramps leading down, and then he guided his beloved horses, outfitted in their harnesses, into their respective graves. From there a local veteri-narian, Dr. A. F. Hill, kindly took over, firing the two shots that did in, dispatched, or undid the old girls.

A cemetery where humans aren't allowed.

Downright depressing, right? Well, it only gets worse. Myra Wallace died just a year later, leaving Eli all alone. In his grief he wrote and published a booklet about his life with Myra, Maud, and Molly titled *When They Were Here,* handing out copies around town. (The Littleton Historical Society has the only two known copies that remain, just in case you're into tearjerkers.) When Eli learned that Maggie, the local butcher's horse, was going to be cashed in, he offered to buy her; instead, the butcher gave Maggie to him as a gift, and she remained with Eli—a source of consolation, we can imagine—until he died on April 1, 1929.

The longest set of instructions in Eli's will concerned arrangements for the perpetual care of the cemetery that contained his beloved girls—Maggie would join Maud and Molly after Eli's death. He bequeathed a third of his estate and forty acres to the Littleton Hospital in exchange for care of the horse cemetery, but over the decades the hospital forgot its obligations and the cemetery was left abandoned and overgrown. It was only a few years ago that the Littleton Historical Society, along with the help of Dr. Richard Hill, the son of Maud and Molly's gun-wielding veterinarian, restored the cemetery to its proper condition. Now the horses rest in well-tended peace, just down an embankment from Interstate 93, a four-lane highway that, local history says, was moved a few feet from its planned course to avoid disturbing the old girls. And that means Eli can rest in peace, too.

The Eli Wallace Horse Cemetery is in the center of Littleton. From Cottage Street, take a right onto Mount Eustis Road (you'll see a green sign for the horse cemetery) and head under I–93; the cemetery will be on your left. The Littleton Historical Society's museum is located at 1 Cottage Street and is open Wednesdays, May through November. For more information call (603) 444–5816 or 444–6586.

Gas Pumps from the Good Old Days of 27 Cents a Gallon
Littleton

If you're not paying attention and catch a glimpse of Don and Ellen Morrow's place out of the corner of your eye, you could confuse it for a gas station from the twilight zone. Colorful antique gas pumps from a number of different eras of American motoring fill the yard, with one whole row stretching at an angle from the front porch toward the road like a line of petroleum sentries guarding the house. On the porch of an outbuilding to the right of the house, you'll see more old gas pumps, and in front of the wooden sheds at the edge of the yard, you guessed it, a few more gas pumps. It's clear the Morrows have a thing for them.

Actually, it's not just gas pumps they're obsessed with, it's everything related to selling gas in the old days: gas signs, gas cans, gas memorabilia—they've turned their whole front yard, and the whole backyard, too, into a kind of outdoor museum of oily Americana. Only none of the artifacts are oily in the least; in fact, even though each and every item looks 100 percent genuine, the gas pumps, the oil cans, and the Mobil, Shell, and Esso signs are all so shiny clean and brightly colored, one starts to wonder if they've ever spent any time at all around a filling station. Don and Ellen Morrow's house is located a mile or two east of downtown Littleton on the north side of Route 116.

Old gas pumps are beautiful, but those old-fashioned prices were downright gorgeous.

REST IN REBELLION

Rare is the individual who causes as much of a ruckus in death as he once did in life, but punk rocker and Littleton native G. G. Allin may very well be one. On June 28, 1993, Allin's career as what he called a "rock 'n' roll terrorist" and one of the most notorious punk rockers of his generation came to an end when he died of a heroin overdose in New York City. He was thirty-six years old. Now buried in Littleton's Glenwood Cemetery, Allin continues to cause trouble, especially on the anniversary of his death, when fans, shall we say, pay tribute to their fallen hero at his gravesite. And the nature of those "tributes" has deeply disturbed some of the locals.

I'll try to put this as delicately as possible, but for readers with uneasiness about the body and its less polite doings, I suggest you stop right here and move on to another entry. Seriously. Because G. G. Allin was perhaps one of the crudest, raunchiest, most id-inspired rock stars in history. Just to give you an idea of how badly he behaved onstage, he was arrested for his antics around fifty times, for everything from allegedly assaulting audience members, to allegedly inserting bananas into impolite orifices, to allegedly going to the bathroom onstage. Number 2, if you must know, and he supposedly hurled it into the audience afterward. When the cops interrogated Allin after that particular, um, performance, he allegedly told them he "didn't think enough came out to bother anybody." He had plans for even more inspired stagecraft yet, pledging that one night he would commit suicide midperformance. Sadly, I am not making any of this up.

The postmortem G. G. Allin troubles peak each year around the anniversary of his death, when fans visit his gravesite to act out their own Allin-inspired antics. Littleton police have had reports of fans going to the bathroom on Allin's gravestone (both 1 and 2), fans burying animal parts at the gravesite, and fans stealing tiny American flags and burning them, among other indelicate, not to mention illegal, acts. Townspeople have not been impressed. In 2003, as the date approached for a tribute concert in town to mark the tenth anniversary of Allin's death, a Littleton reverend is said to have suggested exhuming the rocker and burying him at an undisclosed location to avoid any further problems. G. G. Allin, as his brother noted in an interview, would have loved all the to-do. His remains, however, will remain in Glenwood Cemetery, a troublemaker in perpetuity, or at least as long as his fans feel inspired to flatter his memory with indelicate imitation.

Allin's grave is in the St. Rose section of Glenwood Cemetery on West Main Street, just 30 or so feet from the road.

Isn't It About Time to Fire the Grounds Crew?

North Conway

Without fail, in early September of each year at North Conway's Hog Coliseum, the field conditions are abysmal. No matter what the weather's been like in the Mount Washington Valley, whether heat wave or cold snap, drought or flood, the field of play is virtually unplayable, covered in 14 to 18 inches of soupy, café au lait–colored mud. With such a woeful performance record, you'd think the grounds crew would have been fired years ago, but they seem just about as secure in their jobs as Supreme Court justices. Even more perversely, folks thank them each year for a job well done.

That's because they've properly prepped Hog Coliseum for North Conway's annual Mud Bowl, a three-day-long double-elimination mud football tournament featuring thirteen touch mud football matches, a Saturday-morning Tournament of Mud parade, a Saturday-night Mud Bowl Ball at North Conway's Cranmore Mountain Resort, and, the grimy highlight, Sunday's World Mud Bowl championship

A couple feet of mud? Field conditions are just perfect.

game. Eight gritty teams from as far away as Maine and Massachusetts—including the Mount Washington Valley Hogs, an eleven-time champion, and the Muddas of Amherst, New Hampshire, a record sixteen-time champion—slip, slosh, and slog their way through soupy field conditions at Hog Coliseum. And while it's all in good clean fun, with 100 percent of proceeds going to charity, I can assure you the boys take the games seriously. In 2005 the home-state favorites were stymied by the North Shore Mudsharks of Peabody, Massachusetts, who won the first championship in their team's history, buoyed by the help of at least four off-season draftees from the Muddas' 2004 championship team. Kudos to the Mudsharks' front office . . .

One of the true highlights of Mud Bowl games are the half-time cheerleading shows, wherein the wives and girlfriends of players perform synchronized dance routines in the mud. And even though the Mud Bowl is most definitely a family event (many of the cheerleaders have kids watching in the audience, in fact), the cheerleading teams at the Mud Bowl have been known to get, I hate to say it, a little dirty. It's amazing what a gal will do for charity.

The Mud Bowl takes place each year on the first weekend after Labor Day, in the world-renowned Hog Coliseum, located just off Main Street in North Conway. For more information call the Mount Washington Valley Chamber of Commerce at (800) 337–3364.

Little Church in the Mountains
North Woodstock

People really love tiny buildings. Take, by way of example, very small churches. Maybe people don't love them as much as they love really big churches, like St. Peter's in Rome or Notre Dame in Paris, but still, there's a small but well-established nationwide fascination with

A mini church with a solid foundation.

churches in which you can squeeze five, maybe six, people tops. (Trust me on this one: I've done the research.) And one reason people love them, I imagine, is that a church is supposed to be somewhat big, by dint of its intended function of bringing many people together to pray. That's why the tiny church, in being what it's not supposed to be, wins our rebel-loving sympathies and affection. How's that for a little theorizing?

Of course, another reason people probably feel drawn to a tiny church is that a whole lot less church can happen there, which brings me to the Rock of Ages Church in North Woodstock. Perched on a big boulder and measuring a mere 11 by 11 feet, sources say it has a maximum capacity of twelve and a half people. (And I didn't even know the occupancies of very small buildings were measured in half-people units.) One of the most striking things about the Rock of Ages, though, isn't the fact that it's tiny (I've seen tinier, including a teeny-weeny chapel located at the geographical center of the contiguous United States in Lebanon, Kansas)—it's that the granite boulder upon which the building rests is almost exactly the same size as the church itself. So even though the privately owned church has fallen into disrepair over the last few decades, its foundation will likely remain sound for the next few millennia or so.

Unfortunately, the church isn't open to the public and no services are held there, but it's clearly visible from the road, and if you ask permission the owner might let you take a closer look. From North Woodstock take Route 3 south for about 2.5 miles; just after you pass Meadow Lark Motor Court, the Rock of Ages Church will be on your right.

Forest Gone Wild

Mount Whiteface

If you want to see a really old forest, New Hampshire doesn't have much to offer. Most of the state's been logged, the whole place close to clear-cut (with as much as 85 percent of the land turned to meadow and field) not just once but twice in the last 250 or so years.

The ridge system that connects Mount Whiteface (4,020 feet), Mount Passaconaway (4,043 feet), and Mount Wonalancet (2,728 feet), though, bounds a secluded valley, or cirque, that's never been logged. Known as the Bowl Research Natural Area, these 510 acres of virgin northern hard-wood and spruce-fir forest will give you an idea of what this country looked like before anyone took a saw to it. Research Natural Areas (RNAs) are areas within national forests that the Forest Service has set aside to be permanently protected and maintained in natural condition, so the Bowl RNA will look this way for a long, long time.

These woods are wild.

The Bowl Research Natural Area is located on the eastern slopes of Mount Whiteface in the Sandwich Range Wilderness. The Wonalancet Outdoor Club, a local organization that maintains trails and shelters in the Sandwich Range, can provide maps and trail information. Go to www.wodc.org or call (603) 323–8078. To reach the Bowl RNA, take Route 113 to the Ferncroft parking area in Wonalancet. From the trailhead hike north along the Wonalancet River on the Dicey's Mill Trail for about 3 miles.

The Commute from Hell

Pinkham Notch

"It's certainly one of the more interesting commutes in the state," says Peter Crane of the Mount Washington Observatory, whose calm understatements regarding harrowing circumstances remind me of the way airline pilots speak during emergencies. He's referring to journeys to the top of Mount Washington undertaken by the organization's summit observers in midwinter, when an average day—I repeat, an average day—finds the topmost slopes buried in 10 feet of snow and bathed in thick rime-ice-producing fog, with visibility around 100 feet, the temperature about 4 degrees Fahrenheit, and a wind speed of 50 miles per hour. And you complain about a little freezing rain—for shame!

The Mount Washington Observatory is a private, member-supported nonprofit that permanently staffs a summit observatory on the mountain, where they monitor and record environmental and weather conditions, conduct environmental research and testing, and educate the public about everything from severe weather (they should know) to global warming to alpine ecology. From about mid-May to mid-October, the observatory, located in the state-owned Sherman Adams Building, is open to the public. But in wintertime the only folks allowed inside are the weather observers, who work eight days of twelve-hour shifts and then head down the mountain for six days off before commuting back to the summit.

The tough part of the commute begins at the base of Mount Washington in a high-clearance four-wheel-drive truck equipped with chains on the tires. Partway up the mountain, the big truck with chains no longer cuts it, and observers switch to a vehicle called a snow tractor, with standard features that include a long snowplow blade on the front and dual Caterpillar tracks outfitted with something called grousers to cut through frozen snow. On the way to the top, the driver might bring the commute to a halt to, say, plow a path through a 7-foot snowdrift or wait for visibility to improve to avoid plummeting off the no-longer-discernible edge of the mountain. In summer the 8-mile trip by car up the Mount Washington Auto Road usually takes about twenty-five minutes, but these winter commutes from Hades typically take two to three times as long, with four-, five-, even six-hour trips not uncommon.

In summer the Mount Washington Observatory and its small museum are open seven days a week and accessible by cog railway, car, motorcycle, ATV, and foot. In winter the observatory is closed, as are all other facilities on the summit. You can, however, join one of the observatory's overnight winter Edutrips to the summit (and experience a commute in the snow tractor), where you'll be hosted by staff and taught by experts. For more information call (603) 356–2137 or go to www.mountwashington.org.

Wouldn't It Be Easier to Race *Down* the Mountain?
Pinkham Notch

You might think even one race up Mount Washington is one too many, but there are, in fact, no fewer than three, count 'em, three races up the 6,288-foot peak every summer on the 7.6-mile-long Mount Washington Auto Road. Competitors race by foot, by bike, and by classic car up grades that average 12 percent, with extended sections of 18 percent and more, around hairpin turns, past multiple stomach-churning drop-offs, and up to a summit that's wrapped in clouds or fog more than 300 days a year. Even with the almost mile-high increase in elevation and what's called the "world's worst weather" on the slopes of Mount Washingtion, runners, cyclers, and auto racers still manage to summit faster than you'd ever imagine: the Mount Washington Road Race record stands at 56 minutes and 41 seconds, the Volkswagen Mount Washington Auto Road Bicycle Hillclimb record is 49 minutes and 24 seconds, while the Climb to the Clouds Auto Race record is 6 minutes and 49 seconds, with a mind-boggling maximum-speed-on-the-course record of 133 miles per hour! (The Climb to the Clouds race to the summit ended a few years ago, but the Auto Road still hosts a vintage car race halfway up the mountain.)

Officially completed on August 8, 1861, making it the first man-made tourist attraction in the United States, the Auto Road was once called the Carriage Road, since it was originally built for horse-drawn carriage traffic. In 1911 the Mount Washington Carriage Road officially became the Mount Washington Auto Road, and ever since then, vehicles that make the mile-high ascent up the narrow, mostly paved road, with its breathtaking views and umpteen switchbacks, get bumper sticker bragging rights for the rest of their mechanical lives: "This Car Climbed Mount Washington."

About the Mount Washington Auto Road it could have been prophesied, "Build it and they will try to race up it as fast as they can." Around 600 bicyclists compete in the Volkswagen Mount Washington Auto Road Hillclimb (along with a few unicyclists) in late August, while 1,000 runners attempt the summit in the Mount Washington Road Race, held on the third Sunday in June. After warning runners of the myriad challenges and potential dangers of the race up the Auto Road, race officials like to offer this Pollyannaish bit of encouragement: "Don't worry, there's only one hill!"

Registration for the bicycle race begins in February, while registration for the road race is by lottery in March. The Vintage Car Hillclimb and car show is held in July. For information on all three races (and to register, if you're one of those überfit types), call (603) 466–3988 or visit www.mountwashingtonautoroad.com.

Now Swing Your Partner Round the Diesel Pump!

Randolph

When I stepped into Lowe's Service Station on Route 2 in Randolph, I told a dark-haired gentleman seated at a table just inside the door, by way of introduction, that I was researching quirky, offbeat people, places, and events in the state. "Is this the place that holds a dance around the gas pumps every year?" I asked him.

"Hey, you hear that, Dad?" the man shouted toward the garage. "We're quirky!"

I happened to be talking to the physically imposing Kevin Lowe; his mom, Lucille Lowe, was seated at the table beside him, and his father, G. Alan Lowe Jr., was just then stepping from the garage into the space behind the store's register. Here I was surrounded by Lowes, third- and fourth-generation owners and operators of Randolph's only store, a lone writer/researcher

A square dance where smoking is strictly forbidden.

259

from way down south, and I was afraid they weren't going to take kindly to being called quirky, even in an indirect sort of way.

But, of course, I had nothing to worry about. The Lowe family is well practiced at greeting and politely taking care of all kinds, since they've been doing it for almost a century. Their square dance around the gas pumps, though, is a mere thirty-two-year-old tradition, wherein over 100 folks gather (in a town with a population around 340) to eat, drink, do-si-do around the gas pumps, and have a grand old time.

Back in 1974, townspeople planned an indoor square dance in celebration of Randolph's 150th birthday, but when electrical problems threatened cancellation of the event, the Lowes offered their service station parking lot as a dance hall surrogate. Ever since then, people have been coming to Lowe's on the last Saturday in July to dance with friends and strangers and feast on "whatever we catch," according to Alan. The Lowes serve everything from salmon and trout to moose and venison, all cooked up on the grill out back, while the square dance caller keeps the crowd reeling under the Mobil sign out front. The highlight is the Grand March, when a march song booms from the speakers, everyone grabs a partner, and the caller orders marching twosomes, foursomes, and eightsomes into tunnels and tangles that bring smiles to even the stoniest of Yankee faces.

Lowe's Service Station is located at 908 Route 2 in Randolph. For information about the dance, you can call the Lowes at (603) 466–3950. Whatever you do, though, just don't call them quirky.

White Mountain Charades
Randolph

Outside of your average family, it's rare to find a large group of people willing to act really foolish around each other across multiple generations. But the members of the Randolph Mountain Club have been wearing huge false wooden teeth, cross-dressing as Queen Victoria, and joining heads to behinds to impersonate camels and horses for four generations now, and they don't show any sign of calling it quits in the decades to come. Each year on the third Saturday in August, the Randolph Mountain Club (or RMC) hosts their annual club picnic, the centerpiece of which is an often elaborate and always hilarious game of charades. Held in an RMC-maintained clearing and natural amphitheater called Mossy Glen, the picnic charades attract hundreds of RMC members and Randolph townsfolk, many of whom remember watching their parents embarrass themselves for the merriment of others decades ago.

Founded in 1910, the Randolph Mountain Club is a nonprofit, primarily volunteer organization that maintains a 100-mile network of trails in the heart of White Mountain National Forest. In addition to maintaining trails, the RMC organizes weekly hikes, hosts numerous events, and maintains a series of cabins and shelters open to the public on a first-come, first-served basis.

According to Judith Hudson, a longtime member of the RMC who's at work on a history of the club, the three charade teams of Hill, Midland, and Valley, grouped according to the three long-vanished nineteenth-century Randolph inns where cottage owners once collected their mail, "don't take it [the charades] terribly seriously," with each team gathering only a week before the picnic to choose a word and dream up their performances. When I expressed my disbelief, especially considering the impressive pictures I saw on the RMC Web site—including a photo of a large, elaborately painted model of the torpedoed ocean liner *Lusitania* roped between two trees—Hudson allowed that, well, sometimes "it's a pretty intense week."

For those who've only played silent charades, it's important to know that the RMC version of the game is a much more raucous and theatrical affair, with teams acting out, syllable by syllable, a word like *lubrication,* using sets and props (everything from buildings to gondolas to out-houses, as well as an old bearskin that keeps reappearing), costumes, dialogue, and sometimes even songs. Throw in frequent literary, biblical, and mythological allusions, as well as tongue-in-cheek references to contemporary political events and scandals, and you've got the greatest, not to mention longest-running, show in the White Mountains. A word of warning, though, for audience members seated a little lower, and a little closer to the show, on the hillside: If one of the RMC teams is acting out the word *pie-row-tech-nix,* be on guard for the pie fight in the first act.

The Annual RMC Picnic is held on the third Saturday in August. All are welcome. For more information about the Randolph Mountain Club, its trails, its cabins, and its annual picnic and charades, visit www .randolphmountainclub.org.

AMC Works for Your Weary Body

Sargents Purchase

Taking a multiday backpacking trip is one long lesson in how much back-breaking work it requires to keep yourself relatively safe, moderately warm, marginally comfortable, reasonably well-fed, and minimally sheltered when you willingly forego all the basics of modern civilization. Much of what you do while camping is, thankfully, already done for you back home: For instance, before you cook your meal on the trail, you first have to assemble your stove; before you go to sleep, you first have to erect your house; before you go to the bathroom, you first have to make a toilet by digging something referred to, somewhat mysteriously, as a "cat hole." It's enough to convince a body that his body takes too much darn work.

The Appalachian Mountain Club (or AMC) was way ahead of me when they built their full-service Lakes of the Clouds hut high on the south slope of Mount Washington. The "hut" is really more of a large guest lodge, with lots of windows, wide pine floors and ceilings, and comfy accommodations for ninety tent-shunning hikers in coed bunkrooms, no assembly required. Lakes of the Clouds, and other AMC huts like it in the Presidential Range, make it possible for work-wary hikers like me to head up into the White Mountains without having to hump civilization (or shoddy replacements thereof) on our backs.

Founded in Boston back in 1876, the Appalachian Mountain Club is America's oldest conservation and recreation organization, promoting the protection, enjoyment, and wise use of the White Mountains and beyond. The AMC developed a system of high-mountain huts beginning in 1888 with the construction of a cabin on Mount Madison, and now the club operates a series of eight such huts in the Presidential Range, each separated by about a day's hike, offering bunks and hearty meals to hikers who want to be welcomed into an outpost of civilization at the end of a long day on the trail.

Can you still call this camping?

Well above tree line at 5,050 feet, Lakes of the Clouds remains the highest and most popular hut. Full-service accommodations include a hearty dinner at 6:00 P.M. sharp (including freshly baked bread, salad, entree, side dishes, and dessert); full breakfast at 7:00 A.M.; a bunk; not one, not two, but three wool blankets; and a pillow. (You need to bring your own teddy bear.) The staff not only cook delectable meals, they

263

also educate guests on subjects like low-impact camping and Mount Washington's fragile alpine ecology, provide expert trail information and offer up-to-the-minute weather reports radioed down from the Mount Washington Observatory. They might even serenade you, if you're lucky, to wake you for your full-service flapjack breakfast. Now this, my friends, is wilderness living so good, it might make civilization seem like hard work.

The Appalachian Mountain Club's huts operate somewhat self-sufficiently thanks to composting toilets, solar panels, and wind generators. For more information or to make a reservation, call (603) 466–2727 or visit the AMC Web site at www.outdoors.org/lodging.

Stone Face Happy to Be on the Down and Low

Shelburne

You may not have ever heard of the Old Man of the Valley, but his low profile, or the lowness of his profile, accounts for a good deal of his charm. Located just off Route 2 in Shelburne not far from the Maine border, the Old Man of the Valley (or the O. M. of the V. as I prefer to call him) is a small stone profile, just 4½ feet or so from his slightly weak chin to his very tall forehead, on a granite boulder that sits just a few paces off the road and exactly at eye level among oak, birch, and spruce.

While outright comparison between the O. M. of the V. and the far more famous but now utterly vanished Old Man of the Mountain would be in bad taste, I would like to offer a few words about the Old Man of the Valley in the hopes that it might raise his stature in the eyes of my fellow citizens. First, the O. M. of the V. is a solid guy—he's real, he's grounded, he's like a rock (well, he is a rock). No one could ever accuse him of having his head in the clouds. Even more important, though, is the fact that, no matter who you are and what you do, the O. M. of the V. never looks down on you. In spite of his granite good looks, his little green sign out on Route 2, and the steady stream of visitors who walk the 20 yards down the footpath just to gaze upon his visage, he's never gotten a big head. You know what I'm saying here, I think: The O. M. of the V. has a good head on his boulder.

But don't take my word for it. Go have a look for yourself. Very low maintenance, with no lofty dreams of museums and gift shops and key chains bearing his likeness, the Old Man of the Valley is a stone pro-file for the ages, an O.M. whose M.O. might make him just as fitting a symbol of our state as another far more lofty profile which, out of respect, of course, shall remain nameless.

The Old Man of the Valley is located down a footpath on the south side of Route 2 in Shelburne, just a couple of miles from the Maine border. Look for the green sign that says OLD MAN OF THE VALLEY and a small gravel parking lot.

A boulder profile with his feet planted firmly on the ground.

Pick a Peck o' Pancakes at Polly's Pancake Parlor
Sugar Hill

Occupying the old carriage house of the nineteenth-century Hildex Maple Sugar Farm, Polly's Pancake Parlor has been serving the best pancakes in the White Mountains and possibly the world since 1938, when Polly and Will "Sugar Bill" Dexter first served hotcakes in their carriage house to boost sales of their farm's maple syrup. Why are they so darn good? Well, for starters, they serve their hotcakes with not one but three varieties of Sugar Bill–inspired maple toppings—homemade granulated maple sugar, maple spread, and maple syrup—a simple fact that automatically places Polly's Parlor head and shoulders above a chain of pancake houses that calls itself international.

But the folks at Polly's also stone grind their own grain for the pancakes, mixing up five different varieties to please every pancake palate; plain, corn meal, oatmeal buttermilk, buckwheat, and whole wheat. You can even choose from three different fillings—chopped nuts, blueberries, or coconut—and order a side of country sausage or corncob-smoked bacon or ham. As if that level of delectable attention to detail weren't enough, the same waitress who takes your order and refills your coffee is the one who scoops your pancakes onto the griddle and makes sure they're cooked to golden brown perfection before delivering them to your table with a smile.

Of course, you can order other goodies besides pancakes at Polly's, like sandwiches, soups, and quiche, but pancakes, and the local maple products that you slather upon them, are clearly king here. Long live such a yummy king.

Polly's Pancake Parlor, located at 617 Route 117 in Sugar Hill, is open from the middle of May to the middle of October for breakfast and lunch daily. They don't take reservations, but you can call (603) 823–5575 up to an hour ahead of your breakfast and put your name on a waiting list. To order maple products and pancake mixes, call (800) 432–8972 or visit www.pollyspancakeparlor.com.

A Well-Armed Town Green

Warren

Why settle for just a little old Civil War–era cannon on your town green when you can have, say, a World War II–era tank? And why settle for a little old outdated tank when you can have a retired 60-foot-tall Cold War–era medium-range nuclear missile, the same basic model that delivered a nuclear bomb 38 miles into the atmosphere for the first live nuclear missile test in U.S. history, sent the first American satellite into orbit, and carried Alan B. Shepard, originally of Derry, on his historic suborbital space flight on May 5, 1961?

Such may have been the thoughts of Warren native Ted Asselin when he asked his superiors at the U.S. Army's Redstone Arsenal in Huntsville, Alabama, if he could take home one of those retired nuclear missiles lying in that field over there, since no one seemed to be using them. First deployed in 1958, the Redstone was a highly accurate surface-to-surface missile capable of shooting into space everything from a 1-megaton thermonuclear warhead to 3.75 megatons of TNT to a chimpanzee named Ham to a New Hampshire–born jet pilot turned

Don't mess with Warren.

DOOMSDAY DISAPPOINTMENTS

It seems a peculiar thing to be disappointed about, but when the world didn't end some time between March 21, 1843, and March 21, 1844, as William Miller of Poultney, Vermont, had predicted, he was gravely disappointed. Then, when one of his estimated 50,000 expectant followers came up with a second date for the Second Coming of October 22, 1844, Miller said, "If Christ does not come . . . I shall feel twice the disappointment I did in the spring." As you can probably guess, Miller's high hopes for total destruction were twice-dashed, along with those of his followers, among them a splinter group of Miller-believing Baptists from Sugar Hill who gathered in the town cemetery to await their dilatory maker.

William Miller wasn't always so easily disappointed by the continuation of life on planet Earth. In fact, in his early adulthood he seemed to be a pretty normal nineteenth-century guy, a War of 1812 veteran who was a farmer and a justice of the peace. But by age thirty-four he had joined a Baptist church and become obsessed with marshalling biblical evidence to accurately predict the end of the world, and soon he felt quite certain about an upcoming Second Coming in "about 1843." Miller shared his findings with his pastor, Isaac Fuller, who was so impressed by Miller's scriptural calculations that he encouraged him to spread the "good" news. And spread it

Miller did, publishing numerous articles and a book, journeying around New England to address crowds under his traveling tent, and founding periodicals to communicate with a growing number of 1843 doomsday believers referred to as Millerites.

Although there's no record of Miller visiting Sugar Hill, a significant number of Free-Will Baptists in town were Miller believers. After numerous disagreements with fellow Baptists less convinced by Miller's case, the Sugar Hill Millerites built their own small church in town and started to get their affairs in order for the end of the world. On the appointed day, October 22, 1844, the Sugar Hill Millerites gathered in the cemetery on the hill at the western end of town, cast their eyes toward heaven, and waited. And waited. And waited. If, as certain accounts have it, the group was in fact wearing long flowing white robes, they must have looked like a church choir full of amateur astronomers. One eyewitness account claims that the group looked "very cold and very gloomy" as the sun began to set. And the next day, rumor has it, the Millerites of Sugar Hill were seen up to their armpits in dirty laundry that hadn't been washed in weeks. After all, who worries about ring around the collar when the end is nigh?

The Sugar Hill Cemetery is on a hill overlooking Main Street at the west end of town.

Mercury Project astronaut named Alan B. Shepard. The Redstone missile system was retired in 1964, and by the time Asselin asked for a leftover missile (minus the thermonuclear device, of course) in 1970, the army was more than happy to let it go.

In 1971 the town of Warren voted to accept the Redstone medium-range ballistic missile on the condition that Asselin could figure out how to transport it to New Hampshire (and pay for said transportation) himself. Using a borrowed semitractor and 60-foot trailer, Asselin drove the missile 1,300 miles to Warren, receiving a fine in Ohio for not having a permit to transport a decommissioned nuclear missile across state lines. Getting the missile to stand upright in the launch position, right there beside the church on Warren's quaint town green, was a whole different challenge, but the Redstone was dedicated on Warren's Old Home Day, July 4, 1971, before a crowd of 5,000. Funny, ever since then none of the surrounding towns ever pick on little old Warren anymore.

The Redstone missile is standing right on the common in the center of Warren, just off Route 25. Next to the missile is the Warren Historical Society, open Sunday afternoons, where you can find a letter from Alan Shepard and pictures of the missile's installation.

Not-So-Famous Footprint in Stone

Whitefield

New Hampshire is littered with stone profiles, glacier-carved and water-worn boulders and outcroppings of rock that resemble human faces. And for some reason, the faces people imagine seeing in granite are always old. (I wonder, do people start to resemble rocks as they get older?) It seems like every tourist destination has a least one head giving it a stony stare down: To offer you just a sampling, there's Mount Washington's Old Man of the Cog Railway, Lake Sunapee's Old Man of

WHITE MOUNTAINS

the Lake, the Isles of Shoals' Old Man of the Shore, and Lake Winnepe-saukee's Old Man of Winnepesaukee.

There's no doubt about it—we're crawling with craggy faces. For some reason, though, it's rare for people to imagine they see body parts other than faces in New Hampshire's preponderance of granite. You'd think that with all our rocks and all our daydreaming, we might at least have, say, a Knobby Knee Rock or a Saggy Bottom Boulder, maybe even a Bulging Bicep Mountain. But, no, we only do faces in New Hampshire.

Until now, that is. In a patch of woods on the grounds of White Mountains Regional High School in Whitefield, Marsha Lombardi has uncovered a stone, as yet unnamed, that has what looks to be the impression of a left foot in it. Though upon very close inspection the foot in the stone might actually have one or two extra little toes, in all other respects the impression looks remarkably like it was left there in the granite by a size-11, real-life, bare left foot.

Lombardi heard about the existence of the stone from an elderly man who happened to grow up on a farm where the high school now stands. She's also received information about another foot in a stone on Kimball Hill in Whitefield, but as of yet she hasn't been able to track down that particular track. Of course, one foot in a boulder (should we call it the Old Foot of White Mountains High?) won't do much to balance out all those faces dominating the physical and psychic landscape of our rocky state, but at least it's a step in the right direction.

The foot in the rock is located just off a footpath on the north side of White Mountains Regional High, right near the Whitefield/Lancaster town line. From the village of Whitefield, take Route 3 north toward Lancaster about 4 miles until you see a sign for the school on your left. Head up the access road all the way to the parking area, park your vehicle, and then head for the north side of the school, where you should find a path leading to the school's ski slope. Walk about 200 yards down the path and look to your right to find the 2-foot-tall rock with the foot in it.

GREAT NORTH WOODS

So Just How Good a Lumberjack Are You?

Berlin

So you want to be a lumberjack, but you don't know if you've got what it takes to swing it in the Great North Woods? Well, you may want to test your chopping, sawing, axe-chucking, logrolling, and chain-sawing mettle in the annual Lumberjack Festival and Competition at Berlin's Northern Forest Heritage Park. The park is a three-acre authentic re-creation of a circa-1900 New Hampshire logging camp, with everything from mess hall to blacksmith shop to sleeping cabins, all built with materials near and dear to a true logger's heart: logs. The lumberjack competition takes place just beside the camp in the park's amphitheater, where there's plenty of room to stand clear of flying axes.

The festival gets under way with a logger's breakfast, which, as you might guess, consists of two rice cakes and some lightly scrambled egg whites with a nice low-fat goat's cheese crumbled on top, along with an iced café mocha and perhaps six ounces of organic pomegranate nectar to wash it all down. No, wait, that's the breakfast for the Yuppie Festival and Competition held down in Nashua. The lumberjack breakfast consists of loads of good old-fashioned high-carb flapjacks, sausage, and bean-hole beans, which, just in case you're not the lumberjacking type, are beans cooked in a hole in the ground. Now that's a breakfast to make a tree (or a cabin-mate) tremble in fear.

Caution: Rolling logs.

Then the real fun begins. Competitions include the axe throw; the Jack and Jill crosscut (with a male lumberjack at one end of the saw and a female lumberjack at the other); the open chain saw class, a competition in which "anything goes" (it seems to me chain saws and the words *anything goes* should never be put together); and, of course, the logrolling competition. First, a professional logroller shows onlookers how it's done, and then anyone who's feeling brave and well-balanced can, um, give it a whirl. Of course, the pro makes it look easy, but don't expect to log more than a handful of seconds if you've never done any rolling—and the water in New Hampshire in October can be a little nippy. In fact, forgetting to bring a dry change of clothes to the competition has dissuaded many a would-be lumberjack from buying some thick woolen trousers and a couple of plaid shirts, packing up a chain saw, and lighting out for the Great North Woods.

The Northern Forest Heritage Park is located at 961 Main Street, on the west bank of the Androscoggin River in downtown Berlin. The park is open Memorial Day through October, Tuesday through Saturday, from 11:00 A.M. to 6:00 P.M. You can roll a log at the Lumberjack Festival and Competition in early October of each year. For more information call (603) 752–7202.

MY, WHAT BiG FEET YOU HAVE!

"If I don't answer," the message on Ms. Razz Berry's answering machine said this past fall, "I'm probably out moosin'." Even with all the traipsing through the woods that moosin' entails, Berry, a former reporter for the *Berlin Daily Sun,* hasn't yet spotted the hairy man-creature that sounds suspiciously like the Northwest's infamous Bigfoot right here in our very own Great North Woods. But she knows of at least two people who have, and the experience has left them shaken. One of the gentlemen, a lifelong hunter who almost ran right into a Bigfoot-like creature while he was out tracking deer along an abandoned logging road, hasn't returned to the deep woods since.

Does she believe they saw Bigfoot? I ask. "I believe they saw something. Now whether they saw what some people call Bigfoot or something else, I can't really say." Both sightings occurred, Berry claims, within 15 miles of each other in rugged country to the northwest of Berlin, and both witnesses were what she described as "sensible men who knew their way around the woods and were deeply affected by the sightings."

I don't know about you folks, but that's enough information for me to stay out of the woods in the Berlin/Milan area—after all, there are plenty of other places in New Hampshire to hike and hunt where 8-foot-tall superhairy hominids have never, ever been spotted.

A large portion of the western parts of Berlin and Milan fall in the northern, Coos County section of the White Mountain National Forest. Happy hiking!

Wounded Crucifix Draws Crowds

Berlin

Here's a question they never ask you in the seminary: If the wooden cross in your sanctuary starts oozing a bloodlike liquid, should the fluid be treated as a potential biohazard? If, for example, the cross needs to be removed from the wall to be cleaned, should the priest or deacon don rubber gloves to prevent the possible transmission of blood-borne pathogens? If the crucifix needs to be discarded, should it be placed in one of those red medical waste bags with the scary six-pronged warning symbol bearing a curious resemblance to a martial arts throwing star?

While such questions might seem far-fetched, they may have been on the mind of Father Richard Roberge, the priest of St. Joseph's Catholic Church in Berlin, when, in the spring of 2000, a parishioner discovered that a crucifix on a church wall was oozing a bloodlike substance. Within a few days, word of the potential miracle (and biohazard) had spread and crowds began to gather to bear witness. The Sunday following the discovery, church attendance rose markedly, with some worshippers coming from as far away as Pittsburg and Littleton. You could forgive a Catholic priest for thinking Christmas had come in June.

Of course, no one was willing to claim a miracle until the crucifix was properly investigated, and the priests had their doubts. According to Father Roberge, the crucifix had hung in the same spot for over forty years with absolutely no prior indication of fluid loss, bodily or otherwise. The priests, however, did take a sample of a red material from the wall behind the crucifix (with or without latex gloves, I'm not sure) and delivered it to the Androscoggin Valley Hospital for testing. The crucifix came up HIV, Hep A, and Hep B negative, which was, no doubt, a great relief to all concerned. And, what's more, the substance was definitively proven to be something other than blood. (What it actually was, the hospital didn't, or couldn't, say.)

Whether or not a miracle occurred remains an unanswered question. And, as with most miracles, whether we believe depends less upon our eyes and instruments and more upon our hearts. The question of whether to wear protective equipment when investigating potential blood-based miracles, though, is easier to answer. When in doubt, the Vatican might say, taketh the gloves out. An ounce of prevention is worth a pound of miracles.

St. Joseph's Roman Catholic Church is located at the top of the hill right on Route 16 as you enter Berlin from the north. The address is 633 Third Avenue.

Man-Made Island Mystery

Berlin

If you've driven Route 16 along the Androscoggin River around Berlin, you may have noticed that the river contains a surprising preponderance of small islands. If you're the perceptive type, you've also noticed that the islands share a number of similarities, including: (1) the islands are all more or less the same size, a little taller than a man and as wide as a compact car; (2) they're all located smack-dab in the middle of the river, more or less equidistant from the east and west banks; and (3) even though trees and shrubs have managed to colonize some of the islands, each one appears to be composed almost solely of a large pile of granite rocks, each about the size of a human head.

So, as an ecologist investigating the river might ask: What gives? Over its many millennia of flowing through this fertile forest valley, did the river somehow cough up evenly sized piles of granite rocks at regular, middle-of-the-river intervals the way a cat might send up hairballs every ten days or so? Could the islands be evidence of a Paleo-Indian culture that existed here thousands of years before the arrival of European settlers? Or, if we take our cue from towns along the seacoast, did the Vikings explore the river and give water burials to scads of explorers?

No, no, and, uh, no. The islands are actually things known as boom piers, built over a hundred years ago by two large Berlin paper companies, International Paper and Brown Company, so that they could chain log booms from pier to pier, thereby dividing the river into two distinct channels. In the early part of the twentieth century, these channels enabled the paper companies to separate their respective logs on the river before they arrived at the mills, thus avoiding a great deal of confusion. ("Are you sure that's your spruce log over there, buddy? That looks an awful lot like one of my spruce logs!") A few miles upriver from Berlin, where boom piers are first visible, there was a sorting area where skilled river men in spiked boots used long pick poles to separate the logs, each with its own trademarked company hammer mark, into the appropriate channel. If the river men did their job well, each and every log ended up in the mill of its rightful owner. You've heard the expression "Good fences make good neighbors." Well, in this case, good boom piers made good neighbors.

The boom piers are clearly visible from Route 16 as it follows the Androscoggin River south into Berlin. The town lights beautiful evening fires on the boom piers for their late fall Riverfire Festival. For information call the Berlin Recreation Department at (603) 752–2010. If you're wondering how they built the piers way out there in the middle of the river, just ask a local. (Hint: Berliners certainly aren't afraid of working outside in the dead of winter.)

North Country's Oldest (and Scariest) Ski Jump

Berlin

Berlin's Nansen Nordic Ski Club, named in honor of Arctic explorer Fridtjof Nansen (who was brave enough, or foolish enough, to cross Greenland on skis), was founded by a handful of the city's Scandinavian immigrants in 1872. The group cut some cross-country trails through the woods, built a ski jump on a small hill in the area known as Norwegian Village (around present-day 11th and 12th Streets), and generally went about attending to the essential business of immigrants everywhere: doing whatever they can do to make themselves feel more at home. Apparently, for Berlin's Finns, Swedes, Norwegians, and Danes this involved strapping wooden boards to their feet, tramping through the snow for hours on end in subzero temperatures, and sailing high into the air to see how far they could fly. (At first, you had to be Scandinavian to join the club, and that was, no doubt, just fine with the locals.)

And you thought that half-pipe for snowboarders was scary.

In 1936 it seems the Scandinavians wanted to climb higher and fly farther, so the Nansen Ski Club and the city of Berlin teamed up to build a gigantic steel-frame jump on a hill just north of town. An 80-meter Olympic-style ski jump, it had a 17 ½-foot steel tower, a 225-foot vertical drop, and a descent angle of 37.5 degrees, give or take a degree. (When something's that steep, what's another degree or two?) And just in case those numbers don't mean anything to you, imagine a seventeen-story-tall artificial cliff with a little lip at the bottom for launching skiers skyward.

The jump is still visible today, towering ominously at the top of the hill just across from the Nansen Wayside Area a couple of miles north of Berlin on Route 16. It's impossible to describe in words how frightening the jump looks, even now (or maybe especially now) in its state of disuse and relative disrepair. Even if you remain far below the jump on solid summer ground, with no possibility of ever standing at the top, waiting for the judges to wave you down to the bottom and then clear off the edge with nothing beneath you but your skis and the rushing wind, flying over the sloping hill for a distance of, say, a little less than a football field, still, the sight of the jump alone will be enough to make you groan. For almost fifty years it was reportedly the largest ski jump in the eastern United States and one of the top jumps in the country, the site of many major ski-jumping championships and Olympic-qualifying events.

Praise the Norse gods, the jump is no longer in operation, but the Nansen Nordic Ski Club still maintains a system of cross-country trails in Berlin and Milan and remains the oldest continuously organized ski club in the United States. For information about the club and its trails, call (603) 449–2290.

Bouncing Signals to Bombay

Clarksville

While it's true that Charles Morgan's front yard is strung with enough clothesline-resembling ham radio antennas to hang a whole platoon's laundry out to dry, he assured me that a ham radio operator can communicate around the globe perfectly well going to far shorter lengths with his antenna. One night he even managed to connect with a ham hobbiest in Bombay, India, who, upon discovering he was talking to someone from America, gleefully reported the nature of his rather unorthodox antenna. "I'm in my living room," he told Charles, "transmitting on my curtain rods!"

All those antennas on poles crisscrossing Mr. Morgan's lawn on the east side of Route 145 just south of the Clarksville town offices enable him to talk to ham radio operators around the world, from Germany to Russia to New Zealand. "It's wonderful," he told me. "International borders totally disappear, and you make friends." Like his German friend

Come in, Bombay; this is Clarksville!

DJ8RR, whose name Charles couldn't quite remember because operators generally identify each other by code rather than by name. When I asked him about the quality of the reception he told me, "I can talk to someone in Australia clearer than I'm talking to you right now." I was impressed, but I also decided to speak a little more directly into the phone.

Exactly how Charles communicates with people in far-flung parts of the world was a little harder for me to understand. One thing I did understand, though, is that operating a ham radio puts you in intimate and pretty darn fascinating contact with the workings of the earth's atmosphere in a way that cell phones and e-mail never do. Did you know, for example, that 175 miles above the earth's surface there's a band of charged particles called the ionosphere? If I understood Charles correctly, ham radio operators use the ionosphere as a kind of invisible backboard upon which they bounce their signals to the far corners of the world. And some operators even talk with each other via the moon: That's right, they talk to each other by bouncing their signals off the barren surface of the moon, about 239,000 miles away. If the whole thing weren't so technical, it would almost be romantic, don't you think?

To see Charles Morgan's yard full of ham radio antennas, head south on Route 145 from Pittsburg. Just after you pass the Clarksville town offices, his place will be on your left.

Being in the Wrong Place (and Right Place?) at the Wrong Time
Colebrook

Anyone who's got a three-year-old knows that accidents happen when someone ends up in the wrong place at the wrong time and then, oops, that little someone needs a fresh pair of bloomers. The small monument dedicated to George E. Hodge right beside the road in the Colebrook

Village Cemetery indicates that the poor man died because he was in the wrong place at the wrong time. But it also seems to indicate that he was in the right place at the wrong time.

Confused? Well, poor George's monument reads as follows: "In memory of George E. Hodge, who was killed in this spot by a load of gravel passing over his body, June 13, 1884." Clearly, Hodge wasn't supposed to be standing where a load of gravel could pass over his body, but once the accident happened, it seems George didn't have far to travel to his final resting place. Just what Hodge was doing with all that gravel in the cemetery is another question entirely . . .

Who knew a cemetery could be such a dangerous place?

Of course, things aren't always as they seem. The 2½-foot-tall white marble pillar used to sit on a bank beside Route 26 east of Colebrook, but when the road was widened decades ago, workers moved the memorial to the Village Cemetery for safekeeping. And there it sits to this day, proclaiming a falsehood that makes it seem as if George picked a rather fitting place to have a fatal gravel accident.

The Colebrook Village Cemetery is located on the east side of Route 3 about a mile north of town. To find George Hodge's memorial, take a right at the northernmost entrance, then follow the road past the small outbuilding; the pillar will be on your right.

Reach Out, Reach Out and Touch a Moose
Colebrook

So your favorite moose hasn't called you in a long, long time and you're feeling just a tad bit forgotten? Well, don't just sit there and wallow in a spruce swamp of self-pity. Take the bull moose by the horns and give your old friend a call. Go ahead: Reach out to that big forgetful lug. When you finally see that long face and that big goofy grin again, you'll be glad you did.

But are you the type who always waits for your moose to call you, and now you're not sure how to do it? If so, you should attend Colebrook's annual Moose Festival, a lively end-of-August affair featuring a parade, a guided moose tour to Dixville Notch, a moose burger BBQ cookout, and a one-day, amateurs-only, good old-fashioned moose-calling contest. First, a local expert shows the audience how to call a moose, and then, without much further ado, the mic is open to amateur moose callers of every stripe.

Most moose don't have a landline, let alone a cell, so that leaves you with just a couple of low-tech calling options: (1) you can use the coffee can and string method, or (2) you can employ your voice and your cupped hands to give a shout out to your favorite moose. If you'd like to try the first method, punch a small round hole in the bottom of a three-pound coffee can and then, while holding the can under your armpit, its mouth facing forward, pull a wet rawhide shoelace tied at one end through the hole and all the way out the mouth of the can until the knot stops you. The vibration of the string against the can makes a sound that supposedly will call in a moose, albeit one who's likely got a serious caffeine habit.

Contestants in the festival's moose-calling contest do it au naturel, which makes the competition particularly tough—and, of course, particularly amusing. Where else can you listen to people of all ages (kids give it a whirl, too) stand behind a microphone and attempt to mimic the sound an 800-pound, 7-foot-tall wild animal makes when it's in heat? Moose callers generally attempt to mimic the moans of a moose cow, a sound fairly similar to the mooing of the more common, and easier to contact, barnyard cow, only a little higher pitched and more urgent-sounding. In a recent competition, one contestant sounded like a moose worrying over some profound existential question, another contestant sounded like a moose with a serious chip on her shoulder, and yet another contestant sounded less like a moose than a man in desperate need of emergency medical assistance.

The North Country Moose Festival is held each year at the end of August in the towns of Pittsburg, New Hampshire, and Canaan, Vermont, in addition to Colebrook. For more information contact the North Country Chamber of Commerce at (603) 237–8939.

If You Don't Wear a Helmet, Be Sure to Get Your Hog Blessed
Columbia

If you drive a motorcycle in New Hampshire, you can leave your helmet behind (if you have one at all): There's no helmet law here in the Granite State, so you can cruise the pavement on two wheels at 60 or 70 miles an hour with your cranium uncradled, its three-pound cargo of brain unencumbered by plastic and padding. Ah, the thrill of the open road, the sun on your face, the wind in your hair! Ah, freedom!

Not to rain on your ride here, but our lawyers advised me to mention that your brain contains billions and billions of irreplaceable neurons that control everything from speech to continence, that your brain could very well be the most complex thing in the universe, and that inside your little old skull (no more than a quarter-inch thick in places), your brain has the consistency of the oatmeal you ate for breakfast.

Make you a little queasy? Then you may want to follow the lead of hundreds of other North Country bikers and get your hog a heavenly blessing at Columbia's annual Blessing of the Bikes. Father Levesque performs the ceremony each year for hundreds of bikers at Our Lady of Grace Shrine, a fifteen-acre Catholic sanctuary filled with religious statuary dedicated to Our Lady of Grace, the patron saint of motorcyclists. (In addition to the usual Jesus and Mother Mary sculptures, one of the granite statues features a motorcycle with two riders, sans helmets, kneeling in prayer beside it.)

Attendees drive their motorcycles right onto the lawn and park them in tight rows in front of the shrine's centerpiece: a large granite altar and, behind that, a marble statue of Our Lady of Grace. Space is limited, so be sure to get there early. (If you're a Catholic, think church on Christmas Eve and you'll have a good idea of how crowded it can get.) Father Levesque and the other priests perform the Benediction of the Sacraments at the foot of the altar and then walk among the bikes, asking Our Lady to keep the motorcycles and their riders out of harm's way, and that makes every rider, helmet or no helmet, feel a little

God bless our bikes, every one of them!

more secure. In New Hampshire you can ride without a helmet, you can ride without insurance, but you don't have to ride without a blessing from the Big Guy.

Our Lady of Grace Shrine is located on Route 3, just south of the Colebrook line in Columbia. For information about the Blessing of the Bikes—which coincides with the Great North Woods Ride-In, the region's annual motorcycle rally held each June on the first weekend after Father's Day—call Father Levesque at (603) 237–5511.

The Wild West in Western New Hampshire
Dalton

It's Saturday night and the Dalton Gang heads out for dinner at the Dalton Folk House Restaurant dressed in Wild West cowboy clothes and packing enough firepower to appear downright intimidating. "Yes, these are real guns, and real ammunition," Don Mooney tells a flatlander brave or foolish enough to ask about the two Colt revolvers, one holstered on each hip, that he carries with him up to the buffet line. "A lot of times when we go out, folks from places like Massachusetts will say, 'Can you really do that?' And the fact is we can do it, because we've got what they call an 'open carry' law in New Hampshire," he says. And if Don Mooney says it's legal, and he's got loaded guns on his hips to back him up, well, that's good enough for me.

Besides making frequent unnerving appearances at local eateries, the Dalton Gang, a cowboy action shooting club based in Dalton, holds numerous specialized shooting events and competitions at its Miller Road range. These aren't just your ordinary gun club competitions, though. To begin with, all shooters must wear Old West–style clothes and accessories, like cowboy hats, cowboy boots, bandanas, long leather dusters, buckskin jackets, even authentic reproduction sheriff's badges. Spectators are also strongly encouraged, though not required, to wear cowboy clothes, but by the looks of all the spectators in cowboy hats, strong encouragement from a shooting club is a mighty powerful form of persuasion. In the interests of Old West authenticity, shooters are also required to use vintage (or reproduction) single-action guns, just like those Billy the Kid and Jesse James might have employed to menace a bank teller or two. And members have Western-style aliases to add the finishing touch of outlaw authenticity, like club officers the Melody Kid, Ram Rod, Good Guy, and Slippery Slim.

The original Dalton Gang, a band mainly composed of four outlaw brothers, finished their career by getting ambushed near the town of Coffeyville, Kansas, in October of 1892 as they attempted to rob not one but two of the town's banks at the same time. Coffeyville just happened to be the boys' hometown, and—surprise, surprise—someone recognized them behind their fake beards. This new Dalton Gang is way smarter, and a whole lot nicer: no fake beards, no bank or train robberies, and no murders, indiscriminate or otherwise. But that doesn't stop them from scaring a flatlander now and then.

The Dalton Gang Shooting Club's range is located at 232 Miller Road in Dalton. For information about membership or shooting events, call (603) 444–6876.

Overeager Night Owls Post Nation's First Election Results
Dixville Notch

Drive west on Route 26 from Errol to Colebrook, and you'll soon find yourself cruising through Dixville Notch, a stunningly beautiful and disconcertingly narrow mountain pass flanked by Dixville Peak and Sanguinary Mountain, dizzying spires of rock that seem, to be frank, downright primordial. After one final turn in the notch, the valley opens up and there, beneath a tall ledge of gray granite, a grand old building materializes like a hallucination, a shimmering wedding cake of a hotel reflected in perfect detail in the dark, still waters of the pond at its doorstep.

This is the Balsams, a large hotel and 15,000-acre wilderness resort, one of the few remaining grand hotels in the state. And since 1960 it's here that the nation's first presidential election votes have been cast, counted, and posted for the whole world to see. Every presidential primary and presidential election eve for the last four decades, all the eligible voters in Dixville Notch, an unincorporated village in the town of Dixville, gather just before midnight in the Balsams' second-floor Ballot Room. Each voter receives a ballot and heads for his or her own individual voting booth—that's right, each voter gets a booth to call home—and then, at precisely the stroke of midnight, the Dixville Notchers cast their votes. Polls are closed promptly at 12:01 A.M. (no hemming and

The hotel in the notch where folks get first votes.

hawing over chads here), and in another mere fifteen minutes the votes are tallied and the results are broadcast to the world. In the November 2, 2004, election, twenty-six people cast their votes at the Balsams in the first minute of the day, with George W. winning by a long shot.

Since New Hampshire holds the first presidential primaries in the nation, the Dixville Notch primary vote often makes headlines in election-day newspapers around the country. (The presidential election vote gets decidedly less attention.) Notch voters are of a Republican persuasion, and they can be counted on to choose their Republican candidates presciently: During every primary election since 1968, the Republican presidential candidate who received the most Dixville Notch votes went on to win his party's presidential nomination. (They haven't been so successful picking Democratic nominees. Just to give you an example, the single ballot cast in the 1968 Democratic primary was a write-in vote for Dick Nixon.)

Millsfield, the town just south of Dixville, and Hart's Location down in Carroll County have more recently joined the midnight presidential election madness and tried to steal some of the spotlight from Dixville Notch, but the Notch has bragging rights as the longest-running first election in the nation. And the setting for that election, in a grand hotel surrounded by thousands of acres of spruce and fir woodlands and mountains, well now, that's hard to beat.

The Balsams Grand Resort Hotel is located at 1000 Cold Spring Road in Dixville Notch, just off Route 26, midway between Errol and Colebrook. For information call (603) 255–3400.

Albino Moose Finds Career in Sales Makes Him Stiff

Errol

If you've spent any time in sales, you know it can be tough—the solo road trips to aggressively ordinary locales like Peoria and Sioux Falls, the long boozy client dinners at smoky steak houses just off the interstate, the motivational seminars where you're taught how to become somewhat better than your ordinary self so that you can, at long last, really and truly succeed.

Well, if you think you've got it tough, pay a visit to the Great White Moose at his post in the vestibule of L. L. Cote's Sporting Goods in Errol. A rare albino moose with a great big set of antlers and a tenderly sullen look on his face, think of him as a Great White Wal-Mart Greeter on four legs, a floor salesman with a one-of-a-kind wardrobe, a clerk with a refreshingly hoofs-off approach. Kevin, a manager at Cote's, won't talk about the white moose's actual sales numbers, but he assures me he's been good for business. Real good. "Everybody loves the moose," he tells me. One staff

The Great White Moose puts up good numbers.

member said he'd even seen a kid crawl right up onto his platform and try to grab a hold of a leg. And when you've closed a sale with a kid, the parents are sure to follow.

The Great White Moose has paid the heaviest price for his success, though. Maybe it's because he's all business, all the time, selling the outdoors twenty-four hours a day (even when Cote's doors are closed), that he's become so, well, stuffy. His eyes have an overworked, over-tired glassy sheen, and in spite of his albino charms and winning antlers, he comes across as a little . . . stiff.

Still, there's no arguing with figures, however stiff the figure who puts them up might be. The Great White Moose has been good for business at Cote's, and he's there to stay. In fact, he seems to be assembling his own crack team of salesmen—all albinos, of course. So far there's an albino raccoon and a couple of other albino critters in small glass cases at his feet. Needless to say, the Great White Moose is still in charge.

If you'd like to pay the Great White Moose a visit, he's just inside the front door, along with his albino cronies, at L. L. Cote's Sporting Goods in downtown Errol. Cote's phone number is (603) 482–7777.

Woodn't It Be Nice to Be Together?
Lancaster

John and Abigail Bergin's family tree is a bit more literal than most. If you'd like to have a look at it, you won't have to call up the Bergin family historian or go digging through old records in the dusty basement of Lancaster's historical society. In fact, all you need do is visit Wilder Cemetery in downtown Lancaster. The family tree is there, in the back corner of the cemetery, a great big eastern white pine that's grown up between the couple's early nineteenth-century gravestones.

GREAT NORTH WOODS

Till death and big pines do us part.

The Bergins were some of the original settlers to the area: Abigail died in 1826 and John, an officer in the Revolutionary War, died in 1828. That's given the tree plenty of time to take root, take to the sky, and take over the couple's entire cemetery plot. The tree's gotten so big, in fact, that it's engulfed both stones—John's on the left and Abigail's on the right—and it doesn't show any signs of slowing down soon. The stones have been cracked and broken by the pine's swelling trunk, but they're still in one piece (thanks to repairs), two slate gray saddlebags at the tree's base.

While the Bergins used to sleep in wedded bliss (we can be optimistic about these things, can't we?), now they rest for all eternity in wooded bliss. To see their arboreally conjoined gravestones, just head to Wilder Cemetery—the cemetery overlooking Main Street. in downtown Lancaster—and look for the tree smuggling headstones in its trunk.

The Couple That Gets Alien-Abducted Together Stays Together
Lancaster

Recounted in the 1966 book *The Interrupted Journey* by John Fuller and later turned into the 1975 made-for-TV movie *The UFO Incident* (starring Estelle Parsons and James Earl Jones), Betty and Barney Hill's alleged abduction by aliens while driving home to Portsmouth through the northern White Mountains on the night of September 19, 1961, is considered by many UFO-ologists to be the grandsire of all alien-abduction and close-encounter tales. It's got classic dramatic elements any *X-Files* fan would appreciate: Late evening, early fall, deserted country road in the mountains. A bright light appears on the horizon, moving closer and closer to the couple driving toward home. What is it? A planet? A satellite? A UFO? Barney stops the vehicle, exits it, and takes a closer look at the light with binoculars, only to rush back to the car screaming in utter terror. Soon thereafter, the couple's minds fall under the influence of the aliens, and they're brought on board a disc-shaped craft and examined by way of hair and skin samples and long scary needles pushed into sensitive places, like, for instance, the belly button. After the examination they're released, unharmed and almost totally unaware of the fact that anything unusual has transpired, except for maybe a little soreness in the umbilicus and a lingering sense that things aren't quite right in the world.

The Hills reported their UFO sighting to Pease Air Force Base officials the day after the incident, but it wasn't until months later, after they sought help for anxiety and stress-related problems from Dr. Benjamin Simon, a Boston psychiatrist and hypnotherapy expert, that they recalled they'd also been abducted and examined that evening by 4- to 5-foot-tall aliens whom Betty described as "rugged, not skinny guys." Under hypnotherapy, they recalled specific details of their abduction and examination, including the fact that the aliens had a minor freak-out when they found they were able to remove Barney's teeth (he had dentures). Betty, a social worker, seemed far less afraid of the aliens than her postal worker husband and even went so far as to ask them where they were from. By way of answering, the aliens showed her a star chart, which Betty drew after one particularly fruitful hypnotherapy session with Dr. Simon. (According to some reports, investigators years later produced a match between Betty's map and a cluster of newly discovered stars near Zeta Reticuli.)

Ever since the publication of John Fuller's book, believers and skeptics have been arguing back and forth about the validity of Betty and Barney Hill's abduction tales. But Betty, who gave talks on UFOs and on her abduction for decades, was always a believer. Up until just a few months before her death on October 17, 2004, at the age of eighty-four, she reported that aliens were paying frequent visits to the seacoast area around her home and making good use of a landing spot she had found in Kingston. Believers take solace: Betty assured people that the aliens wished us no harm. All they really wanted, perhaps, was to cruise the seacoast area unmolested. That and easy access to a human belly button now and again.

Betty and Barney Hill first spotted their alien craft on Route 3 just south of Lancaster.

Gravity (Plus Water)–Powered Sawmill
Lancaster

Poor gravity. It takes the fall for shattered dishware, broken hips, and shiny coins down the sewer grate, but it doesn't get any credit where credit is due. To give an example, recent studies on the physics of walking suggest that self-locomotion is best understood as a series of elegantly executed and gently arrested forward falls, one gravity-assisted footstep after another. But when's the last time you heard a marathon winner thank gravity for all its help? His sponsors, yes, family, yes, God, maybe. But gravity? Never.

So it should come as no surprise that water gets all the credit for turning millstones, turbines, or, in this case, the local saw at the mill. (After all, we call it hydro-, not gravi-, electric power.) Water's just that much more sexy, more in your face, more obviously there. At Garland Mill on Garland Brook in Lancaster, water *and* gravity have been doing their work for almost 150 years, supplying the power to turn the huge round saw blade and transform loads of logs into thousands of board feet of lumber.

There used to be hundreds of gravity-powered mills around the state, providing the power to do everything from grinding grain to weaving cloth, before steam and fossil fuel took over. The Garland Mill, listed on the National Register of Historic Places, was built around 1860 and then reconstructed after a fire in 1877.

One of the last gravity-powered sawmills in the state.

At the time it was one of 5 water-powered sawmills in Lancaster and one of about 200 in Coos and Grafton Counties alone. When a logging railroad reached the headwaters of Garland Brook and quickly depleted the area's timber supply, this and many other such mills were abandoned.

Today the Garland Mill is back in operation, turning out timber frames for home and barn construction. This is a real working mill, not a tourist attraction—the equipment is oiled up, you can hear the turbine whirring along as the water rushes by, there are wood shavings on the floor and fresh-cut timbers stacked under a shed by the creek—but folks are welcome to stop by and have a look around. Three cheers for what gravity, and a little water, can do.

The Garland Mill is located at 267 Garland Road in Lancaster.

Where, Oh Where Will the BS Fall?

Milan

By the late 1800s many of New Hampshire's farms were in decline or abandoned entirely, and many of its best and brightest citizens had left the state, gone off to the flatlands in search of better (but certainly not greener) pastures and prospects. All of this spelled financial ruin for New Hampshire, of course: The state was essentially bankrupt, and so were many of its towns. So what did Frank Rollins, the governor of New Hampshire at the time, decide to do in response? He threw a party.

In a burst of nostalgic genius, he inaugurated the state's Old Home Day tradition in 1899, inviting townspeople and, most importantly, all former residents of New Hampshire wherever they might be, to gather in their hometowns and celebrate their heritage, their blessed old New Hampshire homes. "Come back, come back!" Rollins wrote in 1897. "Do you not hear the call? What has become of the old home where you were born? Do you not remember it—the old farm back among the hills, with its rambling buildings, its well sweep casting its long shadows, the row of stiff poplar trees, the lilacs and the willows?" Rollins might have added, "Come back, come back! And remember, oh do remember, to bring your leather wallets full to bursting with their green-hued bills!" But maybe he didn't want to be heavy-handed about the whole thing . . .

Milan, like a number of towns in New Hampshire, continues to celebrate Old Home Day with small-town celebration standards, including a parade, a flea market, a donut-eating contest, hay games (track-and-field-style events using hay bales), and, oh yeah, a game of cow pie bingo. That's right: At Milan's Old Home Day celebration you can come back to your old home, the old farm back among the hills, and place a bet on where Bessy will, uh, make her mark. The cow's holding pen is divided into numbered grids, bettors choose a number, and then the rest is just a waiting game. "Sometimes it takes ten minutes, sometimes it takes three or four hours, and sometimes we have to bring in another cow," says selectperson Gisele Ouellette. "We have no control over that." So, all you wayward sons and daughters of this great Granite State, come back, come back to the old Milan home, to the mountains and pine forests and the deep clear lakes. And if all that's not reason enough, then come back, come back to speculate on where the old home cow will moo-ve her bowels.

The Milan Old Home Day celebration is held in a field off Bridge Street in the village of Milan the second weekend of August. Bridge Street is located on the east side of Route 16 just south of the intersection of Routes 16 and 101B. For more information call Gisele Ouellette at (603) 449–9986.

GREAT NORTH WOODS

A Museum to Make Kermit Proud
North Stratford

Here's a museum for the herpetoculturist in you. (Come on, you can admit it—I know you've got a herpetoculturist somewhere inside of you.) While herpetoculture might sound like a chronic disease, it's merely the name for the hobby of collecting amphibians or reptiles, which together make up the animal group called herps. A boa constrictor is a herp (though I wouldn't say that to his face if I were you), and a bullfrog is a herp, too. But just because they're members of the same group doesn't necessarily mean they'd be fast friends.

That's probably why as herpetoculturists themselves, Carol Hawley and Francis McMilleon only collect frogs—group unity must cut down on intra-herp friction. But what they lack in breadth in their collection, they more than make up for in depth. You won't find the living, breathing, tongue-unrolling-like-a-party-horn kind of frog at the Foolish Frog Gift Shop and Museum, but you will find just about every other variety of frog you can imagine, and many more you couldn't imagine, even in your most twisted herpetoculturist dreams. They've spent decades traveling the world collecting frogs of every color, shape, size, occupation, hobby, and religious affiliation.

There are, according to experts, over 300 different species of common frogs and over 400 species of common toads (which, though we call them toads, are actually frogs), but those experts have never been to see the extraordinarily varied population of frogs in Stratford.

Up on the slope-ceiling second floor of the couple's home, you'll find a shop filled with whimsical frogs for sale, many of which Francis handcrafted himself, including a wonderfully sturdy-looking wooden hobby frog just waiting for a kid to come and ride him. "I had that hobby frog tested by a 300-pound biker," Francis told me with a wink, "so I know it's good and safe." Just beyond the shop is a bedroom-cum-frog-museum filled with so many bug-eyed green critters—on the floor, all over the big queen bed, on the walls—I couldn't even begin to count them all. "We've got 10,000 frogs," Francis told me, "but we don't have room enough to display them all." Surrounded by throngs of their own kind, the frogs don't seem to mind one bit.

The Foolish Frog Gift Shop and Museum is open by chance or appointment, so be sure to call ahead at (603) 636–9843. It's located on the east side of Route 3 about 7 miles south of North Stratford.

Dude, Let's Go Roll Some Snow
Pittsburg

Prior to the era of the snowplow, managing all the snow that accumulates on North Country roadways was a whole different affair. You couldn't really push it—not enough horsepower—and you certainly couldn't shovel it—not enough shovelers—but you could, if you had the right equipment, squash it down a bit. And that's just what the old squashers, I mean old-timers, did.

Enter the curious-looking contraption in Pittsburg's town park right on Route 3. Instead of plunking down a World War II–era tank in their park, Pittsburg has quite aptly chosen to display an old-fashioned snow roller. Don't know what a snow roller is? Think of it as a giant horse-drawn rolling pin for snow. The driver sat above the 5- or 6-foot-tall wooden roller on a seat attached to an axle-mounted frame, and a team of horses pulled the roller and its driver over hill and over dale, flattening the snow as they went. And once the snow was rolled over, residents could use their horse-drawn sleighs to run to the grocery store or do some shopping over at Best Buy.

Don't be too jealous of the old-timers, though—they didn't get out of shoveling entirely. Instead of shoveling snow off the road, they had

Rolling snowbanks down to size.

to shovel it
on—right onto
the roadways of covered
bridges so that sleighs could pass. And yet another reason why jealousy might be misplaced: After a whole winter of packing down foot upon foot of snow over dirt roads, the old timers must have had a ball when the spring thaw finally came. And we think we've got it bad during mud season.

Pittsburg's snow roller is located in the town park on the west side of Route 3. They've placed it under a roof and behind a short chain-link fence so that it doesn't roll away.

LIVE FREE UNTIL THE WHOLE DOUBLE TAX THING GETS IRONED OUT

The North Country of New Hampshire is shaped like a serrated blade with its tip broken off, and the town of Pittsburg is the knife's northernmost, broken-tipped end. Its eastern border is the state's almost arrow-straight boundary with Maine, and its western border is New Hampshire's border with Canada. Stretching as it does from state line to state (and international) line, the town's first big claim to fame is that it is big: At 300,000 acres, or 282.3 square miles, it's reported to be the largest township in the United States. Go Pittsburg!

Its second claim to fame is that Pittsburg was once its own country. That's right, for a little over three years, from 1832 to 1835, the Republic of Indian Stream (named after a small river that runs through town) was an independent constitutional republic consisting of about 300 souls. With so few people in the whole country, just think how easy it would have been to, say, make the Republic of Indian Stream's National Soccer Team, or arrange some face-to-face time with the president.

Just in case you're feeling a little judgmental of the Streamers' lack of patriotism, though, I can assure you they had good reason for declaring independence: double taxation. Twice is definitely not nice when it comes to taxes. As a result of ambiguity in the language of the Treaty of Paris of 1783, which established (or, more accurately, sought to establish) the boundary between the United States and Canada, both governments claimed the town of Pittsburg. And since both governments claimed Pittsburg, both governments felt inclined to tax its poor residents. The ambiguity in the treaty was that it called for the border to run down the "northwesternmost head of [the] Connecticut river," and then along the middle of said river (unnamed in the treaty) to the 45th parallel, where the international boundary would run due west. Look on a map and you'll see at least three interpretive possibilities: a border that runs from the Third Connecticut Lake and down the Connecticut River proper, a border that runs down the more northwestern Indian Stream, and a border that runs down the northwesternmost Halls Stream.

The Republic of Indian Stream voted to be annexed by the United States. in 1835, the U.S. militia came to town, and the boundary dispute was soon resolved in favor of the States. Go Pittsburg! Don't you just love a prodigal town?

No Surprise: An Eskimo Feels at Home in Wintry New Hampshire
Pittsburg

Go to the Indian Stream Cemetery in Pittsburg and search the Hall family plot, and you'll find among the stones the grave of one Minik Wallace, who in 1917, around the age of twenty-five, came to New Hampshire to work as a "shantyboy," or logger. He worked in Pittsburg's logging camps and spent off-seasons with the Hall family for only two brief years before he died from influenza in 1918. A sad tale, but not unusual, right? Not quite. The path that brought Wallace to the Great North Woods is almost unimaginably sad and unthinkably bizarre—so sad and bizarre, in fact, that doing the dangerous work of felling and hauling logs in the brutal cold of the North Woods may have been the best chapter in Minik Wallace's brief life.

In September of 1897 Arctic explorer Robert E. Peary sailed into New York Harbor with six Greenland Eskimos—among them Minik, six or seven years old at the time, and his widowed father, Qisuk—to be studied and placed on exhibit at the American Museum of Natural History. The day after their arrival, 20,000 people reportedly paid 25 cents apiece to board Peary's ship and look at the Eskimos. They were then taken to the museum, where they lived together in the basement, and where visitors continued to come see them until four died from TB, including Minik's father. After the only other surviving Eskimo returned to Greenland, Minik was alone, an Arctic Eskimo orphan in New York City.

William Wallace, the superintendent of buildings at the museum, adopted Minik, but misfortune continued to follow the young boy when, first, his adoptive father was forced to resign from his post after allegations of financial wrongdoing, and second, his adoptive mother died. And it only gets worse. When Minik was still in his teens, he discovered that the famous anthropologist Franz Boas had staged a mock funeral after his father's death, complete with a log wrapped in furs to resemble a corpse. But his father's body, instead of being buried, had been dissected and the bones bleached and then sent back to the Museum of Natural History to be added to its collections.

Minik tried to get the museum to return his father's remains for proper burial, but his efforts were in vain. He returned to his village in northwestern Greenland around the age of eighteen, relearned his native language, and lived there for seven years before coming back to the United States, claiming that he was an exile wherever he went, at home neither in the Arctic nor America. Shortly after arriving back in the States in 1916, Minik moved to Pittsburg, where the logging camps and the locals who befriended him made him feel as much at home as he would ever feel. His good fortune didn't last long, though—Minik contracted influenza in 1918 and became one of the tens of millions worldwide who would die during the epidemic. The Halls nursed him until his death, then buried the young man from the Arctic among their own. The Musuem of Natural History returned Minik's father's remains to Greenland in the early 1990s, but Arctic natives decided Minik should remain in New Hampshire, the place where he had found some peace at last.

The Indian Stream Cemetery is on the north side of Route 3 about 1.5 miles south of Pittsburg. Take a right on Jesse Young Road, and the cemetery will be on your right; the Hall plot is along the fence beside the road.

Who's Afraid of a New Hampshire Wolf?
Pittsburg

Don't panic, but there just may be elusive, natural-born killers roaming the Great North Woods. One of them was hunted down and killed in Maine in 1995, and just recently they caught one in Quebec, a mere 20 miles north of the New Hampshire border, but so far authorities have been unable to gather any definitive proof that they're here in our beloved New Hampshire home. Numerous credible witnesses have reported sightings, though, and experts say it's probably only a matter of time—decades, years, maybe only months—before they're living in our midst. The horror!

Okay, I'm being ridiculous. The woods are actually filled with killers, from frogs to owls to coyotes. The so-called killers I'm picking on are gray wolves, animals native to New Hampshire that were hunted and trapped out of existence beginning with first European settlement and continuing until the last Granite State wolf was killed over a hundred years ago. After successful reintroduction of the gray wolf in Yellowstone National Park, the New Hampshire legislature passed a law in 1999 prohibiting wolf rein-troduction here, which means that if the gray wolf is to come back to its old home, it's got to make it on its own four paws. And, in spite of fears about livestock loss, the idea of letting nature take its course seems to suit most people in New Hampshire just fine.

There's a healthy gray wolf population north of the St. Lawrence River in Quebec, and wildlife experts speculate that if hunting and trap-ping pressures on the group were to ease slightly, younger wolves (called dispersers) might roam southward into New Hampshire in search of new territory. In fact, there are numerous residents in the Great North Woods who think they've already encountered evidence of wolves, from sightings to scat to large tracks. One resident who wishes to remain anonymous even claims the wolf he spotted barked at him in French, thus proving the migration from Canada theory. But in spite of such compelling evidence, whether or not wolves prowl the woods of New Hampshire remains a mystery.

If you think you've found evidence of wolves in the North Country, you can call Peggy Struhsacker, the Northeast Wolf Recovery Coordinator for the National Wildlife Federation, at (800) 229–0650, extension 317.

Mystery Rock on Swift Diamond River
Second College Grant

If you like rocks, and you love unsolved mysteries, then I've got a rock mystery for you. Northeast of the town of Errol on the Second College Grant, there's a mysterious etching on a granite boulder that sits on the north side of the Swift Diamond River. Referred to, not quite accurately I might add, as the Hand on the Rock, it actually consists of what looks like a woman's right forearm and hand, the first finger of which points generally southwest. Under it is the date 1871 in Roman numerals and beneath that the letters WMDOW. Of course, the name Hand on the Rock does have a catchier ring to it than the Feminine-Looking Forearm and Hand above the Roman Numerals and Capital Letters Rock.

Even John Harrigan, the North Country journalist who seems to know practically everything about the woods in this neck of the woods, doesn't know what the real story is behind the Hand on the Rock. "Nothing I know of has been written about this. There's the usual speculation about Viking explorers and such," he told me. "I tend to think that either a river driver got killed there, or someone drowned while fishing, or that someone's family just created the carving because it was a deceased loved one's favorite spot."

The Second College Grant, a 27,000-acre township composed almost entirely of forest, was the second large parcel of land the state legislature gave to Dartmouth College. (Are New Hampshire lawmakers a little less generous now, or am I just being ungrateful?) Dartmouth has used the Second College Grant for hiking and recreation almost since it acquired the land in 1807, so Harrigan, not content to let a mystery rock lie, searched the college's records for a William Dow. He found only one, a young man who survived the Civil War and served as a minister in Portsmouth, but since he lived a long, full life down in Portsmouth, it seems unlikely that the Hand on the Rock is connected

A mysterious hand (and forearm and initials) on a big rock.

HAND ON THE ROCK

PLEASE
HELP
PREVENT
FOREST
FIRES

to him. Of all the
possible explana-
tions for the carving on
the rock, the death of a
river driver seems the most likely,
since the Swift Diamond was a log-drive route,
and the attempt to guide slick, half-ton logs down frigid snowmelt-
swollen waters often proved harmful to a logger's health.

To visit the Hand on the Rock, head north out of Errol on Route 16.
Continue past the Mount Dustan Store, then turn left onto Dead Diamond Road (the grant access road) just before you reach the Went-
worth Location Cemetery. After a half mile, you'll come to a locked
gate. If you're not affiliated with Dartmouth, you'll have to hike or
mountain bike in from here. Follow Dead Diamond Road for 2.5 miles

until you reach Swift Diamond Road. Take a left and proceed along Swift Diamond Road for about half a mile, where you'll see a sign beside the road for the Hand on the Rock. A short trail follows the Swift Diamond River upstream to the rock.

World War II Comes to the Great North Woods

Stark

It was the height of World War II when German prisoners of war landed in the little logging town of Stark, and, as you might expect, they didn't get the warmest of receptions. Their captors told them that the barbed wire fence around their prison camp wasn't so much to keep them inside as it was to keep ferocious bears and half-mad, gun-toting French-Canadian locals out. (Maybe they were right about the Canadians, but, come on, the bears are harmless.) Locals came just to stare. Even the children of Stark tried to taunt the POWs by singing patriotic songs out the windows of their school bus as they passed.

But by the end of the war, unlikely friendships and even romances blossomed between the Germans and the locals, and you can still find people all over the state who cherish the gifts prisoners made for their new Stark friends, from simple children's toys to bone-handled knives to beautiful watercolors. Years later, Allen Koop, Dartmouth professor and author of a book about the prison camp called *Stark Decency*, recalled a Stark old-timer telling him, "Those Germans were the best thing that ever happened to Stark."

How did German POWs end up befriending locals in the tiny town of Stark? The Brown Company in Berlin was in desperate need of workers to meet its wartime wood pulp production quota, so Uncle Sam sent about 250 German POWs to work in Stark as loggers. Under the guidance of Brown Company's civilian foremen, the Germans spent long days harvesting pulpwood in five-man crews using only axes, hand-saws, and horses. And over the many hard months they spent working the woods together, numerous Brown Company employees and German POWs became friends, not only because they shared a common goal of making their weekly quotas, but also because many of the Germans were themselves anti-Nazi, and so from the outset felt more like America's allies than her enemies. (Many of the prisoners at Stark Camp were captured in North Africa, members of a fighting unit composed of anti-Nazi political prisoners and other criminals forced into military service.)

Of course, no matter how good a guy your foreman is, prison camp is still prison camp, and numerous POWs attempted escapes. But who lets an attempted escape get in the way of a beautiful friendship cemented in the woods? To visit the site of Stark's POW camp, head 2 miles east out of town on Route 110 and watch for a historical marker on the right. Not much remains of the camp save for the concrete footings of the watchtowers and some chimney stones.

The "Last" of the Coo-ash-aukes
Stewartstown

In Stewartstown, as in many other New Hampshire towns in the nineteenth century, the poor were "bid off" to locals, who for an agreed-upon sum would care for a needy or dependent individual in their own homes for one year. That's how Chief Metallak, the so-called last of the Coo-ash-aukes, blind and infirm, came to live out the last seven years of his long, legend-filled life (he's said to have lived to the ripe old age of 120) in the homes of various Stewartstown citizens. The once-great chief died in February 1847 and was buried in an unmarked pauper's grave.

The Coo-ash-aukes were the northernmost of the Abenaki tribes, their range extending throughout all of the North Country territory west and north of Umbagog Lake and even into western Maine. One of only a handful of his tribe to survive the smallpox epidemic of 1755, Metallak reportedly led the few remaining Coo-ash-aukes to the Catholic missionary village of St. Francis, Canada, where a long-lasting Indian community was established. (So much for Metallak being the *last* Coo-ash-auke.) He soon returned to his old home around Dixville Notch and Lake Umbagog, and eventually married a woman named Molly Oozalluc, whom he nicknamed Molly Molasses because of her fondness for the sweet.

Not the last of the Coo-ash-aukes.

They had two or three children, one of whom was reportedly killed by a wolf, and it was said that Metallak killed every wolf he could find thereafter, cutting off their heads and putting them up on poles.

There are conflicting legends about Metallak's kindness and/or cruelty to whites, in particular to white babies: One legend has it that he was disqualified as chief for preventing fellow warriors from torturing a white girl, but, according to another report, Metallak bragged about taking "young white papooses and rapping their heads on a tree." He supposedly owned thousands of acres in Coos County up until the end of his life, at which time he was forced to sign over all rights to his land to the government. Surely, most of these surviving stories about Metallak are as much a product of our own fears and fantasies as they are a reflection of the man's actual life. But one thing we do know for sure: He died on the floor (he refused to sleep in a bed throughout his life) in the home of a relative stranger in a land he and his people once called home.

On Umbagog Lake, you can visit Molly's Rock, supposedly his wife's favorite fishing spot. Or you can visit Chief Metallak's grave in the back left corner of Stewartstown's North Hill Cemetery. Take Route 145 south from Pittsburg into Stewartstown, where you'll come upon a historic marker for Metallak's grave on the east side of the road. Turn left on Creampoke Road, follow it up a hill for a short distance, then turn right onto North Hill Road. The cemetery is just up a rise on the right-hand side.

INDEX

INDEX

INDEX

INDEX

INDEX

INDEX

INDEX

INDEX

ÍNDEX

About the Author

A graduate of the University of Iowa's Nonfiction Writing Program, Eric Jones works as a household mover and high school soccer coach when he's not searching for all things odd, unusual, and downright strange in the Granite State. He co-authored *Iowa Curiosities,* published by The Globe Pequot Press in 2005. Eric currently lives in Strafford, New Hampshire.

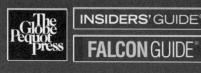